Commentary on Proverbs

Sources in Early Modern Economics, Ethics, and Law

Second Series

General Editors

Andrew M. McGinnis
Junius Institute • USA

Wim Decock
UCLouvain and ULiège • Belgium

Continuing in the line of its predecessor, this series publishes original English translations and editions of early modern religious texts in the disciplines of economics, ethics, and law. Representing a variety of confessional traditions and methodological approaches, these texts uncover the foundations of the development of these and related disciplines.

Editorial Board

Jordan J. Ballor
Center for Religion, Culture & Democracy • USA

Christiane Birr
Max Planck Institute for Legal History and Legal Theory • Germany

Stephen Bogle
University of Glasgow • Scotland

Alejandro Chafuen
Acton Institute • USA

Ricardo F. Crespo
Universidad Austral and CONICET • Argentina

Virpi Mäkinen
University of Helsinki • Finland

Richard A. Muller
Calvin Theological Seminary • USA

Herman Selderhuis
Theological University Apeldoorn • The Netherlands

John Witte Jr.
Emory University • USA

Zhibin Xie
Tongji University • China

Commentary on Proverbs

Philip Melanchthon

Translated and edited by
Derek Cooper and Timothy J. Wengert

Grand Rapids · Michigan

Commentary on Proverbs

© 2023 by Derek Cooper and Timothy J. Wengert

All rights reserved. No part of this publication may be reproduced, stored in a retrieval system, or transmitted in any form or by any means, including electronic, mechanical, photocopying, recording, or otherwise, without the prior permission of the publisher.

ISBN 978-1-949011-12-8 (hardcover)
ISBN 978-1-949011-13-5 (paperback)
ISBN 978-1-949011-14-2 (ebook)

CLP Academic
   An imprint of the Acton Institute
   for the Study of Religion & Liberty
98 E. Fulton
Grand Rapids, Michigan 49503
616.454.3080
www.acton.org

Interior composition by Judy Schafer
Cover design by Scaturro Design

Contents

Abbreviations	*vii*
Introduction	*ix*

Commentary on Proverbs

Epistle Dedicatory	5
Preface	17
Chapter 1	27
Chapter 2	35
Chapter 3	37
Chapter 4	43
Chapter 5	45
Chapter 6	51
Chapter 8*	59
Chapter 10	63
Chapter 11	77
Chapter 12	83
Chapter 13	85
Chapter 14	89
Chapter 15	91

---

*On Melanchthon's omission of Proverbs 7 and 9, see the Introduction, p. xxvii.

Chapter 16	99
Chapter 17	109
Chapter 18	115
Chapter 19	121
Chapter 20	127
Chapter 21	133
Chapter 22	135
Chapter 23	145
Chapter 24	155
Chapter 25	163
Chapter 26	169
Chapter 27	183
Chapter 28	193
Chapter 29	201
Chapter 30	207
Chapter 31	219
Scripture Index	227
Subject Index	235
Index of Authors and Works before 1600	245

Abbreviations

Claus — Helmut Claus. *Melanchthon-Bibliographie: 1510–1560.* 4 vols. Gütersloh: Gütersloher Verlagshaus, 2014.

CR — *Corpus Reformatorum: Philippi Melanthonis opera quae supersunt omnia.* Edited by Karl Bretschneider and Heinrich Bindseil. 28 vols. Halle: A. Schwetschke & Sons, 1834–1860.

CWE — *Collected Works of Erasmus.* 81 vols. Toronto: Toronto University Press, 1985–.

LW — *Luther's Works* [American edition]. 55 vols. Philadelphia: Fortress; St. Louis: Concordia, 1955–.

MBW — *Melanchthons Briefwechsel: Kritische und kommentierte Gesamtausgabe: Regesten.* Edited by Heinz Scheible. 13 vols. Stuttgart-Bad Cannstatt: Frommann-Holzboog, 1977–. The numbers refer to the numbers of the letters. For the texts, see *Melanchthons Briefwechsel: Kritische und kommentierte Gesamtausgabe: Texte*, 14 vols. Stuttgart-Bad Cannstatt: Frommann-Holzboog, 1991–.

MSA — *Melanchthons Werke in Auswahl* [Studienausgabe]. Edited by Robert Stupperich. 7 vols. Gütersloh: Gerd Mohn, 1951–1975.

Abbreviations

PG   *Patrologiae cursus completus. Series Graeca.* 161 vols. Paris & Turnhout, 1857–1866.

PL   *Patrologiae cursus completus. Series Latina.* 221 vols. Paris & Turnout, 1844–1864.

WA   *Luthers Werke: Kritische Gesamtausgabe [Schriften].* 65 vols. Weimar: H. Böhlau, 1883–1993.

WA Br   *Luthers Werke: Kritische Gesamtausgabe: Briefwechsel.* 18 vols. Weimar: H. Böhlau, 1930–1985.

Introduction

Derek Cooper
Timothy J. Wengert

Philip Melanchthon (1497–1560) was one of the most influential interpreters of the Bible in the sixteenth century. Yet in the twenty-first century, his work is hardly as well-known as that of Erasmus of Rotterdam (1466–1536), Martin Luther (1483–1546), or John Calvin (1509–1564). This trend of ignorance began around 1700, when Gottfried Arnold (1666–1714) proclaimed in his *Unbiased History of the Church and Heretics* that Philip Melanchthon had destroyed serious biblical interpretation in favor of his own systematic theology.[1] Arnold's challenge was so significant that a generation later, Georg Theodore Strobel (1736–1794), the first serious Melanchthon scholar, felt constrained to rebut it.[2]

Nevertheless during his own time Melanchthon's work garnered the attention, if not always the approbation and imitation, of many of his contemporaries. Erasmus, upon receiving a copy of the younger man's 1532 Romans commentary, immediately sent it on to Jacopo Sadoleto (1477–1547) so that the latter could respond to it in his own commentary. John Calvin praised the same commentary by

---

[1] Gottfried Arnold, *Unparteyische Kirchen- und Ketzer-historie*, 2 vols. (Frankfurt: Thomas Fritsch, 1699–1700). For a closer look at this book's impact on Melanchthon, see Timothy J. Wengert, "Biblische Übersetzungen und Kommentare," in *Philipp Melanchthon: Der Reformator zwischen Glauben und Wissen: Ein Handbuch*, ed. Günter Frank (Berlin: De Gruyter, 2017), 233–50, here 233–34.

[2] Theodore Strobel, *Historisch-Litterarische Nachricht von Philipp Melanchthons Verdiensten um die heilige Schrift* (Altdorf: Schüpfel, 1773).

Introduction

Melanchthon but then noted that Master Philip skipped verses in his work—an understandable critique from someone trained by Andrea Alciati (1492–1550) in the humanist interpretation of legal texts where omitting texts only gave leave to the opposing party to attack one's arguments. Martin Luther also took note of Melanchthon's work, publishing several of Melanchthon's early lectures on the Bible himself and praising him in prefaces to those works and to the 1529 translation of his interpretation of Colossians, in which Luther famously wrote, "I was born for this purpose: to fight with the rebels and the devils and to lead the charge. Therefore my books are very stormy and warlike. I have to uproot trunks and stumps, hack at thorns and hedges, and fill in the potholes. So I am the crude woodsman, who has to clear and make the path. But Master Philip comes after me meticulously and quietly, builds and plants, sows and waters happily, according to the talents God has richly given him."[3]

Melanchthon's Biography and Biblical Commentaries

Philip Melanchthon was born Philip Schwartzerdt on February 16, 1497, in the town of Bretten in southwest Germany. His father, Georg (1459–1508), was armorer and ordinance master for the Elector of the Palatinate, Count Philip "the Upright" (1448–1508), after whom Melanchthon was named. His mother was Barbara Reuter (ca. 1476–1529), whose father was sometime mayor of Bretten and an important merchant and with whom the young family lived. When her father and husband died in 1508, Barbara could no longer properly keep her sons' tutor in her house and so sent Philip and his brother Georg (1500–1563) to school in nearby Pforzheim, where they lived with a relative by marriage, Elizabeth Reuchlin (ca. 1470–ca. 1545).

From the rector of Pforzheim's Latin school, Georg Simler (ca. 1475–1535), Melanchthon began to learn Greek. When Elizabeth Reuchlin's brother, the famous humanist and jurist noted for his mastery of Latin, Greek, and Hebrew, Johannes Reuchlin (1455–1522), came to Pforzheim for a visit on March 15, 1509, he received from the

---

[3] WA 30/2: 68,12–69,1.

boy a Latin verse and in return gave the budding Greek scholar a Greek grammar inscribed with the Greek equivalent of his German name: *Melan* for *Schwartz* (black) and *chthon* for *Erdt* (earth). In return, Melanchthon and the other students performed one of Reuchlin's plays for him.[4]

After enrolling at the University of Heidelberg in 1509, Melanchthon lived in the house of one of the school's theologians, Pallas Spangel (ca. 1445–1512), and received his bachelor of arts degree in the philosophical *via antiqua*, championed by Thomas Aquinas, on September 17, 1512. A combination of factors led him to change schools and continue at the University of Tübingen for his master of arts degree, achieved on January 25, 1514.[5] As was required, Melanchthon then began to teach in the arts faculty there, but in addition he attended lectures in theology. He also worked alongside the future reformer of Basel, Johann Oecolampadius (1482–1531), at the print shop of Thomas Anshelm (ca. 1470–1522), who was formerly of Pforzheim and later of Haguenau, where his son-in-law, Johann Setzer (d. 1532), a onetime student in Wittenberg, would take over in the 1520s. There Melanchthon edited a collection of letters in defense of Johannes Reuchlin in the controversy over the Kabala with certain theologians from Cologne. The book was titled *Clarorum virorum epistolae* (Tübingen: Anshelm, 1514), for which Melanchthon also provided a preface.[6] By this time, Melanchthon was so fluent in Greek that he was writing poems and couplets in the classical language, including one for Erasmus, who in

---

[4] See Heinz Scheible, *Melanchthon, Vermittler der Reformation: Eine Biographie*, 2nd ed. (Munich: Beck, 2016), 17–18.

[5] Scheible, *Melanchthon*, 24, mentions several reasons for the move, including Melanchthon's young age (he was too young to begin according to Heidelberg's statutes); Spangel's death the same year; the presence of Melanchthon's Pforzheim teacher Simler in Tübingen; and the nearness of Tübingen to Reuchlin, who lived outside Stuttgart.

[6] MBW 1, dated before March 1514. Melanchthon also published, among other things, an edition of Terence (preface: MBW 7, dated before March 1517) and with Anshelm in Haguenau, a Greek grammar (MBW 16, dated ca. March 1518).

an annotation to the first edition of his Greek New Testament praised the young man as one of the few bright (humanist) lights in the Holy Roman Empire.[7] During his time in Tübingen, Melanchthon also delivered and published a speech defending the study of the arts.[8]

All of this, it turned out, was just the prologue for what happened in 1518 as the University of Wittenberg, to show its humanist *bona fides*, began a search for a professor of Greek to fill a newly created position in the arts faculty. When they approached Johannes Reuchlin, he recommended his shirttail relative, Melanchthon, who accepted the position. He arrived in Wittenberg on August 25, 1518, and delivered an inaugural speech on the reform of education three days later—a speech that had the Wittenberg academic community buzzing—including the professor of theology, Martin Luther (1483–1546).[9] Melanchthon began in the arts faculty, teaching Greek and various other courses, including rhetoric and dialectics. Because the university had trouble filling a position for Hebrew, Melanchthon also filled in at various times, teaching this subject until Matthäus Aurogallus (1490–1543) arrived in 1521.

A year later, on September 9, 1519, Melanchthon earned the first degree in the theology faculty, the bachelor of Bible, by defending his theses at a public disputation presided over by Martin Luther.[10] This degree licensed Melanchthon to teach not only on the Greek text

---

[7] See Erasmus, *Annotationes in Novum Instrumentum* (Basel: Froben, 1516), 555 (comments on 1 Thess. 2:7).

[8] For the preface, see MBW 18. The speech may be found in MSA 3:17–28.

[9] For Melanchthon's speech, see MSA 3:29–42. The preface is MBW 30, dated before October 16, 1518. See Luther's review of the speech, filled with extravagant praise, in a letter to Spalatin dated August 31, 1518 (LW 48:78; WA Br 1:192, 11–30 [no. 88]). "Four days after [Melanchthon] arrived, he delivered an extremely learned and absolutely faultless address. All esteemed and admired him greatly, so you need not worry on what grounds you recommended him to us. We very quickly turned our minds and eyes from his appearance and person to the man himself. We congratulate ourselves on having this man and marvel at what he has in him."

[10] MSA 1:23–25. Melanchthon received the degree on September 19, 1519.

(grammar) of the New Testament but also on the text and content of the Latin, where he could combine his knowledge of the text with his developing Evangelical[11] theology.

Although Melanchthon never left teaching in the arts faculty, armed with this Bible degree, he began a series of biblical lectures in the theology faculty that continued, with one brief hiatus, until his death in 1560. He began with lectures on Matthew (1519–1520), Romans (1520–1521), 1 and 2 Corinthians (1521–1522), and John (1522–1523).[12] Upon Luther's return to Wittenberg in 1522 from protective custody at the Wartburg Castle, the older man purloined the younger's lectures on the Pauline corpus and published them in an error-filled printing in Nuremberg with his own preface.[13] Luther followed this book up the next year by publishing, this time in Haguenau with Johann Setzer, Melanchthon's annotations on John, again writing the preface.[14] Enterprising printers managed to acquire and publish Melanchthon's even earlier lectures on Matthew at nearly the same time. This meant that by 1523, the foremost Evangelical interpretations of the Gospels and the Pauline corpus were by Melanchthon—with the exception of Luther's commentary on Galatians in 1519 (second edition, 1523), for which Melanchthon provided both prefaces.[15]

---

[11] To avoid any anachronistic use of the term "Lutheran," we use the word "Evangelical" to denote those adherents to Wittenberg's theology and practice.

[12] For Melanchthon's lectures on Matthew, see MSA 4:133–208. His Romans lectures are not available in a modern edition. For his lectures on 1 and 2 Corinthians, see MSA 4:15–132, and for John, see CR 14:1043–1220.

[13] WA 10/2:305–10; MBW 230, dated July 29, 1522. For the English, see LW 59:18–22.

[14] WA 12:56–57; English: LW 59:43–47, dated late May or early June 1523.

[15] See MBW 54 and 65 (preface and afterword to the 1519 edition) and MBW 283 (preface to the 1523 edition, dated before August). Melanchthon also provided a preface for Luther's *Operationes in Psalmos*. See MBW 47 (dated ca. March 27, 1519). To these books were added publications by Johannes Bugenhagen on the remaining Pauline corpus, by Oecolampadius (by then at Basel) on 1 John, by Justus Jonas on Acts, by Luther on 1 and 2 Peter and Jude, and by Francois Lambert on Luke. These books filled out a "Wittenberg

INTRODUCTION

After a semester as rector of the university, from October 18, 1523, to May 1, 1524, when he revised the arts curriculum along Evangelical and humanist lines, and after travels in southwest Germany to visit his mother, Melanchthon returned to lecturing on the Bible. He eventually filled a newly created, extraordinary position at the university, similar to one held by Luther, which allowed them both to lecture on any topic they wished. It is in this context that Melanchthon first turned serious attention to lectures on the Hebrew Scriptures, beginning with Proverbs.[16] Perhaps as early as 1524, an unauthorized version of his Latin translation of Proverbs with annotations through chapter 27 appeared, which was followed the next year by a publication authorized by Melanchthon.[17] This second translation with notes was republished forty-five times, often with the first, between 1525 and 1560, making it one of Melanchthon's most popular works.

Besides publishing two versions of a commentary on Colossians called *Scholia in Epistolam Pauli ad Colossenses* in 1527 and 1528,[18]

Commentary" on the entire New Testament. See Timothy J. Wengert, *Philip Melanchthon's 'Annotationes in Johannem' of 1523 in Relation to Its Predecessors and Contemporaries* (Geneva: Droz, 1987).

[16] A set of Melanchthon's brief annotations on parts of Genesis and Exodus was published in 1523, but probably represented privately held lectures.

[17] See the note in Claus, 1:170–71 (no. 1524.17); Philip Melanchthon, *ΠΑΡΟΙΜΙΑΙ, sive Proverbia Solomonis filii Davidis, Cum Adnotationibus* (Haguenau: Setzer, [1524?]). For the authorized, altered edition, see Claus, no. 1525.9: *Solomonis sententiae, versae ad Hebraicam Veritatem* (Haguenau: Setzer, 1525). Melanchthon's preface to the latter, MBW 394, dedicated to Duke (later Elector) John Frederick (1503–1554), which also helps clarify the confusing concatenation of annotations and translations, is dated by the MBW editors to April/May 1525, or even somewhat earlier. A German translation of the annotations by Justus Menius (1499–1558), printed with Luther's German translation of Proverbs, appeared in Erfurt in 1526 (Claus, no. 1526.14) with more notes than either Latin edition.

[18] The 1527 edition is printed in MSA 4:209–303. For the history of this commentary, see Timothy J. Wengert, *Human Freedom, Christian Righteousness: Philip Melanchthon's Exegetical Dispute with Erasmus of Rotterdam* (New York: Oxford University Press, 1998).

INTRODUCTION

Melanchthon produced a second commentary on Proverbs in May 1529, *Nova Scholia ... in Prouerbia Salomonis, ad iusti penè commentarij modum conscripta* [New scholia on Solomon's Proverbs written down in the mode of an entirely correct commentary] (Haguenau: Setzer, 1529). This book, which was more a commentary than simply a translation with notes, was printed eight times between 1529 and 1548, including in the 1541 Basel collection of Melanchthon's works.[19] He also published other commentaries on other biblical books in the coming years, including Romans (1529/30, 1532, 1540) and Daniel (1542), as well as on individual psalms.

Shortly after the death of Luther in 1546, the (for the Evangelicals) catastrophic Schmalkaldic War of 1546–1547 followed, bringing about the temporary closing of the University of Wittenberg and the exile of Melanchthon and his family. When the university reopened on October 17, 1547, it was under a new Saxon elector, the victorious but also Evangelical Duke Moritz of Saxony (1521–1553), who had nevertheless fought with Emperor Charles V against his cousin, Elector John Frederick. John Frederick was captured at the Battle of Mühlberg, stripped of his electoral dignity, and placed under a sentence of death, which was later commuted to life imprisonment. But he was released in 1552 in the aftermath of the Revolt of the Princes. After some hesitation, Melanchthon returned to Wittenberg and picked up his lecturing there.

Within a few years, Melanchthon was again producing commentaries. His New Testament works included Romans (1556) and Colossians (1559). Not surprisingly, he also turned his attention back to Proverbs. Indeed, he announced on November 4, 1547, that lectures on Proverbs would begin the following day.[20] Publication of these lectures first appeared in Frankfurt/Main in May 1550 as the *Explication of Solomon's Proverbs, Recently Dictated by Philip Melanthon at the University of*

---

[19] See Claus, no. 1529.8, and for the entire list Claus, 4:2477–80. For a modern printing of the text, see MSA 4:309–464. The new preface (MBW 750), dedicated to Duke Magnus von Mecklenburg, bishop of Schwerin, is dated by the editors of MBW to the end of January/beginning of February 1529.

[20] CR 6:719.

xv

Wittenberg.[21] Melanchthon followed up this book in 1555 with a thoroughly revised version based, according to the title, upon a fresh set of lectures.[22] The latter edition, upon which the present translation is based, is titled *An Explication of the Proverbs of Solomon, Dictated by Philip Melanthon at the University of Wittenberg in 1555*.[23] The 1550 version includes an epistle dedicatory to Duke Johann Albrecht of Mecklenburg, dated by the MBW editors to sometime before April 15, 1550.[24] The 1555 version retains the same letter but omits praise of Andreas Osiander (1498–1552) because in the meantime, Melanchthon and most other Evangelical theologians had engaged in a vicious

---

[21] Claus, no. 1550.17: *Explicatio Proverbiorum Salomonis in Schola VVitebergensi recens dictata a Philippo Melanthone* (Frankfurt/Main: Peter Brubach, 1550). After 1530, in part because a speech impediment made it difficult for him to pronounce "Melanchthon," he spelled his name "Melanthon." The term *dictata*, here translated literally as "dictated," points to the method of classroom lectures where the teacher's comments were read slowly enough to be copied by the students.

[22] See Claus, 4:2414, where Melanchthon does not distinguish the two versions. The 1550 edition was printed four times: twice in Frankfurt/Main (Claus, nos. 1550.17 and 1551.14) and twice in Wittenberg (Claus, no. 1552.69 and 1552.75). The 1555 edition was printed three times in Wittenberg (1555.127; 1556.135; and 1559.127). The latter was also included in volume 2 of Caspar Peucer's (1525–1602) edition of Melanchthon's works: *Operum ... Philippi Melanthonis pars secunda* (Wittenberg: Krafft, 1562), 872–935. From there it made its way into CR 14:1–88.

[23] Claus, no. 1555.127: *Explicatio Proverbiorum Salomonis in Schola VVitembergensi dictata anno 1555 a Philippo Melanthone* (Wittenberg: Peter Seitz's heirs, 1555). Appended to it were two Latin poems of Johann Stigel (1515–1562): "Psalmus quinquagesimus" and "Precatio pro ecclesia Dei." This edition appeared in May 1555, as witnessed by Melanchthon sending copies to several of his correspondents at that time (MBW 7492, dated May 18, 1555, and MBW 7493, dated May 20, 1555).

[24] See MBW 5771 (CR 7:705–10).

dispute with Osiander over justification by faith.[25] Also, the general introduction diverges markedly after the first few paragraphs. The 1555 commentary, while demonstrating parallels to the earlier version throughout, nevertheless differs in many specific ways—a detail that still awaits serious scholarly analysis.[26]

Melanchthon was truly a polymath, publishing major works on Greek and Latin grammar, rhetoric, and dialectics as part of his work in the arts faculty at Wittenberg. In addition to commentaries on biblical books and pagan authors, he produced a history of the world, a commentary on the Nicene Creed, and four editions (three Latin and one German) of his theology textbook, the *Loci communes theologici*. His revision to the curriculum of the arts faculty of 1523/24 included regular orations, many of which he either delivered or wrote for others and that were published either at the time or later. Melanchthon often wrote doctrinal or practical memoranda signed by the entire theology

---

[25] See CR 20:781–84, where the editor cites Osiander's attack on Melanchthon in which Osiander accused Melanchthon of changing his opinion about him based upon the positive things Melanchthon said in the 1550 preface. For this dispute, see Timothy J. Wengert, *Defending Faith: Lutheran Responses to Andreas Osiander's Doctrine of Justification* (Tübingen: Mohr Siebeck, 2012).

[26] Indeed, there has been little to no work done on Melanchthon's interpretation of the Hebrew Scriptures since the dissertation of Hansjörg Sick, *Melanchthon als Ausleger des Alten Testaments* (Tübingen: Mohr Siebeck, 1959), the one notable exception being an article by R. Gerald Hobbs, "Pluriformity of Early Reformation Scriptural Interpretation," in *Hebrew Bible, Old Testament: The History of Its Interpretation*, vol. 2, *From the Renaissance to the Enlightenment*, ed. Magne Sæbø (Göttingen: Vandenhoeck & Ruprecht, 2008), 452–511, esp. 487–511. Given that Melanchthon produced four different commentaries on Proverbs, scholars could well discover just how his interpretation developed from his early work in the 1520s to his mature works in the 1550s and how various external factors shaped his discussion of the biblical text. One could also compare his work on Proverbs to his commentaries on Cicero and Aristotle, in which Melanchthon's development has been brilliantly mapped out by Nicole Kuropka in her award-winning dissertation *Philipp Melanchthon: Wissenschaft und Gesellschaft, ein Gelehrter im Dienst der Kirche (1526–1532)* (Tübingen: Mohr Siebeck, 2002).

faculty, and he contributed several important confessions for the Evangelical Church of Saxony and beyond, including the Augsburg Confession (1530/1540); its *Apology* (1531); the *Treatise on the Power and Primacy of the Pope* (1537); the *Saxon Confession* (1551); the *Examination of Ordinands*, originally for the Mecklenburg church (1553); and the *Response to the Bavarian Articles of Inquisition* (1557). Melanchthon assembled these documents, along with several others, into a forerunner of the *Book of Concord* titled *Corpus Doctrinae* (A body of teaching), which was used as a standard for teaching in several territorial churches until 1580.[27] The preface to the Latin edition was dated February 16, 1560, Melanchthon's sixty-third birthday. He died in Wittenberg only a few months later, on April 19, 1560. He is buried across from Martin Luther in Wittenberg's Castle Church.

Melanchthon's Exegetical Method

Compared to other well-known exegetes of early modern central Europe, Melanchthon represented a unique blend of Renaissance methods and Evangelical (Lutheran) theology. If modern readers simply concentrate on *what* Melanchthon says about particular verses of Proverbs, his overall approach to biblical interpretation can easily go unnoticed, distorting his actual point of view. Even some of his contemporaries, including Erasmus of Rotterdam and John Calvin, complained about his approach to Scripture.[28]

---

[27] See MSA 6 for these works. The 1543/1559 edition of the *Loci communes* was also included in the original *Corpus Doctrinae*.

[28] This brief introduction to Melanchthon's exegetical method builds upon previous work by Timothy J. Wengert: "The Biblical Commentaries of Philip Melanchthon," in *Philip Melanchthon (1497–1560) and the Commentary*, ed. M. Patrick Graham and Timothy J. Wengert (Sheffield: Sheffield Academic Press, 1997), 106–48; Wengert, "Philipp Melanchthon, biblischer Theologe der Neuzeit," in *Melanchthon und die Neuzeit*, ed. Günter Frank and Ulrich Köpf (Stuttgart-Bad Cannstatt: Frommann-Holzboog, 2003), 23–42; Wengert, "The Rhetorical Paul: Philip Melanchthon's Interpretation of the Pauline Epistles," in *A Companion to Paul in the Reformation*, ed. R. Ward Holder (Leiden: Brill, 2009), 129–64; Wengert, "Biblical Interpretation in the Works of Philip Melanchthon," in *A History of Biblical Interpretation*, vol. 2, *The Medie-*

The Biblical Text

Melanchthon was one of the foremost Greek scholars of his time. His Greek grammar was printed over two dozen times.[29] He even oversaw the printing of Martin Luther's translation of the Greek New Testament, the so-called *September Testament*, in 1522. But Melanchthon also knew Hebrew and stepped in to teach Hebrew at several points early in his career at Wittenberg. His translation of Proverbs into Latin and the lemmata in this Proverbs commentary show his use of both the Greek and the Hebrew text instead of reliance on the standard Latin Vulgate. A comparison of this text to these sources and to the German text of Proverbs in the so-called *Luther Bible* of 1534 goes beyond the scope of this work. Nevertheless, it is clear that Melanchthon maintained his humanist commitment of going *ad fontes*, to the (original) sources, throughout his career as he tried to provide his students with what he viewed as the most accurate text of Scripture.

History

The book of Proverbs gives the interpreter scant opportunity to delve into the history of Israel. Yet historical work was crucial to Wittenberg's biblical interpretation, so much so that Melanchthon's student Georg Major wrote an introduction to his own Pauline commentaries titled *Vita S. Pauli, Apostoli* (The life of St. Paul, apostle).[30]

---

val through the Reformation Periods, ed. Alan J. Hauser and Duane F. Watson (Grand Rapids: Eerdmans, 2009), 319–40; Wengert, "Biblische Übersetzungen und Kommentare," in *Philipp Melanchthon: Der Reformator zwischen Glauben und Wissen: Ein Handbuch*, ed. Günter Frank (Berlin: De Gruyter, 2017), 233–50, translated as "Philip Melanchthon on Bible Translation and Commentaries," *Lutheran Quarterly* 33 (2019): 26–45.

[29] Melanchthon's *Grammatica Graeca* was published twenty-seven times in his lifetime (Claus, 4:2461–62), and his *Institutio puerilis litterarum Graecarum* once.

[30] *Vita S. Pauli, Apostoli* was first published by Johannes Lufft in Wittenberg in 1555. See Timothy J. Wengert, "Georg Major (1502–1574): Defender of Wittenberg's Faith and Melanchthonian Exegete," in *Melanchthon in seinen Schülern*, ed. Heinz Scheible (Wiesbaden: Harrassowitz, 1997), 129–56.

Melanchthon had praised lectures on history in his inaugural address at the University of Wittenberg in 1518, and in the 1530s and especially after 1547, he lectured on the world chronicle of Johannes Carion (1499–1537), turning it into his own history of the world from Adam to Charlemagne. Melanchthon's son-in-law, Caspar Peucer, brought the history up to Maximilian II.[31]

But history also plays a role in Melanchthon's commentary on Proverbs in that he takes many of the examples for particular aphorisms from ancient Greek and Roman history as well as from the history of Israel. The astounding breadth of his knowledge of the ancient world and its stories may be seen on every page of this commentary—perhaps more so than in his other biblical works.

Rhetorical Analysis

Among today's biblical interpreters, Melanchthon is best known for his rhetorical analysis of biblical books, especially the Pauline corpus and even more specifically Romans.[32] His interpretations of other biblical books also show his commitment to using rhetoric to analyze the text's structure.[33] His student Georg Major assiduously applied this analytical technique to his commentaries on the entire Pauline corpus.[34]

---

[31] There were at least nineteen printings of various parts of Melanchthon's world history from 1558 until his death in 1560 (Claus, 4:2383). Later it was translated into French and published in Geneva in the early seventeenth century.

[32] Timothy J. Wengert, "Philip Melanchthon's 1522 Annotations on Romans and the Lutheran Origins of Rhetorical Criticism," in *Biblical Interpretation in the Era of the Reformation*, ed. Richard A. Muller and John L. Thompson (Grand Rapids: Eerdmans, 1996), 118–40. Rolf Schäfer provides Melanchthon's rhetorical outline of Romans in an appendix to the 1532 *Commentarii in Epistolam Pauli ad Romanos* in MSA 5:373–78.

[33] For Melanchthon's rhetorical analysis of John, see Wengert, *Philip Melanchthon's 'Annotationes in Johannem,'* 177–82. For Colossians, see Wengert, *Human Freedom*, 48–64.

[34] Wengert, "Georg Major."

Because Melanchthon was convinced that Proverbs is in fact a collection of adages, in the 1555 commentary he does not find any overarching structure in the book. However, in his 1550 commentary we at least find a note at the beginning of chapter 30 in which he claims this chapter is a (rhetorical) summary of Proverbs. As in the 1555 commentary, Melanchthon notes that chapter 30 and the next were added by others, a practice not unusual in a collection of *gnomen* (maxims). He then observes that chapter 30 contains "first a summary rule of all [adages]," namely, to follow the Word of God, which stands in antithesis to the history of the world. The second point emphasizes finding balance in life.[35] The notion that an author—or a later contributor—would summarize a book's main points fits perfectly with Melanchthon's insistence that the human author had a crucial role in shaping these texts.

The introduction to the entire book, "The Preface of Philip Melanchthon in the Proverbs of Solomon," demonstrates how rhetorical analysis directly functions in Melanchthon's interpretation of Proverbs. First he distinguishes two forms of teaching: books that use dialectics to organize a topic (he could have included Romans) and move logically from one theme to another; and books that collect brief comments or aphorisms on a topic in no particular order, such as Proverbs. Then he notes that the Greeks distinguished two types of advice: *gnomon* (Latin: *sententiae*, "maxims") and *paroimiai* (Latin: *proverbia*, "proverbs"), but he notes that the Hebrew language has only a single term for both, so that both may be found in Proverbs. But Melanchthon also insists that Solomon, as a believer, placed faith in God at the center of his thought and that all of his proverbs must be read through the lens of that faith. To ignore Solomon's own theological intention would be to distort his purpose and misread the entire book.

The "Loci Method" of Interpretation

One of the most important aspects of Melanchthon's thought is his use of *loci communes*, literally, "commonplaces," to organize biblical and theological material. In the 1519 second edition of the *Novum*

---

[35] From the *Expositio Proverbiorum* (Frankfurt: Brubach, 1550), 210–16.

Testamentum (the Greek and Latin printing of the New Testament), Erasmus describes such *loci* as *nidulae*, "nestlets," or cubbyholes into which to stick various biblical passages. For Erasmus, these topics included for the most part his most beloved ethical categories and his "philosophy of Christ." Melanchthon, influenced by Martin Luther's theological insight into justification by faith, realized that such an approach reduces the biblical text to "law," that is, into virtues to imitate and vices to avoid.[36] Instead, in 1520 Melanchthon developed a different approach to *loci*, insisting that the categories remain true to and arise from the biblical text itself. Rather than using disconnected cubbyholes, Melanchthon employed a very different, more integrative definition of *loci* gleaned from Rudolf Agricola.[37] He thus viewed *loci* as the central, connected themes of Scripture, and that especially Paul's letter to Romans provides the basic set. Thus in 1520–1521, instead of lecturing on Peter Lombard's *Sentences*, which was the appropriate next step for studies in the medieval theological faculty, Melanchthon lectured on Paul's *loci communes* and subsequently published the first Evangelical textbook on theology, the *Commonplaces of Theological Matters or Theological Outline* (or *Pattern*).[38]

Melanchthon's "*loci* method" of biblical interpretation had two sides. On the one hand, he could use Scripture itself to define the basic theological categories through which one should read the biblical text.

---

[36] A comparison of the introductions of Erasmus and Melanchthon to Romans bears this out.

[37] Rudolf Agricola (1443–1485) wrote a book on dialectics published posthumously as *Rodolphi Agricole Phrisii* [the Frisian] *de inventione dialectica libri tres* (Louvain: Martinus, 1515) that Johannes Oecolampadius gave to Melanchthon while they both worked at Thomas Anshelm's print shop in Tübingen.

[38] *Loci communes rerum theologicarum seu Hypotyposes theologicae* (Wittenberg: Melchior Lotter, 1521). The Greek word *hypotyposes* can mean either "outline" or "pattern." In Quintilian it is a rhetorical term for "a vivid sketch in words." Most scholars recognize that Melanchthon gleaned such topics as grace, faith, sin, law, and gospel from Romans, but other topics come from that epistle as well, including "signs" (sacraments; Rom. 6), love (Rom. 12), government (Rom. 13), and scandal (Rom. 14–15).

On the other, individual passages of Scripture could be connected to an overarching topic within the Bible. This far more integrated approach to biblical interpretation, defined in part by the Aristotelian distinction between genus and species, meant that Melanchthon's commentary on one text could include a wide variety of other passages to imbed the passage at hand into broader topics. Melanchthon's Proverbs commentary demonstrates this method in many places, but no better than in his exposition of Proverbs 31. After examining the acrostic poem in praise of the godly matron and rejecting any allegorical interpretation, which was common in the Middle Ages, Melanchthon appends a lengthy interpretation of 1 Timothy 2:15, a particularly problematic verse for Wittenberg's teachers because it seems to say that women are saved through childbirth rather than through Christ's death and resurrection. The casual reader may imagine that Melanchthon had simply gone "off topic," but contrariwise, this *loci* method forced him to deal with another text within the same locus in order to bring clarity to both texts (species) and the overarching topic (genus).

Theological Premise: The Twofold Righteousness of God

It is tempting to separate Melanchthon's theology from his ethics or philosophy, but this separation ignores a crucial aspect of his thought by which he integrates both into a single, overarching structure. In or around 1521, while Martin Luther was in protective custody at the Wartburg Castle, Melanchthon questioned his absent colleague about the role of government in Scripture, and hence the value of human wisdom in all fields, in the light of the gospel's message of salvation "apart from the law" (Rom. 3:21). From Martin Luther's response to the now lost letter from his younger student and colleague, we hear how Luther's developing notions of the "two kingdoms" or "two governments" allowed Melanchthon to continue teaching in the arts faculty and to reconcile the two fields of study, theology and the humanities.[39] By

---

[39] See Wengert, *Human Freedom*; Wengert, "Philip Melanchthon on Human and Divine Freedom," *dialog* 39 (2000): 262–66; Wengert, "Philip Melanchthon and a Christian *Politics*," *Lutheran Quarterly*, n.s., 17 (2003): 29–62; and Kuropka, *Philipp Melanchthon: Wissenschaft und Gesellschaft*, 1–13.

the time he published the first edition of his *Scholia in Colossians* in 1527, Melanchthon had fully worked out the relation between what he preferred to call the two righteousnesses of God. On the one hand, God works in this world through the law, separate from the gospel, to lead people to earthly wisdom about this life. Here all aspects of human thought and insight have their rightful place. Here free choice rightfully belongs, although always under attack from human sin and the devil. On the other hand, quite apart from (and even contrary to) human wisdom and righteousness, God reveals the gospel of reconciliation in Christ and eternal life. This is the life of faith and trust in God and God's righteousness given in Christ, and it is not based upon human works or righteousness.

This distinction, also referred to as the distinction between civil law and the gospel, played an enormous role in Melanchthon's interpretation of Proverbs.[40] For one thing, when he encountered verses that he viewed as dealing with faith and God's mercy, such as "The fear of the Lord is the beginning of wisdom," he inevitably distinguishes this revelation of God concerning the centrality of faith in God from human wisdom. Thus he criticizes early Christian thinkers, such as Cyril of Alexandria, for not going far enough in their answer to the emperor, Julian the Apostate, who claimed that the works of Phocylides and Theognis were superior to Proverbs. These Christians had argued that because Solomon's work was older, it clearly had precedence over later Greek thinkers. But Melanchthon insisted that the real superiority of Solomon came from his ability to distinguish, and hence employ, philosophy and proper church teaching. Of course Phocylides knew aspects of the law and the consequences for breaking it, but he could not fathom any teaching about the gospel, that is, about the Mediator, forgiveness, reconciliation, prayer, faith, or hope.

---

[40] This distinction also played a role in his commentaries on Aristotle and Cicero, among others, where he always prefaces his comments by distinguishing between the two kinds of righteousness and then excludes the pagan author from making any contribution to the gospel. See Sachiko Kusukawa, *The Transformation of Natural Philosophy: The Case of Philip Melanchthon* (Cambridge: Cambridge University Press, 1995).

For another thing, this same distinction actually permitted Melanchthon to match Solomon's maxims about life in this world with similar statements by pagan thinkers, and even to use traditional terms from Latin and Greek ethics to explain them.[41] This matching is another way the *loci* method worked for him. If, for example, Proverbs makes a comment about greed—separate and apart from any theological point—Melanchthon then could include statements and examples from all kinds of non-Christian sources in addition to similar statements in other parts of the Bible. In so doing, Melanchthon's use of *loci* more closely matches that of Erasmus, in that the topics come from the basic ethical concerns of human thinkers, as described for example in Aristotle's *Nicomachean Ethics*. Indeed, these pagan sources at times helped Melanchthon elucidate what Solomon was trying to say and gave a broader context for his statements. Again, the reason Melanchthon could use these sources arose directly from his distinction of twofold righteousness and his conviction, shared with Luther, that God enlightens human beings about the truths of *this* world, separate and apart from faith in Christ. As the reader will see, this extensive use of extrabiblical sources is one of the most intriguing aspects of this work.

Notes about This Translation

The present translation is based upon the modern version found in volume 14 of the *Corpus Reformatorum*, pages 1–88. We also consulted original copies of the commentary from 1555 and 1559. Because there seems to be no direct relation between the poems of Johannes Strigel placed at the end of the commentary and the commentary itself, we have omitted them here, as did Caspar Peucer in volume two of Melanchthon's *Opera*, first published in 1562.

Melanchthon did not simply use the standard Latin translation but created his own unique lemmata for the commentary. His interest in the translation of Proverbs went back to his original work on the

---

[41] In this translation, we call the reader's attention to the Greek terms by prefacing them with phrases like "which the Greeks call," etc.

text in 1524. Thus in this commentary we have remained faithful to Melanchthon's own Latin translation, not only of Proverbs but also of other Scripture references. The chapters and verses, of course, conform to modern versions, given that versification was first developed in 1555 by Robert Estienne in Paris. Also, Melanchthon did not always cite the chapter. So we have given the specifics in the notes, correcting any mistaken references.

Melanchthon's citations of classical literature sometimes appear to have been from memory; at other times from Renaissance sources, including Erasmus's *Adages*, that have since been improved; and at other times from sources that correspond to present-day texts. The variations are even reflected in different renderings of the same text in different places in the commentary. Thus the translations here may at times vary from modern translations. With the Greek texts, the situation is even more complicated, since sometimes Melanchthon cites only the Greek, other times only the Latin, and still other times both. When he does quote the Greek, we have placed the original text in the footnotes.

Where the *Corpus Reformatorum*, for the most part following the original, uses the upper case for a noun, especially in the case of virtues and vices, we have capitalized the word in this English translation. For translations of Melanchthon's technical language, we have tried to use the same word in as many places as possible, but not when the sense in English would be compromised. *Praeceptum* is translated either as "precept" or "command." *Admonitio* is generally rendered as "admonition," although the Latin is often far milder and may mean (à la Cicero) something akin to "friendly suggestion." *Sententia* is for the most part translated as "maxim" when used over against *proverbium* (proverb) in the introduction, which is almost the only place where the latter term is used. Elsewhere, *sententia* is most often rendered simply as "saying" and hence a synonym of *dictum* (saying). In general, Melanchthon uses *sententia* in a positive sense, unlike *opinio* (opinion), which he thought of as an unsubstantiated idea.

Melanchthon assumed that Solomon wrote the entire book with the exception of chapters 30 and 31. He explains the presence of these later authors in the introduction to chapter 30. As interested as Melanchthon was in literary matters and in the content of the teaching in Proverbs, he did not tie these sayings to the social or historical context of the tenth century BCE. Instead, he was much more eager to connect individual adages to similar sayings in Greek or Latin antiquity—an obvious fruit of his *loci* method described above. Even more noticeable in this commentary, as opposed to his other commentaries, Melanchthon "skipped" not only verses but entire chapters, specifically 7 and 9. To be sure, he had covered some of these omissions in earlier commentaries. But he seemed to assume that the job of the exegete was to provide a scaffold or outline of the text and that the readers could interpret the omitted passages on their own based on his comments. Occasionally, he refers to an omitted text elsewhere in the commentary when a maxim on the same topic appears.

Bibliography

Agricola, Rudolph. *Rodolphi Agricole Phrisii de inventione dialectica libri tres*. Louvain: Martinus, 1515.

Arnold, Gottfried. *Unparteyische Kirchen- und Ketzer-historie*. 2 vols. Frankfurt: Thomas Fritsch, 1699–1700.

Erasmus of Rotterdam. *Annotationes in Novum Instrumentum*. Basel: Froben, 1516.

Hobbs, R. Gerald. "Pluriformity of Early Reformation Scriptural Interpretation." In *Hebrew Bible, Old Testament: The History of Its Interpretation*, vol. 2, *From the Renaissance to the Enlightenment*, edited by Magne Sæbø, 452–511. Göttingen: Vandenhoeck & Ruprecht, 2008.

Kuropka, Nicole. *Philipp Melanchthon: Wissenschaft und Gesellschaft, ein Gelehrter im Dienst der Kirche (1526–1532)*. Tübingen: Mohr Siebeck, 2002.

Kusukawa, Sachiko. *The Transformation of Natural Philosophy: The Case of Philip Melanchthon*. Cambridge: Cambridge University Press, 1995.

Melanchthon, Philip. *Explicatio Proverbiorum Salomonis in Schola VVitembergensi dictata anno 1555 a Philippo Melanthone*. Wittenberg: Peter Seitz's heirs, 1555.

———. *Explicatio Proverbiorum Salomonis in Schola VVitebergensi recens dictata a Philippo Melanthone*. Frankfurt/Main: Peter Brubach, 1550.

———. *Loci communes rerum theologicarum seu Hypotyposes theologicae*. Wittenberg: Melchior Lotter, 1521.

———. *Nova Scholia ... in Prouerbia Salomonis, ad iusti penè commentarij modum conscripta*. Haguenau: Setzer, 1529.

———. *ΠΑΡΟΙΜΙΑΙ, sive Proverbia Solomonis filii Davidis, Cum Adnotationibus*. Haguenau: Setzer, [1524?].

———. *Solomonis sententiae, versae ad Hebraicam Veritatem*. Haguenau: Setzer, 1525.

Scheible, Heinz. *Melanchthon, Vermittler der Reformation: Eine Biographie*. 2nd ed. Munich: Beck, 2016.

Sick, Hansjörg. *Melanchthon als Ausleger des Alten Testaments.* Tübingen: Mohr Siebeck, 1959.

Strobel, Theodore. *Historisch-Litterarische Nachricht von Philipp Melanchthons Verdiensten um die heilige Schrift.* Altdorf: Schüpfel, 1773.

Wengert, Timothy J. "The Biblical Commentaries of Philip Melanchthon." In *Philip Melanchthon (1497–1560) and the Commentary,* edited by M. Patrick Graham and Timothy J. Wengert, 106–48. Sheffield: Sheffield Academic Press, 1997.

———. "Biblical Interpretation in the Works of Philip Melanchthon." In *A History of Biblical Interpretation,* vol. 2, *The Medieval through the Reformation Periods,* edited by Alan J. Hauser and Duane F. Watson, 319–40. Grand Rapids: Eerdmans, 2009.

———. "Biblische Übersetzungen und Kommentare." In *Philipp Melanchthon: Der Reformator zwischen Glauben und Wissen: Ein Handbuch,* edited by Günter Frank, 233–50. Berlin: De Gruyter, 2017. Translated as "Philip Melanchthon on Bible Translation and Commentaries," *Lutheran Quarterly* 33 (2019): 26–45.

———. *Defending Faith: Lutheran Responses to Andreas Osiander's Doctrine of Justification.* Tübingen: Mohr Siebeck, 2012.

———. "Georg Major (1502–1574): Defender of Wittenberg's Faith and Melanchthonian Exegete." In *Melanchthon in seinen Schülern,* edited by Heinz Scheible, 129–56. Wiesbaden: Harrassowitz, 1997.

———. *Human Freedom, Christian Righteousness: Philip Melanchthon's Exegetical Dispute with Erasmus of Rotterdam.* New York: Oxford University Press, 1998.

———. "Philip Melanchthon's 1522 Annotations on Romans and the Lutheran Origins of Rhetorical Criticism." In *Biblical Interpretation in the Era of the Reformation,* edited by Richard A. Muller and John L. Thompson, 118–40. Grand Rapids: Eerdmans, 1996.

———. "Philip Melanchthon and a Christian *Politics.*" *Lutheran Quarterly,* n.s., 17 (2003): 29–62.

———. "Philip Melanchthon on Human and Divine Freedom." *dialog* 39 (2000): 262–66.

———. *Philip Melanchthon's 'Annotationes in Johannem' of 1523 in Relation to Its Predecessors and Contemporaries*. Geneva: Droz, 1987.

———. "Philipp Melanchthon, biblischer Theologe der Neuzeit." In *Melanchthon und die Neuzeit*, edited by Günter Frank and Ulrich Köpf, 23–42. Stuttgart-Bad Cannstatt: Frommann-Holzboog, 2003.

———. "The Rhetorical Paul: Philip Melanchthon's Interpretation of the Pauline Epistles." In *A Companion to Paul in the Reformation*, edited by R. Ward Holder, 129–64. Leiden: Brill, 2009.

Commentary on Proverbs

EXPLICA-
TIO PROVERBIO-
RVM SALOMONIS
IN SCHOLA VVITEMBER-
GENSI DICTATA.
ANNO 1555.

A
PHILIPPO MELAN-
THONE.

VVITEBERGAE
excudebant hæredes Pe-
tri Seitzij.

1 5 5 5.

An Explanation of Solomon's Proverbs,
Lectured upon by Philip Melanchthon at the University of Wittenberg in 1555.
Published in Wittenberg by Peter Seitz's Heirs, 1555

(Image courtesy of the Richard C. Kessler Reformation Collection
at Pitts Theology Library, Emory University)

Epistle Dedicatory

To the Most Renowned Prince and Lord, Lord Johann Albert I,[1] Duke of Mecklenburg, Prince of the famous and ancient Wendish[2] people along the Baltic Sea, Lord of Rostock and Stargard, etc., to His Most Gracious Lord.[3]

To Your Highness, Solomon comes not in splendid attire, as was proper for such a king, and certainly not in robes covered with fine feathers. Instead, I want the voice of the king himself to be both heard and considered. I do not wish for these rags to be looked at, in which I have wrapped them. For I do this only so that Solomon's book may be frequently placed in the hands of the young and may frequently be read again by many.[4]

---

[1] Johann Albert I (1525–1576) was the Duke of Mecklenburg-Güstrow from 1547 to 1556. He was instrumental in the introduction of Protestantism to his realm of northern Germany.

[2] The Wends, or Wendish people, were West Slavs who lived in Germanic regions. They were largely converted to Christianity during the High Middle Ages.

[3] This letter, MBW 5771 (CR 7:705–10), first appeared in the 1550 edition. See the Introduction, pp. xv–xvi.

[4] The 1555 edition omits these opening paragraphs of the original letter in the 1550 edition: "It is exceedingly difficult to translate the maxims and short sayings of a foreign language into another. This is especially the case when it comes to the Hebrew language, which is less well known than Greek or Latin. For there are many stylistic elements [Latin: *phrases*] present in short sayings that are not easily understood, partly because they arise from a language that is less familiar and partly because they refuse, if I may say so, to put on the clothes of a foreigner [cf. Zeph. 1:8]. Because it is very profitable both for the young and for those whom age has matured to be as familiar as possible with Solomon's maxims, I have often wished for the

When Emperor Julian wrote against the church of God,[5] he set Phocylides[6] over against Solomon in order to demonstrate that instruction on the virtues and the separation of good and bad deeds were

---

existence of a Latin translation that is less rough than the common version [the Vulgate] and for an exposition that would add something of light to these weighty maxims of Solomon. In truth, there is no one among the Jews capable of such an undertaking. For even though they may know Latin, they have neither knowledge of nor love for the doctrine of the church of God. For this reason, whether out of ignorance or whether out of malice, they distort many things. And few among them possess enough of judgment to accept advice on matters of the state from this wisest of kings.

"For these reasons, I have asked around in private correspondence, and I similarly ask now publicly, for that distinguished gentleman, Andreas Osiander, to offer some sort of Latin translation on the Proverbs of Solomon that would illumine these obscure oracles in his own treatment of the book. For not only has he been expertly trained in the knowledge of the Hebrew language, but he both comprehends and embraces the doctrine of the church. Through the sharpness and prudence of his innate understanding, which both age and experience have given witness, he sees to which circumstances in life these maxims should correspond. Such a work would be both pleasing to the church and useful to posterity, for it would be very helpful for these maxims to be in the hands of all."

For Melanchthon's attitude toward the Jews, see Timothy J. Wengert, "Philip Melanchthon and the Jews: A Reappraisal," in *Jews, Judaism, and the Reformation in Sixteenth-Century Germany*, ed. Dean Phillip Bell and Stephen J. Burnett (Leiden: Brill, 2006), 105–36. For more on Osiander, who died in 1552 and with whom Melanchthon fought over the doctrine of justification, see the Introduction, pp. xvi–xvii.

[5] Julian (330–363) was the emperor of the Roman Empire from 361 to 363. The Christians gave him the epithet "the Apostate" because Julian dedicated the entirety of his reign to opposing Christianity, the religion of his childhood. Julian wrote a book later titled *Against the Galileans* (in Greek Κατὰ Γαλιλαίων and Latin *Contra Galilaeos*), which only survives today in quotations from his opponents. It was a damning and long-lasting critique of Christianity.

[6] Phocylides (sixth century BCE) was known for his collection of adages.

Epistle Dedicatory

not absent in the writings of the pagan Greeks. Cyril[7] responded to Julian by claiming that Solomon had existed in the generations before Phocylides and Theognis, who both lived contemporaneously with Solon and Thales while Croesus was serving as king.[8] Indeed, according to Cyril, Solomon even lived in an age before Homer and Hesiod, for Homer lived contemporaneously with Isaiah.[9] This comparison of time periods is accurate, and the Greeks themselves write that Phocylides's maxims were collected from other older testimonies remaining from the precepts of the first patriarchs after Japheth.[10] Nonetheless, some other response that is firmer in tone must be offered to counter the wickedness of Julian.

For Julian gets it wrong when he assumes that in the church there is only the teaching of Law and that the church is distinguished from the rest of the world only by its profession of precepts about morals. Thus, even Lactantius only made a comparison of laws.[11] Just as

---

[7] Cyril (378-444) was the patriarch of Alexandria from 412 to 444. Although he lived a generation after Julian, he wrote a refutation of Julian's *Against the Galileans* in a book titled *Against Julian* during his tenure as patriarch because Alexandria was experiencing a resurgence in paganism. The "ten books" that remain from Cyril's refutation are found in PG 76:489-1057.

[8] Phocylides from Miletus and Theognis (ca. sixth century BCE) from Megara, respectively; Solon (ca. 630-ca. 560 BC) was an author and statesman from Athens. Thales of Miletus (ca. 626/623-ca. 548/545 BCE) was an author and philosopher; and Croesus (b. 595 BCE) was a king of Lydia.

[9] Hesiod was active between 750 and 650 BCE. In Melanchthon's time, Homer was thought to have been active in the eighth century BCE.

[10] This reference is to the Japheth mentioned in Gen. 10:1-4, one of the three sons of Noah and ancestor of the Greeks.

[11] Lactantius (ca. 250-ca. 325) was an intellectual who converted to Christianity and served as an advisor to Emperor Constantine. His most influential work was *Divine Institutes*, an apologetic composed in the first decade of the fourth century and divided into seven books. This book was meant to counter the so-called institutes that comprised the civil laws of Rome. See Lactantius, *The Divine Institutes, Books I-VII*, trans. Mary Francis McDonald (Washington, DC: Catholic University of America Press, 1964). Lactantius

we who are born carry a knowledge of numbers with us, so also the knowledge of laws is a light divinely created in the minds of all, even if such knowledge is more darkened because of the depravity of our nature. And God wills that this knowledge remain inside each person, so that God's judgment against one's sin may be acknowledged and one's conduct may be regulated.

Out of this fountain Solon, Zaleucus,[12] and many other good rulers drew worthy laws, and out of this fountain many wise writers drew worthy precepts. This list includes Homer, Hesiod, Pindar, Phocylides, Theognis, Sophocles, Euripides, and others whom I certainly want to be read.[13]

But it must be recognized that the words of the Gospel, which discuss the forgiveness of sins and all of the benefits emanating from the Mediator, offer something altogether different.[14] This type of wisdom was disclosed to neither angels nor human beings apart from divine revelation. Thus, the knowledge of law does not distinguish the church from other nations. Rather, a far different kind of wisdom about the Son of God has been revealed in the promises. Because Julian was

---

wrote in book 4, chapter 8 that Solomon "antedated the fall of Troy by a hundred forty years" (*regnavit, trojanae urbis excidiam centum et quadraginta annis antecessit*) (PL 6:468); and in book 1, chapter 5 that "Homer could give us nothing which pertains to the truth ... Hesiod could, but he gave nothing" (*Homerus nihil nobis dare potuit, quod pertineat ad veritatem ... Potuit Hesiodous ... Sed tamen nihil dedit*) (27; PL 6:131).

[12] Zaleucus was a lawgiver, presumably of the Locrian code, in ancient Greece and a Pythagorean philosopher who flourished in the seventh century BCE.

[13] Melanchthon lectured on all of these pagan authors at the University of Wittenberg. On his commentaries, see for Homer, CR 18:119–54; for Hesiod, CR 18:157–274; for Pindar, CR 19:187–268; for Phocylides, CR 19:1–4; for Theognis, CR 19:5–178; for Sophocles, CR 18:275–78; and for Euripides, CR 18:279–1130.

[14] This basic distinction between Law and Gospel, or the twofold righteousness of God, shapes Melanchthon's interpretation. See the Introduction, pp. xxiii–xxv.

ignorant of the distinction between Law and Gospel, that discussion of his was wrong to the highest heaven.

To be sure, there are many maxims that are only streams flowing from the Law in the Proverbs of Solomon as well as political and domestic precepts that are similar to what the wise men of the [Greek and Latin] pagans handed down. For instance: "It will go poorly for the one who makes a pledge to others."[15] This corresponds with the following saying: "Ruin follows the making of a pledge."[16] Nevertheless, there are many other maxims in Solomon's Proverbs discussing God's will, judgment, mercy, the true invocation of God, proper worship, eternal life, and God's presence and aid in times of our distress. This kind of teaching is not found in the writings of the pagans nor born out of human reason. Rather, it is an exposition of the first table of the Law.[17] Indeed, many such sayings pertain directly to the Gospel, having been drawn from the promise about the Messiah.

These differences must be carefully weighed so that we learn how to make use of Solomon's maxims. In short, it is necessary to observe what distinguishes Solomon from the pagan writers. It is likewise necessary to observe what variety of maxims exists in Solomon's [Proverbs] and to give due attention to the central topics of the church's teaching: Law and Gospel, the worship of God, political governance, and domestic life. All maxims in this book must be thoughtfully interpreted in light

---

[15] Perhaps referring to Prov. 11:15 or 22:26.

[16] The Latin expression Melanchthon uses is *Sponde, damnum praesto est*; in some other renditions of the phrase, *noxa* replaces *damnum*. This expression originated with a Greek saying of Thales found on an inscription at a temple in Delphi dedicated to Apollo: Ἐγγύα πάρα δ' ἄτη. A more literal translation of this Greek expression is something like, "Make a pledge, and ruin is at hand," with the general meaning that bad things happen when one makes rash promises or pledges. See Erasmus, *Adages* 1.6.97; Plato, *Charmides* 165a; and Pliny, *Natural History* vii.119.

[17] The first table is understood to be the first three commandments: "You shall have no other gods; You shall not take the name of the Lord … in vain; Remember the Sabbath Day." (Lutherans did not count the command against graven images as separate from the first commandment.)

of these topics. There is no doubt that this distinction and description through the use of something like classes or groupings is necessary when reading this book.[18] So let the reader understand that the maxims in this book are designed to admonish us about the most important matters in all the duties of life, so that the reader will search out for himself that phase of life to which every saying corresponds: the stages of the human life, dangers, and the kind of specific cases this wisest king may be considering, namely, where he wishes to teach and admonish the reader and where he wishes to console him. For some sayings are didactic, some exhortatory, and others consolatory.[19]

Although the admonition I have just outlined is essential for the reader to recognize in order to distinguish Solomon's maxims into groupings or classes, there is one more admonition that must be added. Solomon himself commenced Proverbs with the following sayings: "The fear of the Lord is the beginning of wisdom."[20] Likewise, "Have faith in the Lord with all your heart, and do not lean on your understanding."[21] Solomon wants to elucidate in all circumstances the knowledge and invocation of the true God, who revealed himself to this very people of Israel by the proclamation of the Law and promises regarding the Messiah. By the use of the name Jehovah, Solomon differentiated this true God from all of the fabricated deities that were worshiped among the nations.[22] Likewise, Solomon made this distinction because it ensured that God was preached in the church of Israel, and Solomon orders the teaching of this God to be heard. And political and familial obedience are pleasing to God when the faith upon which we stand brings to light that God is kind to us on account

---

[18] Melanchthon here describes his *loci* method of interpretation. See the Introduction, pp. xxi–xxiii.

[19] In Greek, διδασκαλικά, παραινετικά, παρηγορικά. See Daniel Gross, "Melanchthon's Rhetoric and the Practical Origins of Reformation Human Science," *History of the Human Sciences* 13, no. 3 (2000): 5–22.

[20] Prov. 1:7.

[21] Prov. 3:5.

[22] At this time, the Christian Hebraists combined the pointing for Adonai with the letters for the divine name YHWH to vocalize the latter as JeHoVaH.

of his Son the Mediator, and on account of him we are heard. And we ask for both families and their homes to be ruled by the Holy Spirit and for the church to be preserved. Let us understand that Solomon embraces this entire teaching in his use of these frequently repeated sayings about the fear of God and faith. And when you hear other political or domestic maxims, let your mind always join them with those preceding things, written as a kind of superscription. Indeed, may your mind regard the very Son of God as already publicly displayed, as crucified, as resurrected, and as reigning at the right hand of the Everlasting Father, and may your mind understand the voice of the Gospel regarding reconciliation and faith. Thereafter may your mind differentiate obedience to the mandated duties of life from that of the pagans, and may it know that such obedience is pleasing to God on account of the Mediator.

Alexander of Macedonia commends the following verse of Homer: "both a mighty king and a strong spearman."[23] And it was such for the first five years [of Alexander's rule]. Nonetheless, he neither acknowledges nor prays to God. Neither does he connect obedience to the illumining of God's glory.[24] Jehoshaphat read a similar maxim among these admonitions of Solomon, from whom he descended: "Lying lips are not becoming for a king."[25] Therefore Jehoshaphat governs the tongue with a greater zeal, offers promises, detests the kind of artifice that resides in so many courts, and restrains sophistical matters in religion and in court cases. Jehoshaphat knows that such diligence is a great honor and is salutary to many, which Solon, Aristides, and

---

[23] Homer, *Iliad* 3.179; *The Iliad*, trans. Robert Fagles (London: Penguin, 1990), 134. The Greek verse Melanchthon quotes is ἀμφότερον βασιλεύς τ' ἀγαθὸς κρατερός τ' αἰχμητής. In this section of the *Iliad*, Helen is describing Agamemnon to King Priam of Troy. The praise is supposedly from Alexander the Great.

[24] Cf. Matt. 5:16.

[25] Prov. 17:7. For more on King Jehoshaphat, see 2 Chron. 17–20.

[Gaius] Laelius also see.[26] In these offices, however, Jehoshaphat has respect for God, acknowledges the Messiah, and admits to having been received on account of this boundless mercy. Moreover, he has known the reasons why the entire nation that he serves has been constituted, and, acknowledging the Mediator, he pleads for and expects help and orients all his labors toward preserving the teaching about him. In this way, Jehoshaphat adds many virtues that are not found in Solon, Aristides, Laelius, and others. In this manner, therefore, all of the political and domestic sayings in this book must be understood as the teaching about good works that the church always includes in the teaching about the Son of God, namely, fear, faith, and true prayer.[27] It is necessary to be reminded of these things at the very beginning of this book. Afterward the reading will be both more useful and sweeter.

Now concerning the maxims themselves, I will not add any commendation other than what is the main point: that these oracles are the voice of the Son of God in the church, that they are in agreement with God's Law and the Gospel, and that they contain the most useful admonitions touching on all the very many duties and dangers of life. Therefore, they should be read on a daily basis among readers of all ages. For both the young and the old will learn many things by reading them. The wisdom will be all the sweeter where the weightiest admonitions receive good and studious consideration.

But why am I trying to invite readers with my own words when the book itself offers its own invitation? For it is not the voice of Solomon alone that calls forth, but the book itself also contains the voice of God: "O men, I call forth to you, and my voice to human sons: Listen ... I have existed from eternity, before heaven, earth, and the abyss came into being. I have always been with the Master Builder ... I play with the globe of the earth, and my delights are to look after the salvation

---

[26] Aristides (530–468 BCE) was an ancient Athenian statesman nicknamed "the Just," and Laelius (d. after 160 BCE) was a Roman statesman and general during the second Punic War.

[27] This statement demonstrates Melanchthon's single-minded adherence to justification by faith alone without works in his exegesis.

of people.... Blessed are those who keep my ways."[28] In this way, divine wisdom invites all people to this very book. Therefore, if readers are not moved by this authority, they are harder to move than all the rocks in the Caucasus [Mountains].[29]

For among our chief duties is to accustom the young to read this in the schools. Therefore, some time last year I again lectured on this book. I know that the fullness of the things mentioned here cannot be comprehended by anyone's exposition. Indeed, our explication is quite gaunt and thin. Nevertheless, I did not object when the printers published it because I thought this new edition would perhaps invite many to read the book of Proverbs.[30]

The reason I have affixed your name to this edition is not only because I know that, given your excellence of temperament and virtue, you will eagerly read the admonitions of this wisest of kings. It is also for this reason: Since I dedicated a former edition twenty years earlier to your cousin, the illustrious Prince Magnus III,[31] Duke of Mecklenburg, I determined to send you this recent edition so that the gift formerly sent to him would remain in your family and in which, as I desire with my whole heart, Solomon's voice may always thereby be heard. Prince Magnus III listened to this voice very devoutly, and since he directed both his private and public attention to the application of these policies, he earned the best from his land. He assisted his wisest father with great reverence in his governing duties, he ordered churches to be rightly instructed, and he was guardian of the two best things: the purity of its teaching and the harmony of those being taught. Prince Magnus III also fostered the study of literature, which

---

[28] Prov. 8:4, 23, 31–32. In traditional Christian interpretation, this chapter has always been connected to Christ.

[29] For a reference to the stoniness of the Caucasus Mountains, see Virgil, *Aeneid* 4.366.

[30] The first version of this book was published in 1550 and as a replacement for Melanchthon's 1529 *Nova scholia*. See the Introduction, pp. xiv–xvii.

[31] Magnus III (1509–1550) was elected bishop in 1516 and began introducing Reformation reforms in the early 1530s. Melanchthon is reflecting on his recent death.

he deeply loved since he was very clearly learned. And since he drew the teaching of the church out of its wellsprings,[32] he constantly read Latin and Greek histories, and from that most learned man, Arnold Burenius,[33] he became accustomed to fashioning a Latin speech so that he could both speak and write Latin correctly and excellently. In short, Prince Magnus III is an example of a good and balanced prince both in his public and his private life.

And so you see not only how much not only his native land but also the neighboring peoples were affected by his ardent yearning. But as the prophet said, "The righteous are summoned out of this mortal life lest they see the bad things coming."[34] In a similar way, God also took the prince into the fellowship of the eternal church, where now among the best princes—David, Jehoshaphat, Hezekiah, Josiah, and similar ones—he enjoys the sweetest vision and conversations of God and our Lord Jesus Christ, which the prince had desired in this life with the most ardent vows. Therefore, let us give thanks for these heavenly blessings.

And because God wishes some in the warfare of this life to be survivors, we pray that the Son of God, the Guardian of his church, our Lord Jesus Christ, would himself govern us, make us a "vessel of mercy"[35] and instruments of salvation, as well as preserve the churches and their friendly bonds. For it is utterly true that these things cannot be preserved by human wisdom alone; rather, they are preserved by the Son of God, who sits at the right hand of the Eternal Father and defends his assemblies, his inheritance, out of his boundless goodness.

---

[32] This phrase of drawing from the founts (*ex fontibus*) or returning to the founts (*ad fontes*) is a typical humanist one.

[33] Arnold Burenius (1485–1566), or Arnold Wormach, studied at the University of Wittenberg, where he befriended Melanchthon. He was the teacher of the duke and later a professor on the Arts Faculty at the University of Rostock in northern Germany.

[34] Perhaps a paraphrase of Isa. 57:1.

[35] Rom. 9:23. Here Melanchthon uses the Greek from the passage, σκεύη ἐλέους, rather than the Latin.

Therefore, may you most eagerly receive from me this book, for in it mention has been made about your cousin. If he were still alive, he would also exhort you to better familiarize yourself with Solomon's Proverbs by reading them.

But concerning my commentary, I shall add nothing more than that I am doing this out of pious zeal so that good books may be in the hands of students. And as far as both this book and all my other writings are concerned, I entrust them to the judgment of the churches and schools of these regions, which have embraced the Confession presented to Emperor Charles [V] at the Diet of Augsburg in the year 1530.[36] For I do not embrace any other kind of doctrine except that very one, which I know to be the everlasting voice of the church of Christ. I wish you a happy and hearty farewell. In the year 1555.[37]

Your Excellency's most devoted Philip Melanthon.[38]

---

[36] Already in 1533, this confession became the standard for teaching and was included in the statutes of the theology faculty at the University of Wittenberg, written by Melanchthon.

[37] In the 1555 commentary, the year was changed from 1550.

[38] In the 1530s, in part because of a speech impediment, Melanchthon changed the spelling of his name to "Melanthon."

Preface

[The Two Methods of Instruction]

It is commonly suggested that there are two methods of instruction. The first is the entire dialectical method, which proceeds in an orderly fashion like the construction of an entire building and which seeks to collect a whole system of doctrine into one. This method is similar to how a doctor first addresses the structure of the body, then its body parts and humors, thereafter the causes and origins of sicknesses, and, finally, the potential remedies.

The second method of instruction consists of the handing down of short maxims such as aphorisms. These maxims often proceed indiscriminately without any particular care to order. In this way, they are like the ethical precepts that Phocylides, Theognis,[1] and others wrote. Such is the collection of maxims here in the book of Solomon, whose title in the Latin edition is *Proverbs*. Although there is now among the Greeks a distinction between the terms *maxims*[2] and *proverbs*,[3] just

---

[1] Phocylides and Theognis were popular Greek poets who lived contemporaneously during the sixth century BCE.

[2] Translating the Greek γνώμας and Latin *sententias* as "maxims" in English.

[3] Translating the Greek παροιμίας and Latin *proverbia* as "proverbs" in English.

as there is in Latin, in Hebrew only one word is used indiscriminately to signify these two.[4]

[Maxims and Proverbs]

A maxim is a short saying containing a precept about customs, or a warning about rewards and punishments, or a description of various consequences in life, which, when contemplated, are also useful as a warning.[5] Examples of precepts include: "Scorn pleasure, for pleasure hurts if it is purchased with pain."[6] "Remember to distrust."[7] "Know yourself."[8] An example of a precept about rewards and punishments is "The best blessings fall on the children of the godly, not the ungodly."[9] And, finally, precepts about consequences include: "Feelings run wild in prosperity."[10] Or "Fate makes a fool out of the one she favors."[11]

In contrast to a maxim, a proverb is a celebrated saying. For the most part, a proverb draws its meaning from the use of metaphor, comparison, image, hyperbole, or irony. Although a proverb may

---

[4] For more on this longstanding Greek distinction, see Sibylle Hallik, *Sententia und Proverbium: Begriffsgeschichte und Texttheorie in Antike und Mittelalter* (Cologne: Böhlau, 2007), 94. The Hebrew word Melanchthon is referring to is מָשָׁל, *mashal*.

[5] Nicolaus the Sophist writes as follows, "Maxim (*gnome*) is a general statement, giving some counsel and advice for something useful in life." In *Progymnasmata: Greek Textbooks of Prose Composition and Rhetoric*, ed. George Kennedy (Leiden: Society of Biblical Literature, 2003), 142.

[6] Horace, *Epistle* 2.

[7] Epicharmus, *Fragment* 250, cited here in the Greek.

[8] This popular Greek saying has been attributed to countless authors, including Socrates.

[9] Theocritus, *Idylls* 26.32. Melanchthon also uses this Greek quotation in a letter written in September of 1557 on behalf of Theophilus Gryneaus. See MBW 8372.

[10] Ovid, *Art of Love* 2.437. Ovid (43 BCE–17/18 CE) was a famous Latin poet during Augustus's reign.

[11] Publilius Syrus, *Sentences* 271.

contain a maxim, it may simply offer some kind of description stated in another way. For example, "To pour words into a vessel with holes in it."[12] "On the first day of the Greek month."[13] "May he go to the crows!"[14] Or "More changing than the moon."[15] These, and many others, do not contain any maxims. Rather, some signify figuratively a time, some a place, or some other circumstances.

Even though there is a difference between a proverb and a maxim, it is nevertheless true that many proverbs are simultaneously maxims. For example, "You have seized Sparta; now adorn it."[16] This is a maxim admonishing each person to recognize his calling (as we say), to maintain his goals before him, and to rightly do those things that are his duty to perform. This is also a proverb, since it has been adorned with a figure of speech and is a very popular saying. Here is

---

[12] Plautus, *Pseudolus* 1.3.135. The Latin expression is [*Ingerere dicta in*] *dolium pertusum*. As it is pointless to pour something into a vessel that will immediately leak, this saying meant something like "to sing before a deaf person's door."

[13] Suetonius, *Ad Calendas Graecas* in *The Twelve Ceasars* 87.1. This common Latin expression, *Ad Calendas Graecas*, referred to a day or time that never occurred since only the Romans, not the Greeks, began their calendar month on calends. In English, it would mean something like "when pigs fly" or "when hell freezes over."

[14] Aristophanes, *Plutus*, line 604, based on the ancient Greek phrase πάει στα κοράκια or ἔρρε ἐς κόρακας. The Latin phrase is, *Eat ad corvos*. Because the ancients associated crows with death (and the eating of flesh), the phrase meant something like "May he go to hell!"

[15] The Latin phrase is *Euripo mutabilior* and is based on the constant waxing and waning of the moon.

[16] This Latin phrase, *Spartam nactus es, hanc orna*, is derived from the Greek expression, Σπάρταν ἔλαχες, ταύτην κόσμει, found in Plutarch, *Morals* 472e and 602b. It is also found in Euripides, *Telephus* § 739; Cicero, *To Atticus* 4.6.2; and Erasmus, *Adages* 2.5.1. It was the phrase that Agamemnon spoke to Menelaus after conquering Sparta. It means that one should make the best out of any particular situation.

another example: "We do not see the knapsack on our back."[17] This is a maxim, and it rebukes the kind of blind self-love[18] that judges others more harshly than we judge ourselves. At the same time it is a proverb since it is figurative and also a very popular saying. Here are examples of other sayings that are both maxims and proverbs: "The judge forgives the crows but harasses the doves."[19] "Turtles conquer strength and wisdom" (in which "turtle" means money).[20] Although there are many such sayings in this little book that are both maxims and proverbs, the title of *Proverbs* is not altogether inappropriate. For whether the title were to be *Maxims* or *Proverbs*, it is necessary to recognize that this collection is a treasure of the sweetest maxims, which contain precepts touching on all of the virtues.

[The Two Tables of the Law]

We often teach that the sum of the teaching about the virtues should be understood in some way as put into the frame of the Ten Commandments. This approach should likewise be taken here so that the classifications of the maxims are organized according to the Ten Commandments. Some maxims speak of the so-called first table of the law, others of the second.[21] These classifications can be understood

---

[17] Catullus, *Songs* 22.21.

[18] Melanchthon uses here a Greek term, φιλαυτίαν, instead of a Latin one.

[19] Juvenal, *Satires*, book 1, satura 2, line 63. This Latin phrase, *Dat veniam corvis, vexat censura columbas*, means that the real culprits are set free while the innocent parties are punished.

[20] Erasmus, *Adages* 2.4.87. According to Erasmus (CWE 33:232–33), the ancient Greek people of Aegina "had a piece of money stamped with the figure of a snail with this motto." The Greek phrase is Τὰν ἀρετὰν και τὰν σοφίαν νικάντι χελῶναι. The Latin is *Virtutem et sapientiam vincunt testudines*. Melanchthon gives both versions.

[21] Following medieval tradition, Melanchthon and Luther counted the first three commandments (having no other gods, not taking God's name in vain, and remembering the Sabbath) as the first table having to do with God, and the remaining seven as having to do with human relations, where the government is included in honoring parents.

as follows: Some maxims are theological, meaning that they preach God and the precepts of the first table of the law. Some are political, meaning that they address the duties of governmental leaders. Some are ethical, meaning that they give instruction concerning the common customs of all. And some are domestic [or familial], meaning that they speak about issues surrounding marriage and the way households should be governed.[22]

To be sure, the maxims spoken from all languages of the world are pleasing, since they concisely offer instruction on worthy matters, and they are as eagerly pursued for the constant counsel they provide on so great a variety of human situations. Nevertheless, a singular sweetness both in the forms used and in the content itself must be recognized in these most ancient sayings of Solomon. For many of these maxims teach about hidden affections of the heart, many about the reasons and causes of the greatest changes in life, and many about the significant upheavals in government, which upheavals are not like the pastoral or bucolic literature [in Greek and Latin thought],[23] as many suppose. How pleasant is the depiction of marriage [in Proverbs] when it portrays the mutual, pure, sincere, and sweet love of a husband and wife—a love displaying nothing of pretense, nothing of mistrust, nothing of acrimony—with the image of a fawn and gazelle![24] How great is the sweetness of a concise precept: "May your fountains be dispersed outdoors," "and may you remain their lord"![25] What is lovelier than fountains and rivers watering both your gardens and those of your

---

[22] For Melanchthon, the political, ethical, and familial maxims all relate to the second table of the law.

[23] This reference to rustic and "Bucolica" matters speaks to the so-called pastoral literature of the classical tradition. While Theocritus wrote *Idylls* in Greek, the Roman poet Virgil did so in Latin. Virgil, in particular, wrote a very influential set of pastoral poems called *Ecloga*, or *Bucolica*, which connected to the bucolic life while noteworthy revolutions were taking place in Rome in the first century BCE.

[24] Prov. 5:19; see also Song 4:5 and 7:5.

[25] Prov. 5:16, 15. Melanchthon is using the Vulgate and Hebrew here in contrast to the Septuagint, the latter of which supplies "not."

neighbors? What eloquent teaching is contained in this saying! Not only does it commend the distinction of powers, but it also advises justice and frugality so that each person may possess his own things,[26] stay away from those things belonging to another, diligently cultivate his own lands, and also exercise benevolence so that he may help others with the fruits of his labor lest he be driven out of the land. Such are the many maxims in this whole collection, which maxims communicate the greatest things in the loveliest images and in the sweetest figures.

[The Maxims of the Greeks and the Maxims of the Church]

It is also necessary at the outset to be reminded of the great distinction that exists between the secular collection of maxims[27] of both Phocylides and Theognis and those handed down by Solomon to the church of God, just as it is said that there is a distinction between other things of this kind and between philosophy and the teaching heard in the church.[28]

Just as philosophy preserves a small part of the law, so, for example, Phocylides says something about the wrath of God and the punishment of the wicked. Though offering many precepts pertaining to the second table of the Ten Commandments, however, he does not say anything about the Mediator, the forgiveness of sins, reconciliation, the true invocation of God, faith and hope, and the presence of God amid our misfortunes. Solomon, by contrast, frequently preaches about the true knowledge and invocation of God as well as the remaining virtues pertaining to the first table of the law. For example, "The fear

---

[26] This statement echoes the traditional definition of justice as "to each his or her own," found in Cicero and Aristotle among others. Here the masculine reflects Melanchthon's view of society, where men owned property.

[27] In Greek, γνωμολογίας.

[28] See Sachiko Kusukawa, *The Transformation of Natural Philosophy: The Case of Philip Melanchthon* (Cambridge: Cambridge University Press, 1995); and Timothy J. Wengert, *Human Freedom, Christian Righteousness: Philip Melanchthon's Exegetical Dispute with Erasmus of Rotterdam* (Oxford: Oxford University Press, 1998).

of the Lord is the beginning of wisdom."[29] Likewise, "Trust in the Lord with all your heart and do not rest on your own understanding; in all your ways acknowledge him, and he will direct your steps."[30] Concerning the cross, Solomon says, "For the Lord chastens those whom he loves,"[31] lest you withdraw from him. And concerning the salvation that follows this life, "The righteous person places hope in his death."[32]

[Law and Gospel]

Emperor Julian[33] set Phocylides against Solomon when he argued that the greater wisdom to be handed down in prophetic and apostolic books was nothing that was not also found in the writings of the pagan Greeks.[34] But when Cyril refuted Julian,[35] he gave preference to Solomon over Phocylides only because Solomon had lived in an age before Phocylides. For Phocylides, who was from Miletus, and Theognis, who was from Megara, lived in the age of Cyrus the Great

---

[29] Prov. 1:7. Melanchthon picks up this same theme in the epistle dedicatory. See pp. 6–10 above.

[30] Prov. 3:5–6.

[31] Prov. 3:12.

[32] Prov. 14:32.

[33] For Julian the Apostate, see p. 6, n. 5.

[34] Here is what Julian wrote: "But has any medical art appeared among the Hebrews, such as that the Greeks know from Hippocrates, or the schools that came after him? Can we say that their wisest man Solomon should be compared to a Phocylides, a Theognis or Isocrates among the Greeks? Surely if you could compare the exhortations of Isocrates with the proverbs of Solomon you would concede, no doubt, that the heir of Theodorus is wiser far than the very wisest king [of the Hebrews]." See Julian, *Against the Galileans*, ed. and trans. R. Joseph Hoffmann (Amherst, NY: Prometheus, 2004), 120.

[35] For Cyril of Alexandria, see p. 7, n. 7.

and Thales.36 But this childish response does not satisfy the magnitude of this dispute. For I said earlier concerning the true wellsprings of teachings that something is either a teaching of Law or a teaching of Gospel. And I conceded that Phocylides spoke about the good part of the Law. However, there is another teaching that is proper to the church, namely, the revelation of God, having been made by clear testimonies about the promises that have been fulfilled, about the Gospel that announces the forgiveness of sins and offers eternal life through the Son of God, and about the comfort found in the cross. Concerning these matters of the highest importance, pagan authors are silent. This distinction must always be kept in view so that it is known what teaching is proper to the church.

[Promises about the Messiah]

In this preface, the following must also be added. Because this book was written in the true church of God, in which the promise about the Messiah was known, let us understand him and his will so that faith may show the way and we may observe the Messiah being referenced in all of the maxims, whether speaking of faith or speaking of works. Proverbs 3 says, "Trust in the Lord with all of your heart."37 You must understand this saying in reference to the Mediator, just as David had taught before: "Kiss the Son"38 and "Blessed are all those who trust in him."39 For Solomon expressly ordered the teaching handed down among this people from God to be embraced. And where there is mention of faith, it is necessary to observe the promises. And when

---

36 Cyrus the Great, or Cyrus II of Persia, founded the Achaemenid Empire. Thales of Miletus was an early philosopher in the Greek tradition. Both men, like Phocylides and Theognis, lived during the sixth century BCE.

37 Prov. 3:5.

38 Ps. 2:12a. This version, "Osculamini Filium," comes from Tremellius, not the Vulgate.

39 Ps. 2:12b.

it says about marriage, "Rejoice with the wife of your youth,"[40] you must understand this saying, with faith showing the way, that these works, which have been divinely ordained, please God because of the Mediator. In this way, therefore, the teaching about the Messiah, which has been handed down more clearly in Psalms and the Old Testament Prophets, must everywhere be embraced. Still, because mention is made about the wisdom of God that was preached to the human race,[41] the wisdom the Son has sent to the church is also signified. And Solomon commands that this teaching, which was handed down to these people by God, must be known. Likewise, when mention is made of faith and eternal life, it is necessary to consider these promises.

---

[40] Prov. 5:18 (Vulgate). Melanchthon will come back to this interpretation in remarks on Prov. 31.

[41] Prov. 8.

Chapter 1

Proposition

"These are the proverbs of Solomon, who was David's son, the king of Israel, who has written them down for you to learn wisdom, instruction, and prudence; to receive intelligence, justice, judgment, and uprightness; so that circumspection may be given to the heedless and knowledge and consideration given to the young."[1]

[The First] Admonition

"The wise will listen and will increase in knowledge, and the intelligent will possess wisdom, and will understand proverbs and the interpretation of the words and the riddles of the wise."[2]

First Precept

The fear of the Lord is the beginning of wisdom. Fools despise wisdom and instruction.[3]

The proposition is clear in which Solomon says that he has collected these proverbs for this great benefit: to admonish the unlearned and the youth so that they might learn and be prevailed upon to gain

---

[1] Prov. 1:1–4.
[2] Prov. 1:5–6.
[3] Prov. 1:7.

discipline in the governance of their behavior toward both God and human beings. Solomon describes such benefits in many words, the appropriate meanings of which are considered below:

- *Wisdom* signifies the knowledge of God with which true fear and true faith shine forth in the heart.
- *Instruction* [*disciplina*], or perhaps *learning* [*eruditio*], is, generally speaking, preparation or the first principles [*institutio*] of education.
- *Prudence* signifies the governance of one's behavior.
- *Intelligence* signifies the type of discernment needed to make a difficult decision after many possible options have been set forth. Examples include the time when, against the opinions of others, Jeremiah recommended surrender and when Zechariah recommended accepting servitude rather than preparing for rebellion.[4]
- *Righteousness*, generally speaking, signifies obedience to all commandments.
- *Judgment* signifies indictment, chastisement, and penalty.
- *Uprightness* is the opposite of hypocrisy, and it could be described as integrity.
- *Circumspection* is the opposite of foolishness, which rushes hastily without consideration.
- *Knowledge* signifies selecting something [better over something else].
- *Consideration* is the same as deliberation. It is what arises in the face of different options relating to places, times, and persons.

---

[4] See Jer. 27–28 and, for Zechariah ben Jehoiada, 2 Chron. 24:20–24.

[The Second Admonition]

"The wise will listen and will increase ..."[5]

Solomon adds to the proposition an admonition that is necessary for the hearer. The wise hearer will increase in knowledge just as the Lord says: "It will be given to the one who has."[6] Likewise, "He will give the Holy Spirit to those who ask,"[7] but not to those who despise and resist the Holy Spirit through a barbaric and cyclopic ferocity. Here he says that those who despise God, such as Epicureans and those like them,[8] do not increase in knowledge, but others, in whom exist the beginnings of the fear of God and who ask to be ruled by God, will. As it is said, "Ask and you will receive."[9]

The First Precept

Solomon now begins [examining] the precepts of which the first is, namely, the fear of the true God. For because he speaks about the JEHOVA who is celebrated among God's people, Solomon leads us first toward the knowledge of the teaching about the true God, and he wants the true invocation [of God] to be distinguished from the worship practices of other nations.

It is customary, however, for the Fear of God to designate the complete and true worship of God rather than an idolatrous worship, or a universal obedience in accord with all the commandments as in the following saying: "Blessed are all those who fear the Lord."[10] This fear first includes the knowledge of true teaching, then fear that is understood through the senses, and finally faith which—when true

---

[5] Prov. 1:5.

[6] Matt. 25:29.

[7] Luke 11:13.

[8] Melanchthon, who knew the origins of this philosophy, often lumped Epicureans with the Stoics and labeled Lorenzo Valla and, at times, Ulrich Zwingli as contemporary fatalists.

[9] Matt. 7:7.

[10] Ps. 128:1 (Vulgate 127:1).

invocation has been added to it—distinguishes this fear from a servile or ungodly fear that flees from and grumbles against God.[11] Likewise included here with the true knowledge of God, true fear, and faith is prayer that asks for and receives reconciliation and that asks and hopes for help in all of life's choices. But this saying about the "beginning" should not be understood as referring just to the onset [of one's faith life] but to its entirety; hence the saying could be stated as follows: "The fear of the Lord is the sum total of wisdom, which governs all choices in both favorable and unfavorable situations."

"Listen, son, to your father's learning, and do not dismiss your mother's law."[12]

Solomon discussed earlier the sum total of teaching and of worship: that "the beginning of wisdom is the fear of the Lord." Now he directs attention to those persons teaching, and he orders them to be heard because it is necessary for there to be a ministry of teaching and a ministry of listening. Thus the first ranking in the order of persons is that of parents. Their primary duty is to correctly hand down the teaching about God to their children, just as it was written to the Ephesians: "Bring up children in the teaching and instruction of the Lord."[13] This saying should be joined to the earlier one: "Listen to your father's learning," namely, his teaching about the fear of the Lord. Listen to the very teaching that sounds forth in the church of Israel,[14] as he called this also by the name "your mother's law," namely, the church's law, which has been handed down by God through the sure and clear testimonies in Israel.

---

[11] This is a standard medieval distinction between *timor filialis* and *timor servilis*. See Heiko A. Oberman, *The Harvest of Medieval Theology* (Cambridge, MA: Harvard University Press, 1963), 475–76.

[12] Prov. 1:8.

[13] Eph. 6:4.

[14] For Melanchthon, this seemingly anachronistic term points to his conviction that the word "church" is defined by the proclamation of God's Word and thus existed from the beginning of the world through Israel to the present.

CHAPTER I

In this way, let us recognize ourselves to be bound to a certain kind of teaching when Solomon says, "Do not dismiss your mother's law." For the church of Israel is signified in the name "mother's." And it is clear that this command has been repeated often so that we would cherish only that kind of teaching that has been handed down to the church in the prophetic and apostolic writings. As the Eternal Father says of the Son: "Listen to him ..."[15] And the Lord says, "Whoever loves me, will keep my Word, and my Father will love that one ..."[16] And just as the Lord adds there the most supreme promise of all to this precept about the knowledge and declaration of teaching, in the same way Solomon adds here a more charming promise—a metaphor taken from childish adornments [namely, a crown and necklace].[17] *Crown* signifies kingdom, or perhaps preeminence, with a meaning as follows: God will place you among sound leaders. He will advance and aid your counsels so that they are salutary for both you and the people with the result that you are "a vessel of mercy"[18] to yourself and to the people like Samuel, David, Jehoshaphat, Hezekiah,[19] but not "a vessel of wrath"[20] like Saul, Absalom, or Ahithophel.[21] *Adornments of the neck* signify eloquence, that is, sound teaching and sound plans. God will adorn you with these extraordinary gifts if only you listen to your mother's law.

---

[15] Luke 9:35.

[16] John 14:23.

[17] Prov. 1:9.

[18] Rom. 9:23.

[19] Samuel was Israel's last judge, David was the king of the united Israel, and the others were kings of Judah.

[20] Rom. 9:22.

[21] For more on Absalom, see 2 Sam. 13–17; for more on Ahithophel and his advice to Absalom, see 2 Sam. 15–17.

"My son, if sinners should entice you, do not consent." [22]

This admonition is aimed against enticements that draw many away from God, namely, against the great number of evil people and their corresponding evil ways.

"The net is spread in vain before the bird." [23]

That is, even though evil people think that they have concealed themselves like bird catchers hiding themselves [in search of their prey], they are not concealed. For God the Vindicator sees all things. As Psalm 58 says, "There is, indeed, a God who judges people on earth."[24] And as it says in Psalm 62, "You repay everyone according to his works."[25] Therefore Solomon urges us, lest aroused by the many examples and corresponding evil ways of the ungodly, we act against God. Then Solomon adds a threat of punishment. Among possible punishments, this is a most grievous one: "Then they will call [upon me], and I will not hear them."[26] But God does not want the lapsed [sinner] to be unable to turn to repentance; nor does he want repentance to be without benefit. On the contrary, he calls us to repentance, and he promises a lessening of immediate punishments as well as the remission of eternal punishment, as it is said in Isaiah: "Even if your sins are as scarlet, you will be as white as snow."[27] However, this is the meaning of the saying: Those who repent are heard before punishment. But when punishment comes, and is already present, [then] if it is bodily punishment, it is lessened for the one who repents; but

---

[22] Prov. 1:10.
[23] Prov. 1:17.
[24] Ps. 58:11 (Vulgate 57:12).
[25] Ps. 62:12 (Vulgate 61:13).
[26] Prov. 1:28.
[27] Isa. 1:18.

if it is eternal punishment, there is no favorable hearing, as in the destruction of Saul and Judas [Iscariot].[28] In short, it is an antithesis: The one who listens or obeys reposes in peace.

---

[28] Medieval theologians often distinguished between the repentance of Saul and Judas and that of David and Peter, a theme also sounded in an early struggle between Johann Agricola (1494–1566) and Melanchthon. See Timothy J. Wengert, *Law and Gospel: Philip Melanchthon's Debate with John Agricola of Eisleben over "Poenitentia"* (Grand Rapids: Baker, 1997).

Chapter 2

The entire second chapter is an exhortation for listening to and putting into practice this teaching that God has handed down to the church. Solomon not only binds us to this teaching, but he commands us to flee from any kind of foreign wisdom that battles against it. For Solomon understands the phrase "the adulterous woman"[1] figuratively as a wisdom that seduces people's minds away from God. For he expressly says that such a roving woman abandons her headmaster, namely, God the Teacher, to whom she had been betrothed. For this kind of mind is like an adulterous woman who, upon abandoning and rejecting her true master to whom she had been betrothed, roves around impudently and frolics about with wicked opinions, as the Epicureans rejoice in their impudence and idolaters rejoice in their worship because they think that they experience great success and all good things on account of them.

Solomon also adds in this chapter both promises and threats. For as the saying goes, "First seek God's kingdom, and then all things will be added to you …"[2] And as it is stated in Psalm 1: "Blessed is the one who …"[3] Solomon also teaches us how we may increase [in knowledge], for he combines two causes: God's aid and our diligence. As it is stated elsewhere, "How much more so will [your heavenly

---

[1] Prov. 30:20.
[2] Matt. 6:33.
[3] Ps. 1:1.

Father] give the Holy Spirit to those who ask."[4] Likewise, "Ask and it will be given to you. Seek and you will find ..."[5] And in Wisdom 6: "Wisdom is easily found by those who love her, and she anticipates those who desire her."[6] These verses promise aid to those who take to heart Solomon's teachings.

---

[4] Luke 11:13.

[5] Matt. 7:7.

[6] Wis. 6:12–13 (Vulgate 6:13–14).

Chapter 3

In the beginning of the third chapter, exhortations have been repeated and a promise inserted: "Mercy and truth will not abandon you,"[1] that is, the mercy of God. This phrase is commonly used to speak about both God and humankind: He has extended mercy and truth, that is, he has offered kindness and faithfulness. For example, Jonathan extended mercy and truth to David by being kind and faithful toward him, which is to say, Jonathan loved him and blessed David without deception or limit. Thus, it is said here that God will bless you [and will do it] faithfully, that is, God will always protect you in accordance with the following saying: "The one who fears the Lord will lack no good thing."[2]

Precepts

[First precept:] *"Trust in the Lord with all your heart."*[3]

Three precepts now follow in this chapter. The first concerns the knowledge, faith, and fear of God; the second, the preservation of the ministry of teaching; and the third, the cross. This teaching is most evident in each of the precepts. Solomon first gives a precept about faith, and then the antithesis is added: "and do not lean on your own

---

[1] Prov. 3:3.

[2] Ps. 34:10b (Vulgate 33:10b).

[3] Prov. 3:5a.

understanding,"[4] which may be understood as referring to these three categories: the knowledge of God, morals, and advice to choose those things which are most profitable. [It is as if Solomon were saying here:] "As you come to recognize God as he revealed himself in this teaching, I do not want you to wander around like pagans, nor invent new deities, contrive new worship practices, or make novel conjectures when it comes to God. Rather, I want you to behave according to what has been prescribed, not allowing your imaginations to run wild like the Spartans who departed from the practice of requiring a marriage contract between a man and a woman. (In fact, the pope also prohibits marriage.) When faced with the choice of profitable outcomes, I want you to follow my precepts and to do what is appropriate. I do not want you to be overly inquisitive.[5] Nor do I want you, whether out of curiosity or out of fear, to try anything that is beyond your calling. May you, instead, be mindful of the saying from Ezekiel: 'Walk in my precepts.'"[6]

[Second precept:] *"Honor the Lord with all your resources ..."*[7]

Solomon commands each and every individual to assist in the preservation of the ministry of teaching in churches[8] as well as in schools, and a most sweet promise has also been added as is also in the Gospel of Matthew: "The one who gives a cup of water to one of the least of my little ones on account of [their] teaching will have a reward."[9]

---

[4] Prov. 3:5b

[5] Here Melanchthon uses the Greek term πολυπραγμοσύνη, which translates to something like "one who conducts too much business." It carries connotations, however, of someone who is a busybody, officious, or meddlesome.

[6] Ezek. 36:27.

[7] Prov. 3:9.

[8] Here Melanchthon uses the Latin word *templis*, ordinarily translated as "temples," but it is clear from context, and precedence in Wittenberg statutes, that "churches" (*ecclesiis*) is what he means.

[9] Matt. 10:42.

Chapter 3

[Third precept:] *"Do not reject the correction of the Lord, and do not despise his reproof."*[10]

Here the entire teaching of the cross must be understood, and a distinction between Philosophy and Gospel must also be made. Philosophy and human reason, for example, think about the causes of death and the causes of human calamity in a way that is decidedly different from the proclamation of the Gospel. To be sure, it is necessary to understand the reasons why the church was subjected to the cross. Thereupon, the philosophical and evangelical topics of consolation may be compared. Indeed, Christian suffering[11] and philosophical suffering must be distinguished.

"Blessed is the one who finds wisdom ..."[12]

Solomon here returns to universal exhortations. He commands us to learn the teaching that has been handed down by God and to obey him, so that we do not give preference to our own wisdom or shrewdness. He also adds promises and warnings. Now, all these things are opposed to human wisdom, which most brazenly plays sport with made-up opinions about God, piety [*religiones*], and worship and does not want to be bound to the Word of God. Likewise, in the counsels of life, this human wisdom shrewdly seeks its own defense; it is not content to remain within the parameters handed down in the Word of God. In this way, Solomon's exhortations agree with the entire psalm: "Blessed are the spotless ..."[13] These commendations of wisdom are rightly understood concerning revealed wisdom, that is, concerning the Word of God as revealed in the church about both the Decalogue and the Gospel. Nor is it improper, however, that the ancients adapted these praises of wisdom to the person who is the Son of God, who is the Revealer of the Word sounding forth in the church, who is

---

[10] Prov. 3:11.

[11] The word *patientia* here could also be translated as "patience."

[12] Prov. 3:13.

[13] Ps. 119:1 (Vulgate 118:1).

efficacious through that Word and shows in it what kind of God he is and what God's will is.[14]

[Additional] Precepts

"Do not keep the one who is able to do good from doing so; and if you are able, do good to yourself also."[15]

That is, you should not get in the way of the callings of other people. Likewise, you should assiduously and faithfully obey your own calling.[16]

"Do not say to your neighbor, 'Leave and come back tomorrow, and then I will give it to you,' if you are able to give it today."[17]

"Do not plot evil against your neighbor, but let him live beside you in peace."[18]

Both this precept and the ones that follow pertain to the precept "Do not murder."[19] Now, evil is done to others in one of two ways: either it manifests itself in violence or in cheating, falsely accusing, theft, and the like. John [the Baptist] prohibited both kinds when he said, "Do not harm or falsely accuse anyone."[20]

---

[14] This statement is reflected in the *Ordinary Gloss* and an interlinear comment there. Its source among the early church's commentators could not be determined.

[15] Prov. 3:27.

[16] The centrality of the callings in daily life may be found throughout the works of Martin Luther and Melanchthon.

[17] Prov. 3:28.

[18] Prov. 3:29.

[19] Ex. 20:13.

[20] Luke 3:14.

"Do not needlessly quarrel with a person when he has done no harm to you." [21]

Here Solomon prohibits every kind of false accusation and unjust disputes.

"Do not envy an unjust person, nor choose his paths." [22]

This is a universal precept given lest, offended by the scandal of the cross and the success of the ungodly, we abandon God and begin to imitate the ungodly in the hope of attaining power, wealth, peace, and other conveniences, as happens with a great many when the church is subject to the ways of the cross and the ungodly take power. One entire psalm preaches against this temptation: "Do not be envious of evildoers ..."[23]

"The exaltation of fools will be a disgrace." [24]

This agrees with the saying [of Claudianus], who wrote: "The unrighteous are raised up high so that they fall down to destruction faster."[25]

---

[21] Prov. 3:30.

[22] Prov. 3:31.

[23] Ps. 37:1 (Vulgate 36:1).

[24] Prov. 3:35b.

[25] Claudian, also known as Claudius Claudianus, *On Stilicho's Consulship* 3.160–61. Claudian, as he is generally known today, was a Greek-speaking Latin poet who wrote this work around the year 400 CE. The immediate section is referring to the pride of Rome. Flavius Stilicho was the son of a Vandal father and Roman mother, and he was a regent of the empire from 395 to 408. Claudian's work was a panegyric that praised Stilicho. Melanchthon uses this saying several times in his commentary.

Chapter 4

Solomon returns once again to universal exhortations, and he commands us to learn this teaching and to be obedient to it. The fourth chapter is a general exhortation geared toward learning teaching, eagerly obeying it, diligently being governed [by it], and remaining circumspect, lest we are ensnared by the examples of the ungodly. Solomon also mentions rewards and punishments.

Although there is obscurity in one saying, "The beginning of wisdom is the acquisition of wisdom,"[1] it is plain that it refers to the manner and the beginning of turning to God, both to heed and truly to desire right teaching, and to ask to be under God's governance. In accord with this teaching is the beginning of turning to God, as it is said elsewhere: "He gives the Holy Spirit to those who ask."[2] And the prophet said, "Turn to me and I will turn [to you]."[3] Similarly, Wisdom 6, "Wisdom is found by those who seek her,"[4] and she comes before those who desire her. And above in Proverbs, "If you seek her … you will find her."[5] James also says this: "If anyone lacks wisdom,

---

[1] Prov. 4:7.
[2] Luke 11:13.
[3] Zech. 1:3.
[4] Wis. 6:12.
[5] Prov. 2:4–5.

let him ask from God."[6] Likewise, "God draws [a person to himself], but only those who are willing."[7]

---

[6] James 1:5.

[7] John Chrysostom, *Hom. XXV in loco N. T.: In Ac. 9:1* (*De mutatione nominum*) III.6 (PG 51:143), glossing John 6:44. At the time this commentary was written, Melanchthon was engaged in controversy with Nicolaus Gallus (ca. 1516–1570), among others, over free choice. See Timothy J. Wengert, "Philip Melanchthon and the Origins of the 'Three Causes' (1533–1535): An Examination of the Roots of the Controversy over the Freedom of the Will," in *Philip Melanchthon: Theologian in Classroom, Confession, and Controversy*, ed. Irene Dingel et al. (Göttingen: Vandenhoeck & Ruprecht, 2012), 183–208; and Robert Kolb, *Bound Choice, Election, and Wittenberg Theological Method from Martin Luther to the Formula of Concord* (Grand Rapids: Eerdmans, 2005), 81–102.

Chapter 5

The fifth chapter pertains to two commandments from the Decalogue: "You shall not commit adultery" and "You shall not steal."[1] For the beginning of the fifth chapter prohibits adultery and all wanton pleasures, and it adds discourses on punishments against such practices since later events will repay breaches to this divine law. Indeed, God will punish both fornicators and adulterers. As Proverbs 6 states, "An adulterer will lose his soul."[2] Both the private and the public stories of David, Troy, and Thebes reveal this [principle] to be true.[3] And although God may greatly reduce the penalty of those who offer repentance, there will, nonetheless, always be certain punitive consequences that follow. In fact, oftentimes one's sins are punished in the offspring, that is, in the lives of one's descendants.

At the same time, Solomon has inserted the sweetest discourse, which approves not just marriage and mutual love, but also the delight of marriage, even though he prohibits adultery. This approval of marriage and mutual love appears in the following proverb: "May you be delighted with the wife of your youth,"[4] that is, the one you married

---

[1] Ex. 20:14–15.

[2] Prov. 6:32.

[3] In these three examples, Melanchthon most likely refers to David's sleeping with Bathsheba (2 Samuel 11), Paris's stealing of Helen from Menelaus (*Iliad*), and Oedipus's marriage to his mother (*Oedipus Rex*).

[4] Prov. 5:18.

while a youth. Solomon proceeds to depict mutual love in the most beautiful of imagery. Love is such that it is compared to a male and female deer or to a male and female goat. In other words, such love is kindled so strongly that it is without deceit or compulsion; it is sweet and free of spite or scorn; it is sincere, without mistrust or pride, with the result that a married couple may find comfort in mutual love so that their love may not be torn asunder or attacked by outsiders. Such a description of ardent love appears in Oppian's[5] writing about deer:

> The hind runs and the stag running with swift feet overtakes her
> And seizes the fugitive and embraces her for his bride.[6]

But the antithesis of this may be demonstrated by means of contrary examples. Emperor Tiberius, for instance, only married Julia reluctantly, and the pretense and coercion of the union produced an unpleasant marriage.[7] Pomponia's marriage to Quintus Tullius Cicero was even more acrimonious.[8] After all, a great part of the nature of men and women is to be suspicious, proud, and distrustful, all of which

---

[5] Oppian of Corycus was a second-century Greco-Roman poet, best known for poems he composed about fishing. But the *Cynegetica* about hunting, although attributed to him, was written somewhat later and is now ascribed to Pseudo-Oppian or Oppian of Apamea.

[6] This verse is cited here in both Latin and Greek. Oppian, *The Chase*. For the exact quote, see *Cynegetica* II.200–201 in *Oppian, Colluthus, Tryphiodorus*, trans. A. W. Mair, ed. T. E. Page (London: William Heinemann, 1928), 72–73. In Greek, ἀλλὰ ποσὶ κραιπνοῖσι θέων ἐκίχανε θέουσαν φεύγουσαν μάρπτει δὲ καὶ ἀγκὰς ἔχει παράκοιτιν.

[7] Emperor Tiberius (r. 14–37 CE) married Julia the Elder, the only biological child of Emperor Augustus, in 11 BCE. Both Tiberius and Julia were previously divorced, and by all accounts, theirs was an unhappy marriage. Most likely, Melanchthon's view of the marriage comes from Suetonius's *The Twelve Caesars* 3.7.2.

[8] Quintus was the younger brother of the more famous Marcus Tullius Cicero, both of whom lived during the first century BCE. Quintus married the sister of Marcus's good friend Atticus. The marriage was regarded as unsuccessful.

fail to foster fairness in interaction. However, all of these vices are removed when we consider the sweet and sincere affection shared between a male and female deer or shared between a male and female goat. Once again, our text offers the sweetest approval of marital love and faithfulness when it says, "Let her breasts intoxicate you,"[9] that is, "May your love be burning and true, and not wandering." The meanings here must be considered, for *breasts* signify "affection,"[10] and *intoxicate* "great love." Then it is said, "May you not know the love of someone," that is, of someone else. Here is the sum of it all: "Truly love your spouse," and "be content with her alone"; such was the law of marriage immediately enjoined in Paradise: "The two will become one flesh,"[11] that is, one male and one female will be inseparably united. For then, too, even if the nature of humankind had remained intact, God would have wanted people to experience sexual purity and to excel in the exercise of obedience by preserving this order, namely, of guarding against wanton pleasures.

Just as the understanding of all virtues has been implanted in the minds of humankind so that the distinction between honorable and dishonorable things would be a testimony that there is a God and would show what kind of God he is and that God is judge, so also God wants chastity to be experienced, and he punishes wanton pleasures most severely. The result of this is that we would know him to possess a pure mind, and, as a result, we would come to distinguish him from natural impurities. Let us also consider this: it is only in the church of God where incorrupt teaching about wanton pleasures has remained. And let us also continually be mindful of the punishments that would ensue. For wanton pleasures are punished in the saddest of ways in this life, resulting in everlasting tortures [in the next], if conversion to God does not occur, in accordance with Paul's saying in 1 Corinthians that "neither fornicators nor adulterers will possess the kingdom of

---

[9] Prov. 5:19.

[10] In Greek, στοργή.

[11] Gen. 2:24.

God."[12] Indeed, let us consider God's judgment both in history and in many everyday hardships.

Concerning the Other Commandment

"Drink water from your own fountains …"[13]

At the same time, Solomon includes commands concerning particular righteousness,[14] abstaining from things belonging to others, and concerning frugality and generosity. To begin with, here this clear testimony against the urging of the monks and Anabaptists may be noted, who praise Platonic community of property.[15] For it is expressly stated, "May you remain master of your own possessions, and not others with you."[16] As stated in the commandment, "You shall not steal,"[17] the distinction of ownership is enjoined, and so we may understand that this distinction is confirmed here when Solomon says, "May you remain master of your own possessions, and not others with you."

Now, concerning frugality, Solomon commands above, "Lest you give your inheritance to strangers, and your years to the callous."[18] Here he calls the callous *leeches* since they feed off the resources of others. This greediness is especially visible in the [princely] courts, and it is portrayed in the story of Actaeon, who was torn to pieces by his own dogs.[19] But concerning generosity and mercy, Solomon states it in

---

[12] 1 Cor. 6:9.

[13] Prov. 5:15.

[14] See Melanchthon's *Philosophiae moralis epitome*, "De iustitia," CR 16:65–67, where particular justice is defined (from Simonides) as "giving to each his [or her] own."

[15] Melanchthon may be thinking here particularly of the Hutterites.

[16] Prov. 5:17.

[17] Ex. 20:15.

[18] Prov. 5:9.

[19] The story of Actaeon and Diana is most famously described in Ovid's *Metamorphoses* 3.206–35. Actaeon, a skilled hunter, was turned into a stag by the goddess Diana (Artemis) after wandering into her in the woods as

such a sweet way: "May your fountains be dispersed outdoors,"[20] and "May you remain master of them,"[21] that is to say, may you increase in fruits and may you maintain possession of your land. In this way, Solomon establishes a measure of generosity: he wishes properties to be preserved intact, and he does not want dispersals and endless divisions of inheritances.[22] At the same time, he also wishes for those in need to be helped by those with means, as the Lord has said, "Give according to your means."[23]

"I was almost in every evil, in the midst of the assembly."[24] This remarkable teaching is illustrated by way of many examples in this chapter. The meaning of it is that contagions of the people harm everyone because the human being is, by nature, drawn to imitation and, in fact, learns by imitation. When, therefore, a person hears the unscrupulous conjectures of the crowd or the great, he [or she] perceives their rites and mores, begins to follow them, and more easily imitates the vices of the wicked. Finally, such practices establish the beginning of lifelong vices. For this reason, there are many sayings commanding us neither to abandon upright examples nor to follow the crowd. For instance, it is expressly stated in Exodus 23: "Do not follow the crowd in committing evil, and do not respond in judgment

---

she bathed. As he fled the scene, Actaeon's hunting dogs chased him down and ate him, not knowing that it was their master.

[20] Prov. 5:16.

[21] Prov. 5:17.

[22] There were a variety of inheritance practices in German-speaking lands, with some places practicing primo- or ultimo-geniture and others dividing the inheritance among all descendants. For the nobility this issue became particularly problematic. In Saxony in the fifteenth century, the division between the Albertine and Ernestine lines of the Wettins was followed by an arrangement between the brothers Elector Frederick (1463–1525) and Elector John (1468–1532) that the former would forgo legitimate heirs so the latter could inherit their lands intact.

[23] Luke 11:41.

[24] Prov. 5:14.

by inclining to the inclination of the many."[25] For we know, especially when it comes to religious matters, how much weight is given to the opinion of the crowd. Against such contagions, let us instead ground ourselves in these sayings: "Your word is a lamp to my feet,"[26] and "Listen to me [you who know righteousness]."[27] For God wants us to be ruled by his Word, not by conjectures and examples that depart from God's Word.

---

[25] Ex. 23:2.

[26] Ps. 119:105 (Vulgate 118:105).

[27] Isa. 51:7.

Chapter 6

The first proverb in the sixth chapter discourages the making of promises of payment. Solomon explains that such promises are dangerous since most of those who make them are ultimately disappointed. As a result, there is a celebrated saying written in an inscription from Delphi: "Ruin follows the making of a pledge."[1] That is to say, if you make a pledge, you will fall into harm's way. Similarly, Homer writes in book 8 of the *Odyssey*, "A pledge for a worthless man is worthless indeed,"[2] meaning that pledges are wicked when they are pledged in behalf of wicked people. But, in general, this saying describes the trustworthiness of those who ensure a pledge. Such persons are rarely honest and trustworthy. On the contrary, many of those who ensure a pledge are unstable, deceptive, untrustworthy, and treacherous, with the result that we read many complaints about them. [Virgil states it this way,] "Nowhere is faithfulness secure."[3] [And Ovid writes,] "Flee

---

[1] On this saying, see p. 9, n. 16.

[2] Homer, *Odyssey* 8.351. The original Greek is δειλαί τοι δειλῶν γε καὶ ἐγγύαι ἐγγυάασθαι. The translation provided comes from Robert Fagles, ed., *The Odyssey* (New York: Penguin, 1999), 202.

[3] Virgil, *Aeneid* 4.373. In this section of the greatest of Latin epics, Dido is reproaching Aeneas for leaving her kingdom and not accepting her offer of joint regency in Carthage.

those you believe to be faithful and you will be secure."[4] We also find in Epicharmus: "Be wise and remember to exercise skepticism, for such is the sinews of the mind."[5] The same is in the Psalm: "Do not put your trust in princes, in the sons of humankind—in whom there is no salvation."[6] Likewise from Jeremiah, "Cursed is the one who trusts in a human being."[7]

Perhaps someone might ask here, "What? Are we not supposed to believe in anything?" Here's my response: First, concerning teaching about God, we must believe in the Word of God since God has, indeed, included illustrious testimonies such as the resurrection of the dead and so forth.[8] However, we are not to believe in that which goes beyond the doctrine handed down [to us] about God, in which people make their own audacious assertions about God. As the saying goes, "Neither add nor detract anything."[9] Second, what is taught in the humanities is certain because of the logical proofs alongside other causes of certainty, since the means of judging[10] and proofs are a divinely instituted order, which God wishes human minds to contemplate. But many things are changeable in matters of this world, especially human wills. Because human wills are often deceptive, a distinction must be made and considered in this passage where and

---

[4] Ovid, *Art of Love* 1.752. Here Ovid is warning about possible seducers and the potential faithfulness of a lover. Not even friends or family are above suspicion when it comes to love.

[5] Epicharmus of Kos was a sixth-century BCE Greek dramatist whose writings only survive in fragments. In Greek, νῆφε καὶ μέμνησο ἀπιστεῖν ἄρθα ταύτα γὰρ ἄρθα τῶν φρενῶν.

[6] Ps. 146:3 (145:3 in the Vulgate).

[7] Jer. 17:5.

[8] On the reliability of Scripture, Melanchthon makes similar statements in his *Loci communes theologici*, and his student Georg Major describes these things in his tract *On the Authority and Origin of the Word of God*.

[9] Cf. Deut. 4:2.

[10] In Greek, κριτήρια. "Probable reason" is a well-known technical term for accepting as true things that cannot be proven through the use of logic. It is similar to the more modern understanding of "common sense."

the degree to which we are to assent to human pledges, and where we should not assent to them.

Now, there is a virtue named Candor that distinguishes between wills. The extremes of the virtue of candor are deception and gullibility. For candor is the virtue most akin to truth approving others' wills using "probable reason" and not generating groundless suspicions arising out of malevolence or maliciousness.[11] Even regarding ambiguous things, candor is the virtue that turns toward thinking the better of something and, in fact, hopes for the best. But still, concerning such changeable things, it thinks that human wills can be changed and that a person may err when it comes to perceiving another's will, especially since the hidden recesses of the human heart are scarcely able to be examined inwardly. For instance, David was inclined to think well of Jonathan since he had probable reason to do so, by what means he hoped his will was steadfast, because he knew Jonathan feared God and was supported with divine testimony. By the same measure, David was not inclined to think well of Ahithophel because he judged that Ahithophel did not fear God.[12] In this way, therefore, we must make mention of the saying in 1 Corinthians 13: "Love believes all things."[13] That is to say, love is pure; it is not suspicious and does not suspect evil of anyone without sound reason and probable cause.

Concerning Work and Diligence

The second precept in the sixth chapter concerns labor, which Solomon also illustrates in an example wherein he orders us to give heed to ants and imitate their diligence. In the first place,[14] therefore, let us learn here that God has arranged ranks of our offices or callings, and that it is a divine mandate that all persons pursue the works of

---

[11] In Greek, κακοηθία.

[12] 1 Cf. 2 Sam. 17.

[13] 1 Cor. 13:7.

[14] As throughout this book, Melanchthon structures his comments around the Evangelical understanding of callings, first developed by Luther in the 1520s.

their own calling and not that of others, but rather that they perform their own with diligence and faithfulness. In this way, the sayings in 1 Thessalonians 4 offer us instruction: "We encourage you to abound more and to be earnest in your lifestyle, namely, that you be peaceful, attend to your own affairs, and work with your own hands."[15] Likewise in Ecclesiastes 9: "Whatever your hand is able to do, do it with absolute earnestness."[16] In the council of God, ranks of our offices have been arranged and delineated, which is manifest from passages such as Romans 12–13 and 1 Corinthians 12, where there are distinctions according to our [particular] ministries. As in 1 Corinthians 7, "Let each person walk in the way he or she has been called by the Lord."[17] Where each is taught, we must come to understand in accordance with the council of God both that the ranks of our offices are distinct and that all people ought to recognize the limits of their office and perform the labors of their rank.

Now, whenever mention is made of labor, the prayer and assistance of God must simultaneously be included according to the following biblical sayings: "I know, Lord, that a person's way is not in himself."[18] "Unless the Lord builds the house, [those who build it labor in vain.]"[19] "Commend your way to God; put your hope in him and he will do it."[20] "Ask and you will receive."[21] "How much more so will your Heavenly Father give the Holy Spirit to those who ask."[22] Additionally, Daniel 2 says, "God gives wisdom to the wise,"[23] just as Colossians 3 asserts, "In everything you do, whether in word or in deed, do everything in

---

[15] 1 Thess. 4:10–11.

[16] Eccl. 9:10.

[17] 1 Cor. 7:17. Although now interpreted quite differently, this text was central to the Evangelical understanding of one's life in the world.

[18] Jer. 10:23.

[19] Ps. 127:1 (Vulgate 126:1).

[20] Ps. 37:5 (Vulgate 36:5).

[21] Matt. 7:7.

[22] Luke 11:13.

[23] Dan. 2:21.

the name of our Lord Jesus Christ."[24] And we have already observed from Proverbs, "In all your ways, consider him, and he will direct your steps."[25] May there always be a combination of prayer and labor.[26]

Such a virtue is [rightly] named Diligence, which may be defined as follows: "Diligence is the virtue by which we constantly and consistently desire to perform the labor that is most consonant with our calling, for God's sake and the sake of the common welfare and with God's help, who has promised aid to those who ask." Examples of diligence include David, who was a diligent soldier, and Paul, who was a diligent teacher. The extremes of diligence are slothfulness and, as the Greeks say, "meddlesomeness."[27] While the slothful person procrastinates too often, the meddlesome person or busybody endeavors to do too many things that are not necessary, or secondary to what is required, such as one who rushes into the callings of others, as we see in the likes of Ahaz, Pericles, and Demosthenes, who instigated wars that were not necessary and could have been avoided.[28] In the same way, the church is often embroiled in unnecessary disputes and struggles, or when teachers rush into civil affairs, having one foot at court and the other at church. Though brief, I believe I have said enough about diligence.

Students should at the same time gather together sayings from the prophetic and evangelical writings as well as other [extrascriptural] wise sayings pertaining to diligence, such as: "You have seized Sparta; now adorn it."[29] In this saying, diligence is commended, just as meddlesomeness is prohibited. Likewise, the following verse from

---

[24] Col. 3:17.

[25] Prov. 3:6.

[26] Note the parallel to the medieval notion of *ora et labora*, "pray and work."

[27] In Greek, *overzealousness* is πολυπραγμοσύνη.

[28] Ahaz was a king of Judah during the eighth century BCE. Demosthenes and Pericles were both Greek statesmen. While the former was a famed orator and politician of the fourth century BCE, Pericles was perhaps the most influential Greek statesman in the fifth century BCE who profoundly shaped Athenian society. All three were involved in avoidable wars.

[29] For this Greek phrase, see p. 19, n. 16.

Gregory of Nazianzus admonishes us to do necessary things: "I say working over and above what is required is scarcely work."[30] This saying of Gregory is an admonition to unity: "Hand in need of hand, foot in need of foot."[31]

"A man of Belial, that is, a worthless person is not only an idler but a troublemaker."[32]

I stated earlier that diligence is the virtue that stands between the depraved extremes of sloth and meddlesomeness, with neighboring vices of ambition and quarrelsomeness. These vices are touched upon in this place because they are exceedingly dangerous to the public good. As Juvenal writes about the corrosive effects of ambition, "Often states have been ruined by a few people's greed for glory, by their passion for praise and for fame."[33] Likewise Claudian says, "For pride, extravagance, vice, and venom have destroyed many kingdoms."[34] Finally, regarding disagreements and the lust for rivalries, we must make mention of this saying: "Small things thrive in unity, while the greatest are destroyed in disunity."[35]

---

[30] Gregory of Nazianzus was a theologian of the fourth century in Cappadocia in modern Turkey. Melanchthon cites the Greek, τὸ μὲν πάρεργον οὐδαμῶς ἔργον λέγω. For a contemporary source, see Hadrianus Junius, *Adagiorum centuriae VIII* (Basel: Froben, 1558), 311. A strict Latin translation of the Greek would be *Extrarium negotium haud opus vocem*.

[31] Gregory of Nazianzus, *Poems* 1.2 (184) (PG 37:941). In Greek, καὶ γὰρ χερὸς χεὶρ καὶ πόδος ποῦς ἐνδεής.

[32] Prov. 6:12.

[33] Juvenal was a Latin poet of the second century CE. Among his extant works are more than a dozen satirical poems divided into five books. This quote appears in his book 4, satire 10, line 142, which discusses how unbridled desire for glory ruins nations. The translation comes from Juvenal, *The Satires*, trans. Niall Rudd (Oxford: Oxford University Press, 1992), 91.

[34] For more on Claudian, see p. 41, n. 25.

[35] Gaius Sallustius Crispus, otherwise known as Sallust, was a Roman statesman and historian living in the first century BCE. The following excerpt comes from his *Jugurthine War* 10. The Jugurthine War occurred in the early

But let us first attend to some definitions. True glory,[36] when sought justly, is the approval of one's own conscience when it judges rightly and the approval of the consciences of others rightly judging. We see the pursuit of this goal in the following proverbs: "A good name is sweeter than gold and silver."[37] "Live without stumbling."[38] "Woe to those through whom scandal comes."[39] "This is our boasting: the testimony of our conscience."[40] "Let all prove their own work, and so they will have glory in themselves only and not from others."[41] Because it is a commandment from God to seek approval of conscience of the one who rightly judges, and of some who judge rightly in the church, it is a virtue to seek this glory in a proper way.

The opposing vices [of the authentic pursuit of glory] are Fickleness and Shamelessness. Fickleness is the inability to form right judgments when it comes to one's conscience or to care about the right judgments of others. As the verse [from Seneca] states, "He is fickle, and the honor of fame does not entice him."[42] Shamelessness, haughtiness, and vainglory are about accrediting to oneself that which is not really there.

Further, in the sixth and seventh chapters, Solomon again delivers a speech concerning chastity, about which I spoke at length earlier.[43]

---

second century BCE between the kingdoms of Rome and Numidia. Jugurtha was the king of Numidia at this time.

[36] In Latin *gloria* can be defined in many ways, including "fame," "honor," "distinction," "pride," and "glory."

[37] Eccl. 7:1.

[38] 1 Cor. 10:32.

[39] Luke 17:1.

[40] 2 Cor. 1:12.

[41] Gal. 6:4 (singular in the Latin).

[42] Seneca the Younger, *Hercules on Oeta* 416.

[43] Melanchthon's use of the *loci* method allows him to omit discussion, in this case of an entire chapter, by simply referring the reader to earlier comments on the same topic. For chastity, see above, pp. 45–48.

And it may be noted that speeches about the penalties of adulterous relationships and other wanton pleasures are taught here and there throughout the Scriptures.

Chapter 8

Solomon recounts the precepts of the Ten Commandments in the beginning of the eighth chapter before returning to a general exhortation urging us to learn and obey them. For he calls this a wisdom presented and revealed by God, a wisdom to which God binds us. Solomon is not speaking here of the wisdom of a Pericles or of an Alcibiades[1] or of anyone whose wisdom is mere shrewdness in the accumulation of power and wealth for any occasion whatsoever, whether accumulated in a just or unjust way. Nor is there any doubt that Solomon is speaking of the revealed Word in the church, that is, the Law of God and the Gospel when he says, "Wisdom calls out from the gates of the city."[2]

However, because the eternal and immovable wisdom, which alone is in God himself, is revealed both in the voice of the Law and the Gospel and also in the Son himself through whom the Father has decreed both the order of creation and the restoration of humankind, the church fathers therefore understood this section about wisdom to be referring to the Son speaking to the church. I approve their

---

[1] Pericles was perhaps the most influential Greek statesman in the fifth century BCE who profoundly shaped Athenian society. Alcibiades was also an important statesman in ancient Greece in the fifth century BCE, though a much younger contemporary to Pericles.

[2] Prov. 8:1, 3. Melanchthon is clearly aware of the allegorical tradition that connects "city" to the church.

interpretation as correct.[3] The Arians,[4] by contrast, falsely chose only those biblical passages that seem to suggest that the Son was a [mere] creature. For instance, when Solomon wrote that "The Lord *took possession of me* in the beginning of his way,"[5] the Arians claimed instead, "The Lord *created me* in the beginning of their ways."[6] However, it must be pointed out from the Hebrew original that the word Solomon used was "possess," not "create."[7] In short, the interpretation of this passage by the Arians is plainly refuted by the use of the verb "possess" as well as the series of verses that follow. As it is written in the Gospel of John: "*In the beginning* was the Word."[8] Likewise, it is sweetly stated in Proverbs: "The Lord took possession of me *in the beginning.*"[9] And also: "*Before the ages were* established."[10] Solomon says that this wisdom was the author or maker of creation, as stated in John 1: "All things

---

[3] This statement is one indication that Melanchthon was reading the biblical text in the light of the tradition. Given his own encounter with those who denied the Trinity, the traditional Christian interpretation of this text, identifying Wisdom with Christ, offered him important counterarguments.

[4] Arius was a fourth-century priest in Alexandria who taught that Jesus was created by God, based partly on passages such as Prov. 8. His teachings became the focal point of the Council of Nicaea in 325, where they were soundly repudiated. Nevertheless, Arian Christianity persisted in the church. In Melanchthon's day, for instance, Arian Christianity was attached to figures like Johannes Campanus and Michael Servetus.

[5] Prov. 8:22.

[6] The Greek Old Testament, the Septuagint, translates this verse as follows: κύριος ἔκτισέν με ἀρχὴν ὁδῶν αὐτοῦ εἰς ἔργα αὐτοῦ, "The Lord created me from the beginning of his ways, before his works."

[7] The Hebrew BHS text reads, יְהוָה קָנָנִי רֵאשִׁית דַּרְכּוֹ קֶדֶם מִפְעָלָיו. The verb used, קָנָה, carries a wide semantic range: "buy," "purchase," "acquire," "create," and "produce."

[8] John 1:1.

[9] Prov. 8:22.

[10] Prov. 8:23.

were made by him."¹¹ We likewise read in Hebrews 1: "Sustaining all things through the power of his word."¹²

The person mentioned in these passages is the same Son through whom we are told that the order of creation and the restoration of humankind were decreed. Therefore here, using the same name, Solomon refers to this Wisdom as creating and bringing to light the Law and Gospel. And it thus follows: "Playing before him at all times, playing in the world, and my delights were with the sons of humankind."¹³ This Wisdom first brings the greatest delight to the Father; second, this Wisdom reveals to the angels and to humankind the Father in the marvelous order of the created world; and, finally, this Wisdom points to and glorifies the Father—in the proclamation of the Word, in the assumption of human nature, in the resurrection, in the restoration of humankind, in the preservation of the entire church, in the flood of Noah, in the Red Sea, and in all other miracles—and this Wisdom rejoices in the bringing to life and restitution of the church. Solomon refers here to all of these marvelous works that are to be marveled upon—the "play" and "delights" of God's wisdom. Devout readers must attentively consider this most sweet sentiment and how this very Wisdom, that is, the Son, outwardly instructs the church by the promulgation of the Word and inwardly sustains, teaches, and enlightens it. And because Wisdom preserves the human race on account of the church, insofar as just actions are wrought in the political realm, they are wrought by Wisdom sustaining and instructing the governing authorities by the promulgated Word and by governing them in a hidden manner. Therefore, Solomon says, "It is through me that kings reign and lawgivers decree justice."¹⁴

Thus, Solomon distinguishes this guiding, divine wisdom promulgated through the Word from human shrewdness. For divine wisdom is fruitful, effective, and redemptive, ultimately bringing delightful

---

[11] John 1:3.
[12] Heb. 1:3.
[13] Prov. 8:30–31.
[14] Prov. 8:15.

results, even though they differ to some degree. But the shrewdness of Pericles, Alcibiades, Demosthenes, and the like is fatal both to their country and to themselves. Therefore the wisdom of God proclaims: "Under my command are counsel and success."[15] In other words, those counsels are righteous that are in accordance with the Word of God and such counsels will ultimately bring delightful results, through the help of the Son of God, who, indeed, desires to be present with those who persevere in the Word that he teaches and who pray to him, invoking him according to this saying: "Commend your way to God, hope in him, and he will act."[16] And as Proverbs 3 states, "In all your ways acknowledge him, and he will direct your steps."[17] Likewise, "God is the one who works in you both to will and to accomplish."[18] Conversely, punishments universally follow unrighteousness, even though for a time in the present either there were agreeable pleasures or power grew.

---

[15] Prov. 8:14.
[16] Ps. 37:5 (Vulgate 36:5).
[17] Prov. 3:6.
[18] Phil. 2:13.

Chapter 10

***"The Lord does not allow the soul of the righteous to go hungry."*[1]**

This basic teaching takes up the topic of providence, which is repeated consistently throughout this entire work.[2] God distinguishes between right and wrong actions through eternal rewards and punishments since it is the order of justice for right actions to be preserved and wrong actions to be destroyed, in accordance with the saying, "God is a consuming fire."[3] For God, by making mention of punishments and rewards, wishes to make a more obvious distinction between righteous and unrighteous matters. The righteous matters conform to God or God's law while the unrighteous fight against God or God's law.

Temporal punishments, however, must be distinguished from eternal ones. Temporal punishments are imposed upon people primarily to call them back to repentance; but for those who do not repent, a second purpose of temporal punishments is to give evidence of the beginning of their destruction and eternal punishments, as seen in the sufferings of Saul, Judas, Nero, and everyone else who has rushed headlong into eternal punishments.

Corporal blessings must also be distinguished from eternal ones. The church will certainly possess eternal blessings. For this reason rational

---

[1] Prov. 10:3.

[2] I.e., Proverbs. Here one can see how Melanchthon uses the *loci* method to define a topic (Latin *communis doctrina*) for a text.

[3] Heb. 12:29.

creatures have been created so that they would be some instrument through which God imparts himself and eternal light, wisdom, justice, life, and joy. But in this mortal life, through God's sure counsel, the church has been subjected to the cross for the time being.[4] Therefore, many members are harshly plagued, some faring better and some faring worse. Nevertheless, because God wants the church to be gathered together in no other way than by the voice of the public ministry in this bodily life, God always conserves some assembly which cannot live without food, drink, or hospitality.[5] In this way, therefore, God lessens the sting of the cross by providing for this assembly the things necessary for preserving bodily life, while also consistently preserving among them these rules concerning the outward life. As the saying goes, "Grave punishments attend grave sins."[6] This is clearly evident in David's adultery and Manasseh's crimes, from which horrible punishments followed.[7] Nonetheless, many punishments can be lessened for the godly, resulting in a course of life that is more peaceful. Because of this, eternal and bodily promises are inculcated here, as is stated in the saying, "The Lord does not allow the soul of the righteous to go hungry."[8] Likewise in Psalm 34, "Lions go hungry, but those who fear the Lord will lack no good thing."[9]

We must always keep in view this basic teaching concerning this distinction, which the eternal and unshakable wisdom of God establishes between righteous and unrighteous actions, and also concerning rewards and punishments. At the same time, the universal teaching about the church, namely, the distinction of eternal and bodily promises along with the teaching about the cross, must also be considered.

There are four particular causes why promises regarding bodily matters have been taught in the church.

---

[4] This paragraph provides an outline of Melanchthon's ecclesiology.

[5] Heb. 13:2.

[6] The source of this quote is unknown.

[7] 2 Sam. 11:1–12:23; 2 Kings 21:1–18.

[8] Prov. 10:3.

[9] Ps. 34:10 (Vulgate 33:10).

First, that these promises may be testimonies of providence against Epicurean assertions, lest we consider these external blessings to be scattered about by chance and particularly in the church, where good externals are given through the exclusive counsel of God and in a singular manner. Indeed, on account of the church, the realm of nature is preserved for the whole human race.

Second, that they would give witness that God's will may preserve the church, even in this earthly life, and that we would recognize the church must originate in this mortal life.

Third, that faith and prayer would be put into practice for every daily necessity in pleading for peace, nourishment, good health, and successful political governance.

Finally, the fourth cause about which these external promises have been handed down to the church is so that these promises would serve as reminders regarding eternal life. For in every petition, faith, which receives forgiveness of sin through the Mediator, ought to shine brightly, and so that we may always believe that the church is preserved in this life, too, because of and through the Mediator, who states, "I will carry you in my bosom just as a shepherd carries his newborn sheep."[10] In short, let us recognize that the promises about good bodily living are not irrelevant. They are confirmed through this divine message, so let us ask and anticipate the necessities of life in our prayer.[11]

"A lazy hand brings about poverty"[12]

Solomon connects promises with the commands about work because God commands both and so that we may perform the works of our vocation and at the same time ask for and expect good outcomes from God, according to this saying, "Commend your way to God and hope in him, and he will act."[13]

---

[10] Isa. 40:11.

[11] Reading *invocatione* for *in vocatione*.

[12] Prov. 10:4.

[13] Ps. 37:5.

"Hatred provokes strife, but love covers all transgressions."[14]

This precept is concerned with what the Greeks call "forbearance,"[15] or fairness, which pertains to the fifth and eighth commandments. Here it is first necessary to recognize common definitions and distinctions of righteousness.

Particular justice is the virtue of "giving to each his [or her] own."[16] Judicial justice, by contrast, is the virtue of granting protection to the just but meting out punishment to the unjust. But because there are degrees of transgressions—such that the devil's wickedness was more heinous than Adam's, or Judas's guilt more heinous than Peter's—levels, severity, and fairness of just punishment must also be distinguished. Both are forms of justice, and they have the same extremes of ruthlessness and leniency. By way of an example, Sulla was ruthless, for he killed a multitude of people indiscriminately even after securing his victory.[17] How true what the poet stated, "The medicine surpassed the malady."[18] Julius Caesar, by contrast, was more lenient; he

---

[14] Prov. 10:12.

[15] In Greek, ἐπιείκεια. Forbearance is an important concept in the ethics of Luther and Melanchthon. For Melanchthon, see Nicole Kuropka, *Philipp Melanchthon: Wissenschaft und Gesellschaft* (Tübingen: Mohr Siebeck, 2002), 58–60. For Luther, see Timothy J. Wengert, *Reading the Bible with Martin Luther: An Introductory Guide* (Grand Rapids: Baker Academic, 2013), 69–91.

[16] This definition of particular justice is found in Cicero and Aristotle and is part of the common definition of *iustitia*.

[17] Sulla (138–78 BCE) was a Roman general involved in many military campaigns. During the Social War in the late first century BCE, Sulla conquered Gaius Marius. The Senate later granted him a dictatorship, and he infamously instituted a series of proscriptions that caused the deaths of thousands of prominent Romans.

[18] Lucan, *On the Civil War* 2.142. This incident comes from a poem written by the Roman poet Lucan (39–65 CE) discussing the Roman civil war between Caesar and Pompey in the first century BCE.

spared Cicero, Marcellus, and others, and he committed no savagery in Rome.[19]

But in Solomon's saying here that "love covers all transgressions,"[20] a distinction must be made between a judge and a private person. For the office of a judge is compelled by a divine mandate to apply the full weight of the law upon those who recklessly transgress it, whether against blasphemy, perjury, murder, corrupt adultery, or lewd sexual misconduct. As Deuteronomy 19 states, "You shall remove evil from among your midst.... You shall not pity the person committing such evil but shall require life for life."[21] For God wants punishments to be completely transparent so that God himself would be recognized as the one who arbitrates between righteous and unrighteous actions and who judges and punishes wickedness so the public order is preserved. At the same time, however, a judge must also take into account those circumstances where punishment is to be mitigated, as even the laws themselves are imposed more harshly upon those who commit premeditated murder than upon those who are involved in an accidental killing. This moderating virtue is called "forbearance,"[22] which is justice, tempering either some laws or punishments due to extenuating circumstances.

Most wisely, many examples of how such softening of the law has been applied have been handed down to us. For example, when David was hungry, he was allowed to eat bread reserved exclusively for a priest.[23] Similarly, Thrasybulus established the practice of what the Greeks called amnesty, which permitted exiled citizens to return to

---

[19] Cicero (106–43 BCE), of course, was the most famous orator in the Roman Empire and also a senator; Gaius Claudius Marcellus Minor (88–40 BCE) was a Roman senator and consul. Like Cicero, Marcellus was largely opposed to Caesar.

[20] Prov. 10:12.

[21] Deut. 19:19, 21.

[22] In Greek, ἐπιείκεία.

[23] 1 Sam. 21:1–6; cf. Matt. 12:1–8.

the land lest future wars arise.[24] In another example, Holy Roman Emperor Conrad III made peace with Welf [von Altorf] in the town of Weinsberg after the women of the town outwitted the terms of the treaty the king had made. For after the king granted permission for the women of the town to take away with them whatever possessions they themselves could carry, they promptly loaded their husbands and sons on their shoulders.[25] In short, these sayings exemplify how a judge must recognize how to apply the law, whether strictly or leniently, as must be discussed elsewhere.[26]

When it comes to private persons and private offenses, there are two matters to consider. The first is that there are situations in which self-defense is justified. The second is that a personal injury outside of self-defense must be forgiven; the slate has to be wiped clean, so to speak, in accordance with the saying, "Forgive and it will be forgiven you."[27] Now, because such injuries naturally befall you over the course your life—and it is foolish to think that these kinds of injuries can be avoided while on earth—let us not suppose that only rare offenses are mentioned in this passage. Instead, let us realize that forgiveness is a necessary component in all areas of our lives, including, of course, private offenses.

We are to offer forgiveness, first, because of God and, second, in pursuit of communal peace. God not only commands this virtue to be practiced but also wants it to be a reminder of God's own forgiveness. Therefore the Lord says, "Forgive and it will be forgiven you."[28] In thinking about and practicing this virtue, God wants us to remember

---

[24] Thrasybulus was an Athenian statesman active in the fifth and early forth century BCE. He advocated for the return of Alcibiades to Athens to prevent a revolt.

[25] The so-called Siege of Weinsberg in Weinsberg, Germany, occurred in 1140 between the Welfs, such as Welf von Altdorf, and the Hohenstaufen, especially Conrad III.

[26] See below, pp. 105–7.

[27] Matt. 6:14.

[28] Matt. 6:14.

his mercy and the Gospel, in which the vast forbearance[29] of the Law is set forth since an incipient, inexact, and inadequate obedience is received and since many grievances are forgiven and penalties daily appeased in accordance with the saying, "By the mercy of God we are not consumed."[30] For it is completely manifest that forgiving and forgetting private offenses is crucial to the preservation of communal peace.

The youth must be warned against allowing a false interpretation of this passage by those twisting this saying toward error, those who imagine that remission of sins is earned through our works. They argue that since "love covers transgressions,"[31] therefore your love covers all transgressions in God's sight. However, this conclusion must be denied since the saying is a political one speaking about forgiveness between human beings, about covering others' transgression, and about rebuking the desire for vengeance. As it is commanded in Leviticus 17: "Do not seek vengeance or hold a grudge against your fellow citizens."[32] For this is expressly stated with reference to citizens so that it means that for the sake of communal peace, many offenses must be overlooked. As such, let our pride and impatience be put to shame since the Son of God not only forgave us our great and grievous sins but also prostrated himself before God, and sustaining punishment on account of our crimes, he bore the punishment in himself

---

[29] In Greek, ἐπιείκεια.

[30] Lam. 3:22, as in the King James Version, adding from the Hebrew, "we are not cut off."

[31] Prov. 10:12. Melanchthon often taught his students about the weaknesses of his opponents' arguments by reducing them to syllogisms and demonstrating their weaknesses such as here in the conclusion, which mistakenly applies a political mandate to theology. See thesis 52 of the theses, all written by Melanchthon, for the doctoral promotion of Johann Marbach, presided over by Luther on February 16, 1543 (WA 39/2:229). The text was indeed used by Wittenberg's opponents to prove that human love, not faith alone, was required for salvation.

[32] Lev. 19:18. Melanchthon, probably citing the passage from memory, writes chapter 17 instead of 19.

for our wrongdoings. Therefore, Christ says, "Learn from me, for I am gentle and humble in heart."[33]

Admonished by this example and command, let us patiently bear it when we come close to being misled about the above passage, since indeed we truly have merited punishments because of many serious sins and may be driven by our impulses lest greater hatred, discord, and wars occur. Let us love this virtue of forbearance[34] for this very reason, so that this very name often reminds us of the Gospel, in which the sweetest forbearance[35] of the divine Law is set forth, as has been said.

Just as severe justice and forbearance[36] are matching virtues, so also are truth, which severely judges the words and deeds of others, and candor. The opposite of truth and candor are flattery and Trickery. However, candor offers the ability to minimize more severe judgments, as when some more careless statements in good writers must be softened by an interpretation that is in agreement with the original intention of the author.

"The mouth of the fool is never far from confusion."[37]

Many of Solomon's sayings are concerned with speaking and the bridling of the tongue. The particular vices related to the tongue are lying, gossip, hastiness, over-inquisitiveness, reproachfulness, slander, trickery, vanity, boasting or bragging,[38] hypocrisy, coarseness,[39]

---

[33] Matt. 11:29.

[34] In Greek, ἐπιεικεία.

[35] In Greek, ἐπιεικεία.

[36] In Greek, ἐπιεικεία.

[37] Prov. 10:14.

[38] Here the Greek word used, θρασωνισμὸς, may be a neologism. Taking a boastful character named Thraso from the Latin playwright Terence's play *The Eunuch*, Melanchthon creates a Greek adjective "Thrasonic," implying that boasting is like "being a Thraso."

[39] In Greek, δυσωπία.

aggression,⁴⁰ shamelessness, love of strife,⁴¹ buffoonery, foulness, mockery, and, finally, flattery. These vices must be kept in mind. We must learn to avoid them with diligence, checking our impulses, and refraining from pouring forth every thought that crosses our minds.

"The blessing of the Lord makes the rich and does not increase sorrow."⁴²

Worldly people think that riches and victories come merely through human industry and human labor. Such people suppose that Alexander the Great was victorious because his army surpassed Persian forces in strategy, labor, and strength, just as the saying commonly goes: "Constant labor overcomes all things."⁴³ Plato also said that happiness consists in this: one's destiny does not depend upon others, but everything necessary for happiness rests upon oneself alone. In the same way, Nebuchadnezzar said, "Is this not magnificent Babylon, which I have built ... by my mighty power?"⁴⁴ Such delusions demonstrate trust in our own cunning and in our own powers, through which haughty people disregard God and undertake what should not be undertaken.⁴⁵ For instance, when Antony saw that he was better equipped than Augustus and hoped to be able to overpower him, he undertook an unjust war. The number of such sad misjudgments is endless.

---

⁴⁰ In Greek, ἀκκισμὸς.

⁴¹ In Greek, φιλονεικία. Melanchthon wrote a letter to Christoph von Carlowitz in 1548 which is found in MBW 5139 (CR 6.880). For scholarly assessment of this letter and the Greek term Melanchthon used to describe Luther, see Timothy J. Wengert, "'Not by Nature *Philoneikos*': Philip Melanchthon's Initial Reactions to the Augsburg Interim," in *Politik und Bekenntnis: Die Reaktionen auf das Interim von 1548*, ed. Irene Dingel and Günther Wartenberg (Leipzig: Evangelische Verlagsanstalt, 2007), 33–49.

⁴² Prov. 10:22.

⁴³ Virgil, *Georgics* 1.145–46.

⁴⁴ Dan. 4:30.

⁴⁵ See Erasmus, *Adages* 1.6.61 in CWE 32:43–44.

The divine message teaches that the reasons why good things happen are due not to human labors alone but to God's aid in such righteous labors, which are simply a combination of human obedience in accordance with one's calling. As a consequence, these negative propositions are taught [in Scripture]: "Unless the Lord builds the house, those who build it labor in vain."[46] Or in Ecclesiastes 9, "The race is not won by the speediest, nor the battle by the strongest, nor bread by the wisest."[47] Or Psalm 33, "It is foolish to put one's trust in a horse for safety."[48] Or Psalm 59, "God does not march out with our powers. Give us help from our trouble, for it is vain to rely on human strength."[49] Or Jeremiah 10, "I know, Lord, that the way of human beings is not their own."[50] Or John 3, "No one can receive anything unless it is given from God."[51] Finally, there is the teaching in John 15: "Without me you can do nothing."[52] These biblical testimonies do not aim to prevent the labor required of one's calling; rather, they teach that good things happen by God's help and are not merely the result of human wisdom alone or human labors alone. Indeed, these biblical testimonies condemn confidence in our own resources.

The divine message subsequently unites these causes of good outcomes: God helping human labors in a calling and our obedience in such a calling. Therefore, God commands just labors in accordance with our calling. See Ecclesiastes 9: "Whatever your hand is able to do, do it in all your strength."[53] Likewise 1 Thessalonians 4: "Diligently work toward leading a quiet life, taking care of your own affairs, and

---

[46] Ps. 127:1 (Vulgate 126:1).

[47] Eccl. 9:11.

[48] Ps. 33:17 (Vulgate 32:17).

[49] Ps. 60:10–11 (Vulgate 59:12–13).

[50] Jer. 10:23.

[51] John 3:27.

[52] John 15:5. Either Melanchthon, citing the passage from memory, writes chapter 5 instead of 15, or this is a typographical error.

[53] Eccl. 9:10.

Chapter 10

working with your hands."[54] Genesis 3: "In the sweat of your brow will you eat your food."[55] Psalm 127: "You will eat the labors of your hands; you are blessed and it will be well for you."[56] And, finally, Proverbs 10: "The hand of the diligent will become rich."[57] In short, it is necessary to recognize that our labors are blessed and that good outcomes follow when God helps our labors in accordance with our calling.

As a result, promises about divine aid and commands about prayer have been handed down so that God is acknowledged and, likewise, so that his presence is acknowledged in the governance of matters both private and public. See Psalm 36: "Be subject to God and pray to him."[58] Likewise, "Commend your way to God; put your hope in him and he will do it."[59] Psalm 33: "Those who fear the Lord lack nothing."[60] Psalm 54: "Cast your care upon God and he will sustain you."[61] Psalm 90: "I will protect him because he has known my name; I am with him in tribulation."[62] Daniel 2: "God gives wisdom to the wise and knowledge to the understanding."[63] Proverbs 16: "The human heart plans one's way, but God directs one's steps."[64] Proverbs 21: "The horse is prepared for the day of battle, but God gives the victory."[65] Proverbs 20: "The eye may see and the ear may hear, but God made

---

[54] 1 Thess. 4:11.

[55] Gen. 3:17.

[56] Ps. 128:2 (Vulgate 127:2).

[57] Prov. 10:4.

[58] Ps. 37:7 (Vulgate 36:7).

[59] Ps. 37:5 (Vulgate 36:5).

[60] Ps. 34:9 (Vulgate 33:10).

[61] Ps. 55:22 (Vulgate 54:23).

[62] Ps. 91:14 (Vulgate 90:14).

[63] Dan. 2:21.

[64] Prov. 16:9.

[65] Prov. 21:31.

both."[66] Isaiah 46: "I have made you and I will carry you in old age."[67] Isaiah 40: "I have carried you as a shepherd carries nursing lambs."[68] Deuteronomy 30: "For God is your life and the length of your days."[69] Deuteronomy 8: "A person does not live on bread alone but on every word that proceeds from God's mouth."[70] Exodus 19: "I have carried you on the wings of eagles."[71] And, finally, also from Deuteronomy 8: "Don't say, 'My [own] strength and hands have given me all things,' but rather be mindful of the Lord your God because it is God who has given you strength."[72]

It is profitable to keep these and similar biblical testimonies in view to cast out any worldly speculation from our minds, lest we begin to rely on our own intelligence and strength; let us believe sincerely that our labors are only blessed when they are helped by God and when we solicit the aid of God, as many [biblical] sayings attest. For instance, in the Psalms: "Commend your way to God; put your hope in him and he will do it."[73] And Proverbs 16: "Commend your works to God and your thoughts will be directed."[74] We are to give heed to this rule of life in all of our plans and endeavors, performing the labor of our calling while soliciting and expecting aid from God. This teaching about praying to God here is to be joined to teaching about divine promises.

It is also necessary to keep in mind that even pagans are forced to admit from experience that those who are stronger and wiser [than their opponents] often suffer defeat, namely, when they do unjust things such as undertaking unnecessary things by trusting in their own strength. In many cases, such trust resulted in destruction, as it

---

[66] Prov. 20:12.

[67] Isa. 46:4.

[68] Isa. 40:11.

[69] Deut. 30:20.

[70] Deut. 8:3.

[71] Ex. 19:4.

[72] Deut. 8:14.

[73] Ps. 37:5 (Vulgate 36:5).

[74] Prov. 16:3.

is said about Ajax. When he said that he was even able to be victorious without God, on account of this ungodly trust in himself, he was punished, knowingly killing himself in a rage.[75] For instance, the story of Milo of Croton is often told.[76] While attempting to tear apart a tree trunk, he got stuck and was torn to pieces by wolves. Then there's the story of how Bellerophontes was dismounted by Pegasus while trying to enter Mount Olympus.[77] And, finally, there's the story of how Perseus destroyed Medusa's head.[78]

---

[75] Ajax ultimately killed himself after failing to win the battle gear of Achilles in a competition with Odysseus. In a rage, he killed himself as a result of his loss of honor.

[76] Milo of Croton was a sixth-century BCE Greek wrestler who was renowned for his strength.

[77] In Greek mythology, Pegasus was an untamed winged horse and the offspring of the god Poseidon; Bellerophontes (also called Bellerophon) was a great hero akin to Heracles or Perseus. With the aid of the goddess Athena, he captured Pegasus but later died by falling off the creature when riding to Mount Olympus, as mentioned here.

[78] Perseus and Medusa are two other famous characters in Greek mythology. Perseus, a famous hero like Bellerophontes, was the offspring of Zeus. He killed Medusa, one of three Gorgons whose hair was made of poisonous snakes and whose faces turned onlookers into stone.

Chapter 11

"The Lord detests a dishonest scale, but a fair weight pleases him."[1]

This precept has to do with particular justice and truthfulness in contracts. It also pertains to the saying in the Ten Commandments: "You shall not steal."[2] This threat is often repeated. Here it must be understood as returning to a precept already discussed, namely, that grave sins are punished by means of grave punishments, even in this life.[3] As the sayings go, "The one who lives by the sword dies by it,"[4] and, "Woe to you who rob, for you will be robbed."[5] It is in consideration of this order that God wants himself to be acknowledged and wants this order to be understood as divinely sanctioned.

Let us also recognize that marriages, political matters, contracts, judgments, and penalties are all works of God's wisdom and justice, and that they are preserved by God in a powerful way to the extent that a modicum of order remains, even while great storms are set in motion by the devil and the devil's instruments. As a shepherd may safeguard some sheep, although wolves snatch some of the flock, so Solomon says below about political order in the sixteenth chapter:

---

[1] Prov. 11:1.

[2] Ex. 20:15.

[3] See Melanchthon's comments on Prov. 5 and 10:1–3.

[4] Matt. 26:52.

[5] Isa. 33:1.

"The weights and balances are God's judgment, and all weights on the scale are God's works."[6] This admonition is necessary to oppose the madness of the Manichaeans and Anabaptists, as it is stated in other places with frequency and at length.[7]

"When pride comes, disgrace comes afterward; but in the humble there is wisdom."[8]

It is common for people to become more careless in prosperity. For, after having fortified their defenses, they begin to show less fear and discomfort, and as a consequence, their prayer to God becomes weaker, as it is said in [the books of] Moses: "The people sat down to eat and drink and then got up to play."[9] Likewise, "Feelings run wild in prosperity."[10] For after the fear of God is extinguished and people become careless, swelling in their own sense of power and stepping into many things beyond their calling, they become injurious to others. This is when punishments follow by means of the divine order in accordance with the sayings, "God resists the proud, but gives grace to the humble."[11] Likewise, "God has dethroned the powerful, but exalted the humble."[12]

Experience forces pagans to admit that through the divine order, punishments follow unavoidably upon pride, when it goes to ruin beyond the bounds of their calling. The Greeks gave this order the name *Adrasteia*,[13] which was a sign of ruin following an extraordinary

---

[6] Prov. 16:11.

[7] Regarding the Anabaptists, Melanchthon particularly opposed their notions of communal property. See above, p. 48.

[8] Prov. 11:2.

[9] Ex. 32:6. The apostle Paul also quotes this passage in 1 Cor. 10:7.

[10] Ovid, *Art of Love* 2.437. For Ovid, see p. 18, n. 10.

[11] Prov. 3:34 and James 4:6.

[12] Luke 1:52.

[13] Adrastea, in Greek ἀδράστειαν, "the Inevitable," was a title in Greek mythology for Nemesis and for the nymph who took care of Zeus when he was a child in hiding from his father Cronus.

arrogance, in line with the saying of Claudian: "The unjust are raised up so that they may be hurled down ..."[14] This is exactly what Solomon means in this passage. In contrast, however, he says that wisdom exists among the humble. As Peter said, "God gives grace to the humble."[15] And it is spoken by Isaiah: "Where does the Lord live?... Among those with a contrite and humble spirit who keep my words."[16]

It is important to provide definitions for Humility and Pride. Humility, or "lowliness of mind" in Greek,[17] is acknowledging and confessing one's own weakness in the fear of God, not reaching beyond one's calling, but rather, in the hope of divine aid, serving God within the confines of one's calling, neither looking down upon nor seeking to outdo others, but yielding to the individual level into which they have been ordered, both understanding that they, too, can be salutary instruments of God and not becoming angered when God punishes. An illustrious example of the virtue of humility is Jonathan.[18] But the best example is the obedience that God's Son manifested in his calling. As he himself said, "Learn from me, for I am gentle and humble in heart."[19]

Pride, by contrast, is being secure and living without the fear of God, relying upon one's own strength, arrogantly breaking loose from the duty of one's calling, wishing to enlarge one's own sense of power, "despising and oppressing" others,[20] obstinately giving preference to one's own wisdom as the best advice, and being angry with God and

---

[14] Claudian, *Against Rufinus* 1.21–23.

[15] 1 Peter 5:5.

[16] Isa. 66:1–2.

[17] In Greek, ταπεινοφροσύνη.

[18] See, for example, 1 Sam. 18:1–5.

[19] Matt. 11:29. See also Phil. 2:5–11, which uses a form of the same Greek verb.

[20] Quintilian, *Institutes of Oratory* 11.1.16. Quintilian, whose full name was Marcus Fabius Quintillianus, was a Roman who was perhaps most famous for the composition of this twelve-book work on rhetoric.

other people when one's plans end in misfortune, as in the case of Pharaoh, Goliath, Saul, Ahithophel, and others.

"If there is retribution on earth for the righteous, how much more so for the ungodly and sinner?" [21]

This is a sobering admonition, out of which the following saying of Peter is derived: "For it is now time for judgment to begin with the house of God. And if first with us, what will be the outcome of those who do not believe in the Gospel? And if the righteous are barely saved, what will become of the ungodly and the sinner?"[22] This teaching has to do with repentance and the judgment coming upon the ungodly, but it also has to do with the consolation that comes from the scandal of the cross. This is an example of an *argumentum a minore [ad maius]*, "an argument from the lesser to the greater."[23] Since we know that the just are afflicted in this life even though they seek to improve, how much more so will the ungodly be punished who obstinately and stubbornly persist in their crimes. Therefore, it is necessary that after this life there remains another judgment, so that, although David was punished [in this life] for adultery and murder, other worse people, such as Dionysius and Tiberius,[24] will doubtless be punished [in the future]. Although they experienced peaceful deaths in this life, there therefore remains another judgment.

Here, however, two rules clash, and a resolution must be offered. The first rule is this: Severe sins are punished in severe ways in this life. This coincides with the order of justice in God. And because this generally happens, the congruity of these examples testifies to the providence and presence of God in this world.

---

[21] Prov. 11:31.

[22] 1 Peter 4:17–18.

[23] This lesser-used logical argumentation originated in Aristotle's *Topics*.

[24] The Dionysius mentioned here is probably Dionysius I of Syracuse, a Greek ruler of the fifth and fourth century BCE who was commonly regarded as evil and cruel. Tiberius was the emperor of Rome during the entirety of Christ's ministry. Ruling from 14 to 37 CE, Tiberius was regarded by Roman historians as corrupt and depraved.

The other rule is this: The church has been subjected to the cross, and [worldly] tyrants assail her in a cruel way.25 This does not appear to coincide with the [divine] order of justice, causing Reason to ask whether providence exists. But the church responds as follows: In the first place, it does coincide with God's order of justice for even the church to be punished [in this life] since sin clings to her. And the church has known many reasons why it has been subjected to the cross. When it comes to tyrants, another true rule obtains, namely, that they also are often liable to punishments in this life, in accordance with the saying, "Few kings go down without murder or blood to the son-in-law of Ceres [that is, Hades]. Few tyrants meet a bloodless death."26 Although tyrants flourish for a time, in other words, they will eventually be driven from power.

In the second place, [this punishment] exists so that the church may come to conform to God's standard of justice, as God punishes crimes not only with present and temporary punishments but also eternal ones. Thus, the church may respond to the following argument: "It goes well for the righteous but evilly for the unrighteous. The church is righteous, and tyrants are unrighteous. Therefore it must go well for the church but evilly for tyrants." The church responds to the major premise as follows: It indeed goes well for the righteous and evilly for the unrighteous in accordance with the declaration of the Gospel, which teaches why the church has been subjected to the cross in this life. Nevertheless some remnant is always preserved by

---

25 With the defeat of the (Evangelical) Schmalkaldic League in 1547 and the resulting harsh measures enacted against some of their churches and pastors, this theme becomes especially important for Melanchthon's ecclesiology.

26 Juvenal, *Satire* 10.112. Juvenal was a Roman poet of the second century CE. In this tenth satire, Juvenal mocks human desires and speaks of the ills of those seeking their own aggrandizement. Ceres was a popular Roman goddess. Ceres's son-in-law was Pluto (or Hades in Greek mythology), the god of the dead. Incidentally, and Melanchthon does not mention this, but this tenth satire of Juvenal's includes the famous expressions *mens sana in corpore sano*, "a healthy mind in a healthy body," and *panem et circenses*, "bread and circuses."

God, and afterwards the church will possess eternal blessings while the ungodly will be in eternal punishment. Indeed these very examples are testimonies of the coming judgment. For Abel was killed by Cain, even though the righteous God had formerly shown that he loved Abel.[27] In addition, to the minor premise it must be responded: The church is righteous by [divine] imputation and only in an initial way, not yet in a completed one. Therefore the church is assailed at this time so that she would recognize God's judgment against sin, as it is stated in Isaiah: "Chastisement acts as discipline to them so that they cry out to you."[28] Therefore this is the conclusion that follows: Tyrants are often punished in this life, but in the afterlife there will always be eternal punishments. Although the church is afflicted, it experiences mitigation of such affliction in this life and will later possess eternal blessings.

---

[27] Gen. 4:1–16. Melanchthon is interpreting the notion in Genesis that God accepted Abel's offering and not Cain's (4:4–5) as demonstrating God's love for Abel. Based on the verbs used in the Hebrew (וַיִּשַׁע), Greek (ἐπεῖδεν), and Latin (*respexit*) versions, the key verb may be translated variously as God "gazed upon," "looked with favor upon," or "regarded" Abel's sacrifice. For a similar interpretation, see Luther's lectures on Genesis (LW 1:257–59).

[28] The reference for this quotation is unknown.

Chapter 12

There are many sayings in the twelfth chapter. Regarding God's providence statements are repeated that the unjust are going to be punished. Likewise, there are topics regarding labor as well as vices of the tongue, such as lying, sophistry, trickery, boasting, and bragging. However, it is especially important for the reader to remember the following saying: "Lying lips are an abomination to the Lord."[1] Let us acknowledge the command to love and maintain diligent care for the truth, as it relates both to teaching about God and to the arts, and as it relates to all trustworthy agreements and contracts. And because truth is among the most distinguished and illustrious virtues, the contrary vice of using a harsh word is condemned and called an "abomination," that is, an evil which God detests in sweeping terms, in the same way that an idol is also called an "abomination" in Greek.[2]

---

[1] Prov. 12:22.

[2] In Greek, the term is βδελυγμία. This is the word used often in the Septuagint, which the Vulgate renders as *abominatio*, and is seen most clearly in the passage Melanchthon is discussing: Βδέλυγμα κυρίῳ χείλη ψευδῆ (Prov. 12:22), "lying lips are an abomination to the Lord."

Chapter 13

"Among the proud lies contention, but wisdom is found among those who deliberate."[1]

There is a saying in Greek that "one mountain is not connected to [another] mountain," by which is meant that "two people of equal stature do not associate with each other."[2] Indeed, although discord is caused by many things, oftentimes the main cause is pride. That is to say, it must be noted that when there are two personalities that regard themselves highly and want to be superior to the other, they will seize upon any occasion of strife whatsoever, undaunted by either the largeness or smallness of the matter, fighting for reputation and for popular applause. Afterward, what evil things result from public discord! It is out of this context that the following sayings arise: "At that time, the glory of a few overthrew the land in the desire for praise

---

[1] Prov. 13:10.

[2] Erasmus, *Adages* 3.3.45 (CWE 34:296), which also provides word-for-word the explanation Melanchthon uses.

and commemoration."[3] Likewise in Claudian, "For pride, extravagance, vice, and venom have destroyed many kingdoms."[4]

Thus, there are two human qualities that are especially bitter: desire for glory, and rage or a desire for vengeance. These qualities are exemplified in the lives of Gaius Marius and Sulla, and of Pompey and Caesar,[5] and others. It is for this reason that the Son of God explicitly commanded in the most severe terms that these two qualities must be bridled: "Learn from me, for I am gentle and humble in heart."[6] Here the virtue of humility counters pride while that of gentleness counters desire for vengeance.

Now, gentleness is the virtue that in the first instance is included in justice, so that it does not fight unnecessary battles. But even when it is necessary to fight, gentleness restrains any anger, showing leniency by giving the benefit of the doubt even when anger is justified or punishment is due. But because in this passage "deliberation" is contrasted with "contention," it signifies that souls hindered by ambition, anger, or other such human emotions either do not perceive what is true or, when they do, they nevertheless do not want to appear to be conquered,

---

[3] Juvenal, *Satire* 10.142–143. In this section of the satire, Juvenal is discussing how mighty leaders and figures have been more concerned about their own fame than with virtue. The word translated here as "commemoration," *titulus*, is referring to an inscription or epitaph celebrating a leader's glory and memory, which were common in the Greco-Roman world. As the next line in Juvenal's satire indicates, the immediate reference is to an epitaph engraved upon one's tombstone.

[4] Claudian, *On Stilicho's Consulship* 3.160–61. The immediate section Claudian is referring to is on the pride of Rome. For Claudian, see above, p. 41, n. 25.

[5] These are four of the most important statesmen and generals in Roman history who lived in the second and first centuries before Christ. Each of them held the consulship and were celebrated generals of their times, dominating Roman politics and waging countless battles during their lives.

[6] Matt. 11:29.

as it is said, "A friend will frequently lend gold, wealth, and a security; but the one who agrees to forfeit a *talentum* [of silver] is rare."[7]

For this reason, we recognize "in deliberation"[8] that truth must be sought out of its own sources, and inquiry must not be impeded by waves of the emotions. The following sayings must also be considered: "Truth is lost in too much arguing."[9] Likewise, "Whoever is not very wise, he is wise."[10] "Believe me, to be wise is not to be very wise."[11] The mind, having discovered the truth, is satisfied, gives thanks to God, and applies the truth to its proper use in life, as was stated above: "Lying lips are an abomination to the Lord."[12]

"Abundant food in the tillage of the poor, while others amass it without measure."[13]

This precept for the household[14] has to do with moderation and attentiveness in preserving one's resources in a moderate way in accordance with the saying, "Praise large estates, [but] cultivate a small

---

[7] Martial, *Epigram* 8.18. This poem was written to Cirinius. Martial paid a compliment to Cirinius for not publishing his own epigrams so that they would not compete with Martial's.

[8] Prov. 13:10.

[9] This common expression was used in law and was one of which Melanchthon was especially fond.

[10] Martial, *Epigram* 14.210 reads as follows: *Quisquis plus iusto non sapit, ille sapit*, "Whoever is not more than wise enough, is wise." Here Martial is mocking a foolish person. It is possible that Melanchthon is borrowing this phrase from Martial, especially since he certainly quoted from him a few lines above. The Latin verb *sapere* has a broad range of meaning, for example, "to know [information]," "to be able," "to find out," "to taste," and "to smell."

[11] These words of Socrates are from Plato's *Apology* and seem to be a summary of Socrates rather than a direct quotation.

[12] Prov. 12:22.

[13] Prov. 13:23.

[14] For Melanchthon, there are several "precepts." See discussions in previous chapters.

one."[15] The meaning here is that it is better to be in possession of moderate resources—overseeing them capably and enjoying them in peace and quiet than to amass great riches, because it is not possible to amass them without misfortunes.[16] Here the saying of Paul pertains well: "Those who desire to become rich fall into foolish and dangerous temptations."[17] To these sayings another must be brought to bear: "It is better to be in charge of something small—and maintain it—than some great thing that we are less able to maintain in excellence."[18] The following little verse must also be noted, which Aristotle cites in book 4 of *Politics* out of the writings of Phocylides: "Those in the middle [class] often have the best, which is why I think it is best to be in the middle [class] of the city state."[19]

---

[15] Virgil, *Georgics* 2.411–412. Here Virgil is possibly reversing a saying from Hesiod in *Works and Days* 643: "Praise a small ship, but put your cargo in a large one." Hesiod's Greek phraseology, νῆ' ὀλίγην αἰνεῖν, μεγάλῃ δ' ἐνὶ φορτία θέσθαι, is just as succinct as Virgil's Latin: *Laudato ingentia rura, exiguum colito*. Virgil is referring to the toilsome labor it takes to work a farm.

[16] Here Melanchthon is working out of language and concepts—such as the "mean" and "moderation"—that are most often associated with Aristotle. Melanchthon will subsequently quote directly out of Aristotle's *Politics*, where Aristotle argues that a happy life is one that is lived according to the mean and moderation—where one is neither too wealthy nor too poor. Melanchthon accepts this argument, believing that one should be in charge of just the right amount of resources in accordance with one's calling, possessing or overseeing neither more nor less.

[17] 1 Tim. 6:9.

[18] The source of this quote is unknown.

[19] Aristotle, *Politics* 4 (1295b.33–34). Aristotle begins the section by stating, "In all states therefore there exist three divisions of the state, the very rich, the very poor, and, third, those who are between the two." Phocylides was a sixth-century Greek poet, most of whose writings have only been preserved in fragments. The Greek cited is πολλά μεσοισιν άριστα μέσος θέλω εν πόλει είναι.

Chapter 14

"There is a way that seems right to a person, but whose end nonetheless is a way toward death."[1]

This admonition is about the weakness and feebleness of human judgment as well as many great errors contained in human advice, since it is quite clear that people err frequently in matters of judgment and deliberations. Such people are deceived by their own imaginations, by the poor examples of others, or by custom and the like. And by being so greatly deceived, they rush forward headlong, becoming ensnared by the devil, as it was written of Judas: "Satan entered his heart."[2] In this way, a great multitude has approved of and assents to ungodly worship, and heretics tenaciously attempt to cling to monstrous dogmas. For instance, both Pompey and Josiah erred in their consideration of war.[3] There are existing complaints concerning this prevalent infirmity and weakness according to the following sayings: "The number of fools is infinite."[4] "Everyone is a liar."[5] Likewise, "Not one human being is

---

[1] Prov. 14:12.

[2] Luke 22:3.

[3] Pompey was a celebrated Roman general who was involved in several wars, so it is difficult to know to which war exactly Melanchthon refers in this passage. As for Josiah, however, Melanchthon most likely refers to his decision to go to war with the king of Egypt in 2 Kings 23:28–29.

[4] Eccl. 1:15 (Vulgate).

[5] Ps. 116:11 (Vulgate 115:11); Rom. 3:4.

wise in all things."[6] Likewise, "Looks can oftentimes deceive."[7] And, finally, Simonides says, "Fame constrains the truth."[8] Against such evils, there is only one remedy: devoutly discerning the Word of God and prayerfully doing all things in accordance with that Word of God. As these sayings indicate, "Your word is a lamp to my feet."[9] Likewise, "Commend your way to God; put your hope in him and he will do it."[10] Finally, Deuteronomy 4, "This is your wisdom, namely, to walk in my commandments."[11]

---

[6] Theognis 902 (cited in the Greek).

[7] Theognis 128 (cited in the Greek).

[8] Simonides, *Fragments* 598 (cited in the Greek).

[9] Ps. 119:105 (Vulgate 118:105).

[10] Ps. 37:5 (Vulgate 36:5).

[11] Deut. 4:6.

Chapter 15

"A mild response diminishes anger, but a harsh word provokes it."[1]

The entire law of God is a description of God's character—God's qualities. This law has been revealed to human beings so that we would come to know both God's qualities and that he wants us to be conformed to him. For example, God gave the command "Do not murder"[2] because God is not the God of destruction but of salvation, as God also attests: "As I live, says the Lord, I do not wish for the death of the sinner but rather for the sinner to have a change of heart and live."[3] Due to these statements describing God's qualities, many precepts have been handed down about peace that pertain to the precept cited above about not committing murder. Those who disturb peace without a just cause violate this precept. Therefore, these sayings must be duly noted: "Blessed are the peacemakers because they will be called the children of God."[4] And Romans 12 states, "As much as you are able, maintain peace with all people."[5]

---

[1] Prov. 15:1.

[2] Ex. 20:13.

[3] Ezek. 33:11. This is an important text for Melanchthon in his insistence on the effectiveness of God's promises over against what he viewed as a too harsh an understanding of predestination in John Calvin and others.

[4] Matt. 5:9.

[5] Rom. 12:18.

Precepts about how to retain peace have also been handed down. First, let no one injure another. Second, it does not suffice merely to refrain from generating unjust strife but rather there must also be a way to oppose wrongdoings "in defense,"[6] as they say in Greek. For there is no resistance worse than injuring someone. As it is stated, "Let not defending [oneself] be the same as [going on] the offensive."[7] If it is a contention over words, and awful accusations are made, you should respond moderately with words. If, however, the words are not awful accusations, then it is oftentimes a virtue to keep quiet about these things, to forgive for the sake of common peace, and to refute them more so by the testimonies of one's life than by recrimination. As Cicero said, "It sits poorly with me if speech convicts me more so than my life."[8] Similarly, Demosthenes said that he was not going to respond to personal aspersions [about his character] since his [open and public] life opposed such accusations: "If you know me to be such a person as [Aeschines] himself alleges, rise up immediately and condemn me."[9] Finally, David said, "They were disparaging me, but I was praying."[10]

---

[6] In Greek, ἐν τῷ ἀμύνεσθαι. Thucydides, *Peloponnesian Wars* 2.43.1. For Melanchthon's translation into Latin of orations contained in Thucydides, see CR 16:1019–1112; for 2.43.1 in particular, see 1045–50.

[7] The source of this quote is unknown, but it seems to be a standard Latin adage, reflected in Justinian's Code, bk. 4, tit. 3, eclog. 14.1, regarding moderation in response to an injury.

[8] Among other sources, according to Cornelius a Lapide, *Commentaria in Epistolam I S. Petri* (Naples, 1859), 502, this reference to Cicero comes from Lactantius, *Divine Institutes* 3.15–16. If so, it is not explicitly stated there.

[9] Demosthenes, "On the Crown," in *Orations* 18.10, a famous speech delivered by Demosthenes in Athens in 330 BCE. In the excerpt that Melanchthon quotes here, Demosthenes is referring to Aeschines, who had accused Demosthenes of violating Athenian law. For more, see a Latin translation of *On the Crown* (*De Corona*) in reference to the passages cited in Philip Melanchthon, *Interpretatio Orationis Demosthenis De Corona* (CR 17:806).

[10] Ps. 109:4 (Vulgate 108:4).

This moderation pertains to the following virtues: gentleness, patience, and the duty owed to the church or to the preservation of public peace. However, the extremes are, on the one hand, "love of strife,"[11] as the Greeks say, which is otherwise known as eagerness for contention, and on the other hand, tenderness. Still, many commit a sin in their love of strife, since this evil is much more pernicious.

Indeed, love of strife ignites wrongful disputes and unnecessary controversies arising out of pride, ambition, a capricious temperament, jealousy, irritability, or excessive fear; or it arises out of a need to respond without concession, refusing to back down in anything, wishing only to conquer and seize upon the occasion of inciting hatred from all sides, as Lucan says, "[Fate] found excuse for drawing the sword."[12] Likewise in Lucan, "[But Caesar] wandered [through the troops] adding fury to the souls already flaming [with the rage of war]."[13] By nature, many tribunes are restless and quarrelsome. In fact, there are as many heretics in the church as there were tribunes in Rome. This recalls an old saying compiled by Stobaeus, asserting that

---

[11] In Greek, φιλονεικία. This word means "love of strife," "love of victory," "contention," or "quarrel." Already in the 1550s, Melanchthon was attacked for calling Luther a lover of strife. This matched his understanding of heroes, who were allowed to have characteristics not proper for lesser folk. In this context, Melanchthon may be criticizing his own Lutheran opponents. See p. 71, n. 41.

[12] Lucan, *The Civil War* (*Pharsalia*) 1.265, trans. J. D. Duff (Cambridge, MA: Harvard University Press, 1928), 23. Lucan was a Roman poet who lived from AD 39 to 65. His most famous surviving work, *The Civil War* (also called *Pharsalia*), poetically describes the war between Caesar and Pompey. In the section quoted, Caesar is crossing the Rubicon, signaling war against his enemies in Rome. This reference would seem to be Melanchthon's indirect rebuke of the attacks by his intra-Lutheran opponents, especially Matthias Flacius.

[13] Lucan, *The Civil War* VII.559, trans. Edward Riley (London, 1905). In this section, Caesar is attacking the senators.

eagerness of contention is the cause of excessive damage: "Great evils come into being from nothing other than love of strife."[14]

Since, therefore, this vice must be avoided, Solomon delivers an admonition in this manner. "A mild response diminishes anger,"[15] that is to say, not only should you not offend anyone by wrongdoing, but even when responding to someone, you should strive to soothe the situation to some degree. There are many such similar precepts advising us not to fight in anger, for instance, "Do not stir up a fire with a sword."[16] The following verses of Euripides are also to be lauded: "When two people are saying angry things to the other, the one who does not become contentious with his words is wisest."[17]

But some will object here, saying, "Rebuke in season and out of season ..."[18] Such zeal serves as a pretext for private hatred, pride, and other such affections. Yet let those who reason soundly recognize in this matter that regulations handed down by God must be followed.

Teachers rightly teach in this instance—and how necessary this kind of teaching is—that fools should not instigate foolish fights over words, nor should they argue over nonessential matters or things not

---

[14] In Greek, τὰ μεγάλα κακὰ οὐκ ἄλλως ἢ ἐκ φιλονεικίας συνίσταται. Johannes Stobaeus, *Anthologium*, vol. 3, section 121, ed. Curtius Wachsmuth and Otto Hense (Berlin: Weidmannsche, 1894), 252. Stobaeus was a Greek writer in the fifth century CE. His compilation of known Greek sayings, called *Anthology* in English, but *Eclogues* in Greek (and so titled in the first volume) and *Florilegium* in Latin (and so titled in the second volume) has not yet been translated into English. All translations by Derek Cooper.

[15] Prov. 15:1.

[16] This proverb, here written in Latin, has roots in Greek, πῦρ μαχαίρᾳ μὴ σκαλεύειν. Variations of this proverb appear frequently in the classical Latin and Greek traditions, many with connections to Pythagoras. Essentially, this proverb means that it is not prudent to incite a person who is already angry, similar to pouring oil on a fire.

[17] In Greek, δυοῖν λεγόντοιν θατέρου θυμουμένου ὁ μὴ ἀντιτείνων τοῖς λόγοις σοφώτερος. This saying is another compiled by Johannes Stobaeus, possibly coined by Euripides. It appears in *Anthologium*, vol. 1, section 18, ed. Thomas Gaisford (Oxford: Clarendon, 1822), 146.

[18] 2 Tim. 4:2.

germane to one's calling.[19] Inquiring disciples should [instead] respond concerning this teaching as Peter said, "Be ready to give a response to all who inquire, with gentleness."[20]

"The sacrifice of the wicked is an abomination to the Lord, but the prayers of the just please God."[21]

This teaching was frequently enjoined in the prophets, particularly relating to three kinds of works: regarding ceremonies, morals, and faith. This assembly of topics encompasses the entirety of Psalm 50: "I will not command the flesh of bulls ..."[22] On the contrary, the psalmist rebukes the way these ceremonies were abused. Likewise, it is said in Jeremiah 7, "I did not command you to make sacrifices."[23] And in the last chapter of Isaiah it is said, "Slaughtering a sheep is like strangling a dog."[24] Ecclesiastes 4 teaches, "Obedience is better than the sacrifice of fools who do not know what they are doing."[25] In Hosea 6, "I want mercy and not sacrifice, and the knowledge of God more than burnt offerings."[26] And John 4, "True worshipers will worship the Father in Spirit and in truth,"[27] that is, through the true knowledge according to the Word of God in the stirrings of the heart

---

[19] In Greek, the word for "fights about words" is λογομαχίας; and the word for "nonessential matters" is πάρεργοις. In both cases, Melanchthon is again reflecting his struggles in the early 1550s with other Lutherans over adiaphora, in which he deemed most of the debates to be merely a war of words.

[20] 1 Peter 3:15.

[21] Prov. 15:8.

[22] Melanchthon, using the Vulgate, cites Ps. 49 here and in the section below. Melanchthon's citation comes from 49:13 in the Vulgate (50:13 in modern Bibles).

[23] This verse is summative for the *locus* of the chapter in Jeremiah, not necessarily a direct quote; however, its language is most connected to 7:22.

[24] Isa. 66:3.

[25] Eccl. 4:17 (Vulgate).

[26] Hos. 6:6.

[27] John 4:24.

in fear, faith, and hope. These and similar sayings are known most readily to all, and the youth must particularly come to recognize the following three ranks of works or acts of worship.

The first kind of works is religious ceremonies, that is, external signs. God has established certain religious ceremonies for two reasons. The first is so that they would represent signs of promises, and the second is so that they may strengthen those gathered for public worship. For God does not want the church to be hidden in a corner but rather to be seen and recognized by all nations in word and in religious ceremonies.

However, it must be wisely considered in what way religious ceremonies are to be used. For people are inclined toward false worship, particularly the abuse of religious ceremonies. But once the knowledge of the promises is lost and the light of faith is extinguished, people turn their eyes toward religious ceremonies, assuming that these external acts merit the forgiveness of sins and constitute righteousness before God. This notion has been paraded about far and wide at all times and in every human society. Not only did the Gentiles feel this way about their sacrifices, but so, too, did a large portion of the people in Israel. Likewise, the Pharisees were teaching the same notion, as did monks about Mass, vows, and other religious ceremonies.[28]

However, the prophets sharply rebuke this common error. This is apparent in what I cited from Psalm 50 as well as in many other biblical passages. In fact, even the pagan Gentiles censured this superstition, which pays attention to religious ceremonies without good, moral works. As Plato stated, "It is proper to worship God—not pretending to do so out of a feigned sense of duty but truly honoring in a virtuous way."[29] Nonetheless, this pagan Gentile censure is not enough. For even though it is true that there ought to exist in human beings

---

[28] As Peter Fraenkel has argued in *Testimonia Patrum: The Function of the Patristic Argument in the Theology of Philip Melanchthon* (Geneva: Droz, 1961), 52–109, Melanchthon viewed the history of God's people to be a continuing struggle between ceremonialists and believers.

[29] Melanchthon begins with a Latin translation before shifting to the Greek, οὐ σχήμασι τεχνάζοντας ἀλλὰ ἀληθείᾳ τιμῶντας ἀρετήν. See Plato, *Epinomis* 989c.

the righteousness of a good conscience, nevertheless we know in the church that there must not simply be teaching about law-centered doctrine but also about the Mediator, the promise of grace, and faith. For knowledge of the Redeemer and the promise and trust in the Mediator ought to shine light on all moral and ceremonial works, so that our hearts may believe that they are accepted and heard on account of the Mediator, however undeserving we are, and by this faith approach God, just as the Lord says: "No one comes to the Father except through the Son."[30] Likewise, "whatever you ask the Father in my name, he will give it to you."[31]

God requires this kind of faith in prayer and in all of life. God also requires hope and anticipation when pleading for help, in accordance with the saying, "Because it [a vision] is coming, it will come, and it will not delay ..."[32] Likewise, "Make a sacrifice of righteousness and hope in the Lord."[33]

Second, good, moral works are pleasing to this end: not that they merit forgiveness of sins, but so that we may obey God, and that others may learn this teaching, and that they may praise God, and that the devil may not triumph in us against God.

Finally, religious ceremonies established by God are pleasing [to God] to this end: not to merit the forgiveness [of sins], but because they are signs, reminding us about God's promises with the result that faith is ignited, likewise because they are signs of confession [of faith], and likewise because they display the strength of the congregation. In the church, these true goals ought to be understood, and ungodly opinions ought to be eradicated.

---

[30] John 14:6.

[31] Melanchthon does not explicitly cite this verse, but it probably refers to John 15:16 or 16:23.

[32] Hab. 2:3. It may be that Melanchthon reads this verse to be about Christ: "The one coming will come and will not delay."

[33] Ps. 4:6 in the Vulgate (4:5 in modern English Bibles).

Chapter 16

"It belongs to the human being to prepare the heart, but the response of the tongue comes from God."[1]

A similar saying comes up below in this same chapter: "The human heart plans its way, but God directs one's steps."[2] These sayings do not take away freedom of the human will or of choice.[3] Rather, they signify that there are certain choices of the human will—both of those who are not reborn, for instance, Pompey, and of those who are reborn, for example, Joshua, David, and others. But when making these choices people sometimes make mistakes, for instance, as when Josiah waged an unnecessary war against the king of Egypt.[4] Although Josiah's will enjoyed free choice in the matter, his choice proved wrong, and an unfavorable outcome ensued.

And it must be carefully considered that it is one thing that a choice is in our purview, but success is quite another thing. For even if we make a favorable choice, it is necessary for God's assistance to be added in two ways: first in the decision itself and then in directing the outcome. For unless our judgment is governed both by the Word of God and by divine light, many errors will occur. For instance, Josiah,

---

[1] Prov. 16:1.

[2] Prov. 16:9.

[3] Instead of using the technical term for choice (*arbitrium*), Melanchthon uses a more general one (*electio*).

[4] See 2 Chron. 35:20–27.

Zedekiah, Demosthenes, Pompey, and Cicero all made the mistake of choosing to go to battle, resulting in disaster, because they were not helped by God. In fact, sometimes even when the mind does not err in judgment, God nevertheless does not step in to help those involved due to other reasons, as in the battle against Benjamin; unfavorable results befell the Israelites because they trusted in their own strength.[5]

Therefore, let us recognize that the cause of favorable outcomes does not arise only from human choice and diligence. As Jeremiah says, "I know, Lord, that a person's way is not his [or her] own."[6] This means that a person who makes plans without requesting divine assistance makes frequent errors and is unable to acquire favorable outcomes. Therefore, it has been written, "Unless the Lord builds the house …"[7] Likewise, "No one can receive anything unless it is given from God."[8] And also, "Without me you can do nothing,"[9] which is to say, "Without my assistance, you are not able to achieve favorable outcomes."[10]

God wants us to acknowledge this weakness of ours. Similarly, God wants us to be governed by God's Word in our calling, to fear God, and by faith to request divine assistance, according to this saying: "Commend your way to God; put your hope in him and he will do it."[11] Likewise, "Ask and you will receive."[12] And also, "When we do not know what to do, our eyes are directed to you."[13]

---

[5] See Judg. 20.

[6] Jer. 10:23. Note that Melanchthon cites this and the next three biblical verses here and in chapter 10. The topic here is very similar to the one found there and is a good indication of how *loci communes* (common topics) functioned in his exegesis.

[7] Ps. 127:1 (Vulgate 126:1).

[8] John 3:27.

[9] John 15:5.

[10] In all of these cases, Melanchthon takes texts often used in debates over predestination and applies them to human affairs.

[11] Ps. 37:5 (Vulgate 36:5).

[12] Matt. 7:7.

[13] 2 Chron. 20:12.

Therefore, this rule of life, which Solomon also repeats here, must be noted: "Commend your works to God, and then your thoughts will be confirmed."[14] In other words, follow the commands of God according to your calling and ask for assistance from God; once you do so, then there will be favorable outcomes for you and for the people.

This teaching must be frequently reflected upon, so that we would kindle in ourselves forethought to be governed by the Word of God and to be seeking divine assistance, and so on. These sayings must be accommodated to this specific use and not to the Stoic opinions about necessity.[15] For it does not logically follow: The outcome did not prove favorable to Zedekiah [in rebelling against Babylon], therefore Zedekiah did not freely will to go to war. On the contrary, there is no doubt that Zedekiah wanted to go to war, and that he willed it with neither the command nor the invocation of God; as a result, the outcome was not favorable.[16]

"God does all things because of himself, even [preparing] the ungodly for their day of wrath."[17]

The proverbs above were maxims about seeking assistance from God. This saying preaches about providence, about which there are many gloomy doubts that fill human minds. There are two kinds of

---

[14] Prov. 16:3.

[15] Melanchthon had in mind, for example, the arguments of John Calvin, whom he nicknamed "our Zeno," after the founder of Stoicism.

[16] The story of Zedekiah principally appears in 2 Kings 24:18–20; 25:1–7; and Jer. 52:2–3. He was the last king of Judah before the kingdom was destroyed by the Babylonians. After Jerusalem was conquered, Zedekiah was captured, his sons were killed in his presence, his eyes were gouged out, and he was taken as a captive to Babylon. Although this story was not specifically cited by Calvin, nevertheless, Proverbs 16:1 was, so that Melanchthon was assuredly going after the Genevan's "Stoic" position, as argued in the 1543 *The Bondage and Liberation of the Will: A Defence of the Orthodox Doctrine of Human Choice against Pighius*, trans. G. I. Davis, ed. A. N. S. Lane (Grand Rapids: Baker, 1996), especially 223–25.

[17] Prov. 16:4.

situations. The first are good things, in which order is evident; and the second are bad things, which involve the destruction of order, such as evil deeds and disasters.

Concerning good things, the mind is moved to consider that good things either do not arise by chance or are preserved by chance, but assenting to this reality[18] is nonetheless confused. For many philosophers dispute that the substance of heaven and earth has to exist in a certain way by necessity, and that it has always existed in such a way, and that this substance has generated other forms of matter—such things neither having been freely created by an eternal mind nor freely preserved by it.[19]

This discourse draws us away from these Cycloptic ragings back to the first article of faith concerning creation. No, Solomon says, such things do not occur by chance. Instead, God is truly wise and good, and God has most freely created good things and continues to preserve them. Namely, these good things are ordained by God: heaven, earth, the succession of time, the fertility of the earth, the creation of animals in their individual species, human society, the political order, the church, God's gifts in the good minds of individuals (wisdom and virtues), and the countless rescues of those who pray.

All these realities were carried out and came into being most freely by God so that they would serve as testimonies both to God's existence and to God's role as a wise and good God who creates and orders. This is what Solomon means when he says that God created "for himself."

But the Epicureans object by citing all the disorderly things [in the world]. They say that if God really wanted order, then where do evil, wickedness, and disasters come from? Solomon responds that they are punishments. In fact, even punishments are testimonies of providence, because it is universally [true] that severe sins are punished in severe

---

[18] Here Melanchthon is using a technical term from Ciceronian philosophy, *assensio*, "belief in the reality of sensible appearances." See Charlton T. Lewis and Charles Short, *A Latin Dictionary* (Oxford: Clarendon, 1879), ad loc. See Cicero, *De Fato* 40.

[19] Melanchthon has in mind Greek philosophers' insistence on the eternality of matter.

ways, even in this life in accordance with the saying, "The one who takes up the sword will die by the sword."[20] It is also universal that death and all disasters are punishments of original sin and of other sins in accordance with this saying of Paul: "Death came through sin …"[21] At the same time, it is true that God neither wills, nor executes, nor endorses sin. However, after people have wasted away their lives by their own freedom, God's justice becomes evident in this order of things because compensation for sin comes in the form of punishment.

What is more, in the proverb at hand, the syntax of the word *facit* must be considered.[22] Solomon does not say, "[God] *makes* the ungodly." Rather, he adds to the predicate: "[God] *makes* for the evil day." That is to say, God drags away for punishment the one who is ungodly—who sins by his [or her] own choice irrespective of God's will. This, too, is a testimony of providence. It is as when we say, "The sculptor made a figure of Alexander out of marble."[23] This sculptor did not give birth to the marble, but he is the fabricator of the figure. In the same way, God is by no means the cause of ungodliness, but through the order of justice punishes and destroys the ungodly.

Therefore, this entire proverb is a warning about providence. It admonishes us to acknowledge that God freely acts and preserves good things, and also that God most freely punishes in accordance with Psalm 32: "The Lord looks down from heaven, and he sees all the children of humankind."[24] And Psalm 61, "You repay all according to their work."[25]

---

[20] Matt. 26:52.

[21] Rom. 5:12.

[22] The verb *facit* means both "he makes" and "he does." It is one of the most common verbs in Latin, capable of many translations having to do with performance and activity.

[23] It is assumed that Melanchthon is referring to a statue of Alexander the Great. He is playing on the fact that in Latin the phrase *facere ex*, "to make from," can mean to generate something.

[24] Ps. 33:13 (Vulgate 32:13).

[25] Ps. 62:12 (Vulgate 61:13).

***"All the proud in heart are an abomination to the Lord. Though hand is clasped to hand, the haughty will not go unpunished."*[26]**

This saying is also cited in Luke 16: "That which is precious among human beings is an abomination before God."[27] And the author of Sirach says, "The beginning of all sin is pride."[28] The above-mentioned definitions must be pondered, and the opposing examples of Jonathan and the triumvirate of Antony must also be considered.[29] Finally, we must always have in mind the following saying: "God resists the proud but gives grace to the humble."[30]

***"Iniquity is atoned for by mercy and truth, and one is restrained from evil by the fear of the Lord."*[31]**

This admonition about distinguishing various forms of worship has been repeated, as in the saying above: "The sacrifice of the wicked is an abomination."[32] And also in Hosea 6, "I desire mercy and not burnt offerings and the knowledge of God more than sacrifices."[33] Here Solomon asserts in the same way that people do not achieve righteousness through sacrifices, but by possessing fear of God, God's mercy, and God's truth. The total sum of this doctrine has been sum-

---

[26] Prov. 16:5.

[27] Luke 16:15.

[28] Sir. 10:13 (Vulgate 10:14).

[29] Melanchthon is probably referring here to the second triumvirate during the first century BCE of the Roman Republic consisting of Octavian, Antony, and Lepidus. The alliance of the triumvirate is seen as the exact opposite of the kind of loving and humble covenant relationship between Jonathan and David (1 Sam. 18:1–5).

[30] 1 Peter 5:5.

[31] Prov. 16:6.

[32] Prov. 15:8.

[33] Hos. 6:6.

marized as follows: "Fight the good fight,"[34] and "Retain the faith and a good conscience."[35]

Fear of the Lord signifies true conversion to God in which there is fear and faith, just as it is said expressly elsewhere about faith.

This figure of speech about the pure and unfeigned love among people is common in Hebrew. This love is illustrated in the way that Jonathan exemplified mercy and truthfulness with David. That is, Jonathan blessed David and did so faithfully, without pretense, but with unswerving constancy. Such love appears in a proverb below in chapter 20: "Mercy and truth preserve the king, and his throne is strengthened by clemency,"[36] meaning that kindness and faithfulness are also the strength of royal rule. But if "truth" is understood here in relation to God, then it signifies true knowledge of God, which is faith.[37]

"Prophecy is on the lips of the king; his mouth will not err in judgment. Weights and balances are judgments of the Lord, and all the weights in the bag are his work."[38]

These sayings affirm that the entire political order—government officials, laws, the distinction among powers, contracts, judgments, punishments—are works ordered among the human race by God's wisdom. And even though the devil and human beings attempt to unsettle this order by many acts of unbridled rage; nevertheless, so that the human race not be completely wiped out, some element of political order remains. Let us understand that it is powerfully preserved by God, just as Daniel said, "God takes away and establishes

---

[34] 1 Tim. 6:12.

[35] 1 Tim. 1:19. In 1561 Melanchthon's commentary on 1 Timothy was published, based upon his lectures from 1550 to 1551, where he discusses this passage at length and connects it to 1 Tim. 6:12.

[36] Prov. 20:28.

[37] Unusual for this commentary, Melanchthon gives an alternative interpretation here of Prov. 20:28. He may be doing this against the interpretation of Nicholas of Lyra, who insists that truth and mercy are human virtues (not faith) and help atone for sin.

[38] Prov. 16:10–11.

kingdoms."[39] Therefore, once we recognize the political order to be the work of God, let us love it, strive to give attention to our callings, obey the ruler in a kindly manner for God's sake, and give thanks to God for preserving it. And let us recognize that the ragings of the devil and of people who only seek to unsettle the political order displease God. This doctrine is recited at great length in Romans 13.

But why does Solomon say, "Prophecy is on the lips of the king; his mouth will not err in judgment"? These parts must be combined. This saying speaks about a king and judgments, not about a tyrant and calumnies.[40] The voice of the king is prophecy when he judges according to the laws. Therefore, Solomon calls the laws themselves and judgments made in conformity with the laws "prophecy," because the laws demonstrate divine wisdom. For the font of all worthy laws is the Ten Commandments, which is the summation of all natural laws. It is for this reason that God has originally and principally placed government officials in command of the human race so that they would echo the voice of the Ten Commandments and would be those who administer punishment. Moreover, God has also armed government officials with the responsibility to enact their own laws, which do not conflict with the Ten Commandments but are instead derived from the Ten Commandants using either proofs or common sense.

So that those who rule may perceive these grounds for enacting laws, God moves the minds of some kings and makes them exceptionally inspired[41] (as some skilled craftsmen possess exceptional inspiration) because God wishes to preserve the human race in this way, governing the minds of salutary leaders and excellent craftsmen. As the

---

[39] Dan. 2:21.

[40] This limitation is found throughout Melanchthon's thought. See David C. Steinmetz, "Calvin and Melanchthon on Romans 13:1–7," *Ex Auditu: An Annual of the Frederick Neumann Symposium on Theological Interpretation of Scripture* 2 (1986): 74–81.

[41] Melanchthon uses the Latin term *motus* much in line with Ciceronian anthropology (cf. *De officiis* 1.36.130: *motus animorum duplices sunt, alteri cogitationis, alteri appetitus*).

saying goes, "God made both the eyes for seeing and the ears for hearing."[42] Such was the exceptional inspiration of Solomon in reckoning which of the two was the mother.[43]

The more recent judgment of Gonzaga, the Milanese governor of Gonzaga, offers an exceptional example.[44] When the Spanish prefect of a city under his authority took a nobleman captive, the captive's spouse petitioned for his freedom by offering a large sum of money. The Spaniard then demanded to sleep with her, so that when he got his way, he killed the captive and returned him to her dead. Gonzaga subsequently learned of this incident, captured[45] the Spaniard, and forced him to marry that woman. After he married her, the prince judged the Spaniard guilty of a capital crime, had him put to death, and gave the Spaniard's possessions to the woman.

---

[42] Prov. 20:12.

[43] See 1 Kings 3:16–28.

[44] The noble family of this name ruled in northern Italy for centuries during the Middle Ages and Early Modern period, especially in Mantua, not Milan. In a variant of this story, Melanchthon and Luther refer to Duke Charles of Burgundy. See Luther's *On Temporal Authority*, LW 45:128–129 (WA 11:279–280) and a "table talk" of Melanchthon in CR 20:531. According to *Martin Luther: Studienausgabe*, vol. 3, ed. Hans-Ulrich Delius (Berlin: Evangelische Verlagsanstalt, 1983), 71n489, this latter version was based upon a contemporary ballad of Hans Folz.

[45] Here *cepit* is understood for *coepit*.

Chapter 17

"Whoever keeps another's offense secret acquires a friendship, but whoever reveals them tears apart princes."

"Rebuking the wise causes more torment than a hundred blows to a fool."

"The evil person seeks only discord, and a cruel messenger will find them."

"It is better to encounter a bear bereft of her cubs than a fool in his stupidity."[1]

These connected sayings all pertain to the order of rendering judgment. This is understood in the saying of Christ: "If your brother [or sister] should sin against you, point out the fault only between the two of you."[2] Pastors and others, especially those who possess the office of teaching, when learning of someone's error or of some injustice committed, should first admonish the accused privately. If the ones admonished do not amend their ways, however, then the one admonishing should make a public accusation.

However, let Truth and Candor accompany those making the admonishment; they should not seek to distort what they seek to amend.

---

[1] These quotes come from Prov. 17:9–12, respectively. They are based upon Melanchthon's own translation, where in verse 9, he reads *aluph* as *aleph*, the first ones.

[2] Matt. 18:15.

The admonishment given should be gentle, not antagonistic. Under no circumstances should there be what the Greeks described as "love of strife,"[3] that is, an evil desire for contentiousness. The precepts given in this passage apply both to the one admonishing and to the one being admonished.

Unfortunately, evil persons seek only controversies. Rather than seeking the truth and salvation of the church, they—like Cleon and Alcibiades in ancient Greece who frequently spread the seeds of war—stir up trouble to no limit.[4] The Cynics and philosophers of the Academy of ancient Greece spoke against all kinds of things.[5] They are the ancient equivalents of Valla, Cornelius Agrippa, Karlstadt, Osiander, Stancaro,[6] and many others who have contentious natures.

---

[3] In Greek, φιλονεικία. See p. 71, n. 41.

[4] Cleon and Alcibiades were important statesman in ancient Greece in the fifth century BCE, younger contemporaries to Pericles. The "war" referred to is the Peloponnesian War, fought in the fifth century between Athens and Sparta. Cleon and Alcibiades were opponents of Pericles; unlike Pericles, they sought war against Sparta. Melanchthon, who lectured on portions of Thucydides's *Peloponnesian Wars*, doubtless has in mind attacks against him by so-called Gnesio-Lutherans, especially on matters of adiaphora and free will.

[5] The Academy was a school founded by Plato. Melanchthon would have understood not simply later Platonists but also especially skeptics.

[6] All these men were churchmen and academics. Lorenzo Valla (1407–1457) was an Italian humanist who first published criticism of the Latin Vulgate Bible on the basis of the original Greek text. Melanchthon often mentioned him in attacking determinism. Cornelius Agrippa (1486–1535) was a Cologne-trained humanist and theologian, some of whose writings—on the superiority of women and defending women accused of witchcraft, as well as *De occulta philosophia libri tres*—occasionally brought him into conflict with authorities in the Roman Church. Melanchthon, however, may have in mind Agrippa's 1527 broadside *Of the Vanity and Uncertainty of Arts and Sciences*. See Charles G. Nauert, *Agrippa and the Crisis of Renaissance Thought* (Urbana: University of Illinois Press, 1965). Andreas Bodenstein von Karlstadt (1486–1541), an erstwhile professor at Wittenberg, opposed both Luther and Melanchthon after 1522, writing on baptism and the Lord's

These people do not seek truth, but rather skillfully pervert those things expressed rightly, or they insolently stir up unnecessary battles, and when warned, do not concede, but, on the contrary, rabidly defend their errors. About such people, Solomon writes in this place: "It is better to encounter a bear bereft of her cubs than a fool in his stupidity," as when a bewitched Papist manifests errors.

Thus, these sayings condemn slander, the evil desire of strife, and stubbornness in clinging to such errors. On the contrary, they prescribe the preservation of order in offering admonishments, and command the application of truth, candor, and what the Greeks call "forbearance,"[7] as well as the caveat that admonishments should be gentle. These all accord with the saying, "Stop doing wrong."[8] Likewise, "Repent and believe the gospel."[9] This is why it is said here, "Whoever keeps another's offense secret acquires a friendship." In other words, the one who admonishes error in conformity with order restores the person admonished, does not publicly make an uproar, preserves that person, and fosters public peace. Conversely, the neglecting of such order by seeking controversies leads to dissensions among rulers, wars, and desolations in keeping with a verse from Empedocles: "The one noising abroad vain things occasions savage killings through discord."[10]

Supper among other topics. Andreas Osiander (1498–1552) and Franciscus Stancaro (1501–1574) were both involved in different ways in the so-called Osiandrian controversy of the 1550s, with Stancaro accused by Melanchthon of Arianism. See Timothy J. Wengert, *Defending Faith: Lutheran Responses to Andreas Osiander's Doctrine of Justification* (Tübingen: Mohr Siebeck, 2012).

[7] In Greek, ἐπιείκεια.

[8] Isa. 1:16.

[9] Mark 1:15.

[10] In Greek, Φοιτᾷ δὲ βροτολοιγὸς ἔρις κενεὸν λελακυῖα. Empedocles was a fifth-century BCE Greek philosopher. Among other teachings, he taught that love and strife explain the structure of the universe. This saying was later attributed to Timon of Phlius (ca. 320–230 BCE) in one of his poems. See Friedrich Wilhelm Sturz, *Empedocles Agrigentinus* (Leipzig: Göschen, 1805), XXXIV. Melanchthon provides his own Latin translation here. A

These sayings also level a punishment against controversies elicited by slanderers and those who admonish them. "A cruel messenger will find them," which is to say that those who spark calumnies or encourage discord will eventually undergo punishment because even though the truth is repressed for a while, the truth will prevail in the end. Demosthenes said it well: "The truth is powerful."[11] What's more, Paul ordered that heretics should be avoided after a "first and a second admonishment," writing that "they sin and are 'self-condemned.'"[12] Although they may not appear so, they are convicted by their conscience and have already condemned themselves by their testimony.

You may ask, How can a person be convicted? I respond: In civil matters, a person may be convicted by a lawful verdict and a judge's sentence. In philosophy it happens through common norms and occurs in one of three ways, falling under the label of what the Greeks called "the means of judging."[13] There are three: universal experience, first principles, and understanding of the logical outcome. In the teaching of the church about the law and the articles of faith, a person is convicted through testimonies properly cited from the prophets and apostles as well as by the creeds. For the church's teaching of the fundamentals is unambiguous.

But it must be understood that it is a divine commandment that, when recognizing the truth, we would take pleasure in it on account of God, would give thanks to God because God has shown forth God's light, and would apply it to its proper use, as it is commanded in Zechariah 8: "Love truth and peace."[14] Those who do not assent to the truth about God violate both the first and second commandments of the Decalogue: "You shall have no other gods," and "Do not take the

---

literal translation of the Greek would be, "But the one plaguing people with frenzy, screaming empty strife."

[11] In Greek, Ἰσχυρὸν τὸ ἀληθές. Demosthenes was a fourth-century BCE Greek statesman. See *On the False Embassy* [19].208.

[12] Titus 3:9–11. The Greek term used is αὐτοκατάχριτοι.

[13] In Greek, κριτήρια.

[14] Zech. 8:19.

name of the Lord your God in vain."[15] And to resist acknowledging the truth about God is blasphemy, about which it is stated, "Blasphemy against the Holy Spirit will not be forgiven."[16] In other matters, this other commandment is violated: "Do not give false testimony."[17]

---

[15] Ex. 20:3 and 20:7.

[16] Matt. 12:32.

[17] Ex. 20:16.

Chapter 18

"The righteous are the first to accuse themselves; only then do they ask about others."[1]

Among the foolishness of the human race, the source of many sins is that which the Greeks called "love of self"[2] and pride. These sins are the ones that please us the most and lift us above others. We thus fawn over ourselves, being in love with what the Greeks referred to as "flattery."[3] Not adequately assessing our own faults, we also want others to be seen as inferior to us, and we judge them severely. However, largely sparing ourselves, we nonetheless rush to become the critics and Faultfinders[4] of others. In short, we are blind to our own faults, but are ever the Lookout[5] in recognizing the faults of others. We prove ourselves to be discerning in public, but inside our own homes we are not. The following sayings apply here: "What each person possesses is beautiful to that person."[6] And Cicero wrote in *Letters to Atticus*, "Every person has his [or her] own spouse, but mine for me; and

---

[1] Prov. 18:17.

[2] In Greek, φιλαυτία.

[3] In Greek, κολακεία.

[4] *Momus*, the Latinized Greek word for "faultfinder," is often personified.

[5] *Lyncei* is the plural form of Lynceus, the sharp-sighted companion of Aeneus.

[6] This slogan was popular in both Greek and Latin. Similar wording is found in Cicero, *On the Nature of the Gods* 3.38.

every person his [or her] own lover, but mine for me. How shrewdly put."[7] Concerning this topic is a fable about two knapsacks, about which Catullus says,

> We all are surely deceived [the same way], nor is there anyone
> In whom you are not able to see, a Suffenus,[8] in some way.
> To each, one's own error has been assigned;
> but we do not see the knapsack on our back.[9]

Horace says, "When you look at your own faults, your eyes are blind and glazed over. Then why, at the faults of your friends, do you have such an acute sense of sight?"[10] Meanwhile, Persius writes, "As no one—no one—is tempted to descend into himself, the knapsack on the back of the one in front is observed."[11] And Persius also states, "Live with yourself, and you will discover how poorly furnished your house is."[12]

Likewise, in the Gospel, the hypocrite is severely judged for having a plank in his [or her] own eye while wanting to [first] remove a speck of sawdust from another's.[13] Against such "love of self," as well as such harshness of judgments, this admonition must be held in view, which is handed down in this saying as follows: "The righteous are the first to accuse themselves; [only then do others follow]," which is to say that the righteous recognize their infirmities and lapses of judgment because it is right to begin judgment with ourselves in accordance with the saying, "Shame on the learned when their faults return to them."[14]

---

[7] Cicero, *Letters to Atticus* 14.20.3. Cicero wrote a series of letters under this title to his friend Titus Pomponius Atticus from 68 to 44 BCE.

[8] Suffenus is someone that Catullus regards as a poor writer.

[9] Catullus, *Songs* 22.18–21.

[10] Horace, *Satires* 1.25–26.

[11] Persius, *Satires* 4.23.

[12] Persius, *Satires* 4.52.

[13] Matt. 7:3–5.

[14] Dionysius Cato, *Distichs of Cato* 1.30. Cato was a Latin author of the fourth or fifth century CE whose collection of proverbs and adages, frequently called "Cato" as well, was highly influential in the Western tradition.

In addition, even the righteous have some faults. This conforms to the saying, "There is no one righteous on earth who does not sin even when doing good."[15] But because such people are righteous, they confess those things that are true, do not defend their faults or lapses, grieve over them, and are the first to punish themselves and to seek to amend their ways. Only then do they ponder when and in what way they may be the judge of the faults of others, not judging out of petty suspicions but out of sound convictions.

Therefore, the text has a sense of the word in Latin, "he will investigate," stating, "But let every person prove his [or her] own work so that the glory will be his [or her] own and not another's,"[16] which is to say that if one follows his [or her] own office appropriately, the person will have a peaceful conscience[17] and will not rely upon the approval of the crowd. There are many sayings pertaining to this concept. For instance, "It is right to measure ourselves by our own standards of measure."[18] And likewise, "Those who weigh their burdens can bear them ..."[19]

The Greek translator of Solomon has employed a notable word. He states, "The righteous accuses himself 'in the opening remarks.'"[20] The Greek phrase "opening remarks" is a legal term; it is the address of the plaintiff delivered before the defendant is heard. It is difficult, however, to completely remove from minds a first impression, as Demosthenes says.[21] Indeed, consider how many critics there are everywhere and the kind of hypocrites this picture paints—those who have a plank in their eyes but still want to remove a speck of sawdust from another's.

---

[15] Eccl. 7:20.

[16] Gal. 6:4.

[17] Here and elsewhere, Melanchthon uses the term *conscientia* not so much to designate a particular part of the soul, as in medieval thought, but rather the person's entire mind.

[18] Horace, *Letters* I.7.98.

[19] Martial, *Epigrams* 12.98.8.

[20] In the Greek Septuagint, this sentence is δίκαιος ἑαυτοῦ κατήργος ἐν πρωτολογίᾳ.

[21] See Melanchthon's translation of Demosthenes, *De corona* 7 (CR 17:806).

There are many vices involving such perversity of judgments that converge: "love of self," pride, "meddlesomeness,"²² and cruelty, that is, when hypocrites spare themselves and mete out their rage upon others. But let each of us come to recognize our most salient faults, let us be moved in mercy toward those who can be cured, and let us be eager to correct these faults in accordance with our calling. And let us be mindful of the words of Gregory of Nazianzus: "If you are conscious of a debt owed you, apply mercy. For with God compassion is weighed by compassion."²³

***"The one who finds a wife finds goodness and will draw pleasure from the Lord."*²⁴**

The phraseology here must be noted. In this instance, the word means "to wed happily," which in Greek is "happily being happy."²⁵ In this way, the saying indicates an exceptional gift of God, a marriage that is simultaneously happy, peaceful, and godly, in which there is mutual love, and spouses are like-minded in the church and together calling upon God according to the verse, "May there be one mind and one love in God."²⁶ Therefore, in the next chapter, Solomon will add, "A prudent wife is from the Lord."²⁷

---

22 In Greek, πολυπραγμοσύνη.

23 Gregory of Nazianzus, *Poems* 33.59–60. In Greek, εἰδέ οἶδας ὄφλων καὶ πρόχρησον τὸ πρᾶον οἴκτω γὰρ οἶκτος τῷ θεῷ σταθμίζεταὶ.

24 Prov. 18:22. In Greek, προτωλογία.

25 In Greek, εὐτυχώς εὐτυχὼν.

26 Johannes Franciscus Ripensis, "Domino Martino Themmio et Dorothea Sponsae," 45, in *Epistola de Coniugio* (Wittenberg: Johannes Krafft, 1553). Franciscus, also known as Hans Frandsen (1532–1584), was a Danish author and former student of Melanchthon. The quote comes from the last line of a wedding poem to the couple mentioned in the title. To learn more about Melanchthon's influence on Danish Neo-Latin wedding poetry, see Pernille Harsting, "From Melanchthonism to Mannerism: The Development of the Neo-Latin Wedding Poem in 16th Century Denmark," in Thomas Haye, *Humanismus in Norden: Rezeption antiker Kultur und Literatur an Nord- und Ostsee* (Amsterdam: Rodopi, 2000), 289–302.

27 Prov. 19:14.

At the same time, sayings such as these offer ample testimony that marriage is pleasing to God. The verse at hand also provides this particular emphasis: "[He] will draw pleasure from the Lord," as if to say, "There are many dangers in this life, and we all experience many troubles. Nevertheless, God will be the protector of such married couples who harmoniously pray to and rejoice in God because they know that God cares about their marriage." Examples from the marriage of Zechariah and Elizabeth as well as other holy couples illustrate that God miraculously protected them when armies of the worst sort frequently wandered throughout Judea. When Lamyrus killed thirty thousand Jews and forced the captives to eat the dead bodies of their Jewish brothers, for example, God protected Zechariah, Elizabeth, Mary, and her parents in the same way that God preserved the three men in the furnace in Babylon.[28] From these examples we may recognize what it means "to receive pleasure from the Lord."

It is worth noting the use of the verb in Latin "to draw [particularly water]," which alludes to fountains or springs, thereby signifying manifold, powerful, and sweet consolation almost like that of re-creation. We must also note the teaching here on Purity and Marriage. God has created male and female, because God wills that the church consist of the human race. For God joined together male and female [in marriage] through a fixed law. God has set limits on marriages and prohibited wanton lusts so that there would be an understanding of purity within the human race. God wants it to be understood that the mind should be pure, and that in prayer this purity should be separated from natural impurities. For it is necessary for us to recognize what we pray for. And because we do not embrace God with our arms—but instead approach God through our mind—we must come to understand the nature of God and where God is best revealed.

---

[28] Lamyrus, also called *Lathyros,* meaning "the Buffoon," is the surname of Ptolemy IX (sometimes counted Ptolemy VIII), ruler of Egypt from 116–107 and 88–81 BCE. He was deposed in 107 and seized Cyprus, from where he invaded Judea. Another massacre of Jews in Alexandria is attributed to Ptolemy I Soter, who ruled from 303 to 282 BCE. The account of the men in the furnace is in Dan. 3:1–30.

Therefore, we say, "Almighty God, Eternal Father of our Lord Jesus Christ, Creator of heaven, earth, angels, and people, who together with your Son our Lord Jesus Christ and your Holy Spirit, you who are a wise, good, true, just, and merciful judge, in your purest and boundless way, have mercy on us on account of your Son Jesus Christ, whom you willed to become a sacrifice on our behalf, 'both mediator and supplicant.'[29] Justify us on account of him and through him, and sanctify us by your Holy Spirit in truth and in purity ..."[30]

Therefore, we must take note of the teaching about purity, particularly keeping in mind the most severe divine warnings recorded in Leviticus 18 and 1 Corinthians 6: "Neither fornicators, nor murderers, nor adulterers will possess the kingdom of God."[31] Likewise, in Hebrews, "God will judge fornicators and adulterers."[32] We are, likewise, to keep in view the examples of punishments expressly outlined in Leviticus, namely, that the Canaanites were destroyed because of their unlawful sexual practices.[33] There is no doubt that a large part of the calamities upon the human race are punishments for sexual lusts.

Therefore, let us become more ardent in requesting Chastity from God, because God is very angry by such iniquity, and the devil greatly inflames human beings. God much rather wants to protect us when we plead for chastity. Let us also preserve this rule: "Avoid sin by avoiding all appearance of sin."[34] Likewise, "Walk carefully, not like fools do."[35] And finally, "If you put to death the deeds of the flesh by the Spirit, you will live."[36]

---

[29] In Greek, καὶ μεσίτην καὶ ἱκέτην. Possible allusions to Heb. 8:6 and 5:7, respectively.

[30] Melanchthon employs prayer in many aspects of his theological works: in speeches, in his exegesis, and especially throughout the second and third Latin editions of his *Loci communes theologici*, 1535 and 1543, respectively.

[31] 1 Cor. 6:9.

[32] Heb. 13:4.

[33] Lev. 18:1–30.

[34] 1 Thess. 5:22.

[35] Eph. 5:15.

[36] Rom. 8:13.

Chapter 19

"Pleasures are not worthy of fools. Nor should servants rule over princes."[1]

All people who have infirm natures only become more careless in prosperity, as it is customary to say, "Feelings run wild in prosperity."[2] Likewise, "Fate makes a fool out of the one she favors."[3] And also, "The people sat down to eat and drink and then got up to indulge in pleasure …"[4] It is for these reasons that this warning has been repeated often in writings because when hearts are not distressed, they pray less often to God and are generally less intent to do those things needing to be done. But when a person's nature lacks a fixed goal and becomes inclined toward pleasures and vices, it shows no interest in performing necessary tasks but hastens toward depravity, as Cato said, "People who do nothing end up learning to do evil."[5] Likewise, "If you remove idleness, Cupid's bow will be unstrung; his torch, now despised, will shed no light on the industrious."[6] And also,

---

[1] Prov. 19:10.

[2] Ovid, *Art of Love* 2.437.

[3] Publilius Syrus, *Sentences* 271.

[4] Ex. 32:6. The apostle Paul also quotes this passage in 1 Cor. 10:7.

[5] Attributed to Cato the Younger (95–46 BCE). No such saying can be found in Erasmus's *Adages*; it is equivalent to "An idle mind is the devil's workshop." See also Sir. 33:29: "Multam enim malitiam docuit otiositas."

[6] Ovid, *Love's Cure* 139.

"Idleness is deceiving, causing damage to those who put confidence in it."[7] David, for instance, surrendered to and inflamed the passions of love when idle.[8]

Solomon, therefore, writes here that "pleasures are not worthy of fools," meaning that those who are not disciplined and restrained beforehand will only become more careless and uncontrolled afterward. For example, Rehoboam became more arrogant after he became king and began living a life without worries.[9] Likewise, many vices developed in Alexander [the Great] after the large string of victories that he won.

Therefore, we have been universally commanded about discipline in Sirach 33: "As fodder, a rod, and a burden are for the donkey; so bread, discipline, and work are for the servant."[10] This saying means that people should not be idle but should instead be occupied with an honest day's labor. But nevertheless, there must be a limit, so let them have nourishment and let them have supervisors that are overseers of the work—what the Greeks called "taskmasters"[11]—that they may urge them to work and punish the obstinate, so that others may be restrained in their office by fear of punishments. This commandment is a warning both about each person's body and about economic governance and regulations; for kingdoms should not simply torment the population but also feed the inhabitants and take care that they provide an honest day's labor in addition to punishing the obstinate.

Nowadays, the greater part of discipline is neglected, and the resources of the city are exhausted by unscrupulous plundering with the result that the average person does not have the necessities of life and is taken up with the charge of raising and educating offspring. But the divine message has foretold that in the old, doddering age of

---

[7] Ovid, *Art of Love* 1.238.

[8] Melanchthon is referring to the story narrated in 2 Sam. 11, when David became idle while his country was at war.

[9] 1 Kings 12:6–11.

[10] Sir. 33:25.

[11] In Greek, ἐργοδιῶκται.

the world, kingdoms will only become more deformed. This divine message orders us, therefore, to petition God for a lessening of both public and private punishments and for some preservation of decent society and the church.

"When the mocker is struck down, the ignorant will become more attentive."[12]

After the human mind was plunged in sin, destruction—namely, Death—followed because human nature has ceased being the home of God as it was before in accordance with the saying, "In him was life."[13] For humanity lived through the Word dwelling inside a person. Consequently, when that Word had been cut off, God was likewise cut off and no longer served as judge and life-giver, and death resulted. However, because God wanted to gather together the eternal church out of the human race because of the Son, our first parents were not immediately destroyed but were once again made alive through the Word dwelling in them by means of the promise made known to them.[14]

Since, therefore, the human race exists, many sins are present, punishments are piled up, and innumerable afflictions precede death. Natural philosophers say that the cause of death and many afflictions is matter, which withers or rots by its own nature. They also say that some miseries are summoned by human errors and desires. They speak accurately about the immediate causes. But why is the nature of humankind currently like this? Where do ignorance and the depravity of the will come from?

In this matter, the teaching of the church demonstrates the principal causes, namely, sin. Once the Word of God has been cut off, a person also cuts off God as judge, and other sins emerge, because out of that original sin innumerable, actual sins arise. There is, however, an order

---

[12] Prov. 19:25.

[13] John 1:4.

[14] Gen. 3. Here Melanchthon is echoing the standard interpretation of Gen. 3:15 as a promise of the coming Messiah.

of justice in God, so that natural guilt is destroyed, as it is written, "God is a consuming fire."[15] For this reason, punishments follow sin.

There are, however, four causes of punishments that we must particularly consider.

1. The first cause has to do with the order of justice found in God, for it is just for a guilty nature to be destroyed.
2. Then come the final causes. God wants the difference between the honorable and the base to be recognized, for God's basic qualities to be acknowledged, and for God's role as judge and avenger of wrongdoings to be understood. This, therefore, is the second cause of punishments: that they serve as warnings, testifying to God's existence and essential qualities. For instance, we learn from God's destruction of Sodom that God is both chaste and a lover of chastity, and that God is exceedingly angered at incestuous lusts.[16]
3. The third cause is practical in nature. In short, punishments preserve the human race. For if there were no punishments for crimes, there would be no end to misconduct.
4. The fourth cause is so that others may be warned by example and may be restrained out of fear with the result that some would be converted to God. This fourth cause applies to the passage at hand: "When the mocker is struck down, the ignorant will become more attentive." For example, when all the neighboring nations were being destroyed, the Gibeonites became more attentive and sued for peace.[17] Likewise, the punishment that Sisamnes received made his son Otanes more attentive, for Sisamnes's skin was used to cover the seat upon which Otanes sat, as Herodotus describes in *Histories*.[18]

---

[15] Deut. 4:24 and Heb. 12:29.

[16] See Gen. 19:1–29.

[17] Josh. 9:1–27.

[18] Herodotus, *Histories* 5.25. According to Herodotus, Sisamnes was a corrupt judge living in sixth-century BCE Persia. The ruler, Cambyses II, ordered Sisamnes's punishment for bribery, and Sisamnes's son Otanes took his place as judge. Cambyses placed the skin of Sisamnes on his son's judgment

The saying at hand states expressly that "mockers are struck down," that is, horrible criminals. When punishments are postponed, they mock admonishments in a kind of Epicurean contempt, becoming even more enraged, with the result that their punishment becomes more conspicuous. As it is said, "They [the unjust] are raised up higher, so that they may be guilty of a worse crime"[19]

The other half of this saying states, "Correction for the wise increases knowledge."[20] This means that not all have to be deterred by examples of punishments. Rather, some, who are not so enraged, accept admonishment and take the warning to heart.

---

seat as a reminder for Otanes to judge rightly. Melanchthon uses the Latin word *Terpsichore* to refer to the pertinent section of Herodotus's *Histories*, since later editors had divided this work into nine chapters that represent each of the nine muses in ancient Greek mythology. Terpsichore was the muse representing the fifth chapter of *Histories*.

[19] Claudian, *Against Rufinus* 1.21–23. See p. 41, n. 25.
[20] Prov. 19:25.

Chapter 20

"God made the ears for hearing and the eyes for seeing."[1]

For the felicitous ordering of governance, two things must come together: good counsel from those who govern and obedience of the people. And both, says Solomon, are a gift of God. For instance, Jeremiah was a good counselor, but he did not have the compliance of King Zedekiah; therefore, Jerusalem was destroyed.[2] Conversely, [King] Hezekiah did comply with the counsel of Isaiah, and therefore the city [of Jerusalem] was preserved.[3] This is the principal meaning for this sweetest of sayings: "God made the ears for hearing and the eyes for seeing."

Solomon urges that the political spheres and the household be governed by more than just human wisdom, but that assistance from God be sought in giving, in counsel, in bending human wills toward obedience, and in guiding the results, as Jeremiah said, "I know, Lord, that a person's way is not in himself."[4] Likewise, "Unless the Lord builds the house, those who build it labor in vain."[5] And, "Commend your way to God; put your hope in him and he will do it."[6]

---

[1] Prov. 20:12.

[2] Jer. 37–39.

[3] 2 Kings 19.

[4] Jer. 10:23.

[5] Ps. 127:1 (Vulgate 126:1).

[6] Ps. 37:5 (Vulgate 36:5).

Otherwise, Solomon's saying may also be applied in general to all excellent artisans whose minds discover and observe many things in the arts through divine insight that others do not discern, just as it is said in Daniel, "God gives wisdom to the wise and understanding to the knowledgeable."[7]

"Buyers complain, 'this is unfair, this is unfair,' but after their purchase they leave and boast ..."[8]

Let us consider how great our faults are able to become so that we might in some way begin to correct them. For, by nature of our birth, we bring forth many vices. Among these vices is a loathing for present good things. This loathing arises from either the fickleness or capriciousness of the mind, or from weariness or impatience that emerges whenever we are put out by some inconveniences and long for change. Many sayings reprove this kind of loathing. For instance, "The lazy ox envies the horse's saddle, but the horse envies the ox's plow."[9]

Aesop's fable about the donkey also reproves this mindset in which the donkey's condition only becomes worse.[10] Likewise, there are the verses of Sophocles in [the Greek tragedy] *Ajax*: "Foolish men do not recognize the good in their hands until they have lost it."[11] Finally, individuals observe such loathing of their present condition in themselves, just as it is written in Terence: "We are dissatisfied with our

---

[7] Dan. 2:21.

[8] Prov. 20:14.

[9] Horace, *Letters* 1.14.43. The general meaning of this saying is that the ox wants what the horse has, and the horse wants what the ox has; in other words, they both want what the other has, similar to "The grass is always greener on the other side of the fence."

[10] In this famous fable, a donkey eventually falls off a bridge and drowns because the owner and his son capitulated to the changing opinions of every passerby about how the donkey should be used. The moral of the story is that you cannot please everyone. See Aesop, *Fables* 721.

[11] Sophocles, *Ajax* 134.

lot."[12] And, as stated in Thucydides, it is exceedingly common for present kingdoms not to endure too long before coveting after other kingdoms: "The present always weighs heavy."[13]

It is against this instability of minds that many divine commands have been handed down about patience. For instance, "Humble yourselves under the mighty hand of God."[14] Likewise, "Do not grumble against God."[15]

Consider how the philosophers understood moderation of the mind: "Endure present realities."[16] Likewise, "Be content with whatever you are, not wishing for anything more."[17] And in one of Pythagoras's verses, "Accept whatever your fate is, and do not become resentful."[18] In Stigel, "If you be a donkey, a bitter lot follows every kind of donkey whatever; the one who bears this burden calmly is wise."[19] Likewise, "Each day has enough trouble of its own."[20] And Pindar warns us most charmingly when good and evil are mixed together that the good is to be chosen and cherished while the evil is to be countenanced: "Immortals dispense to humans two calamities for every blessing. Fools cannot bear this in stride, but the good can by turning it inside

---

[12] Terence, *Phormio* 1.3.20.

[13] Thucydides, *Peloponnesian Wars* 1.77.5. In Greek, τὸ παρὸν αἰεὶ βαρύ.

[14] 1 Peter 5:6.

[15] 1 Cor. 10:10.

[16] Herodotus, *Histories* 9.117.1. In Greek, Στέργειν τὰ παρεόντα.

[17] Martial, *Epigrams* 10.47.12.

[18] Pythagoras, *Golden Verses* 18. In Greek, Ἢν ἄν μοῖραν ἔχῃς. πράως φέρε μηδ' ἀγανάκτει.

[19] Johann Stigel (1515–1562) was a former student of Melanchthon's who taught Latin and wrote many Latin poems. Melanchthon is referring to one of his epigrams.

[20] Matt. 6:34.

out."[21] We must put this necessary skill into practice in our lives. For to embrace the present good with gratitude is constitutive of justice. And prudence and tolerance are exercised when we temperately bear certain misfortunes, lest we call forth additional evil through our foolish impulses, as Periander warns, "Do not attempt to remedy evil by evil."[22]

This saying of Solomon should also be applied to this teaching, where he rightly censures loathing the good things in the present, and he signifies that when those things have been lost, they may again be desired and sought after. This saying should also be applied to the common place[23] on loathing the present and on patience, which is wishing to obey God in the midst of onerous undertakings, which God commands us to endure, and at the same time to request and expect assistance from God, just as Paul makes this connection: "Rejoice always, give thanks always, and pray always."[24]

"An inheritance gotten hastily in the beginning will lack a blessing in the end."[25]

This precept is about waiting in one's calling. For example, Absalom could have become king if he had waited for the death of his father. However, because he sought to seize power precipitously and without sufficient calling, he was cast out and eventually overwhelmed with

---

[21] Pindar, *Pythian Odes* 3.82–83. In Greek,
ἓν παρὰ ἐσθλὸν πήματα
σύνδυο δαίονται βροτοῖς
ἀθάνατοι τὰ μέν ὧν οὐ δύνανται
νήπιοι κόσμῳ φέρειν ἀλλ'
ἀγαθοί τά καλά τρέψαντες ἔξω.

[22] Herodotus, *Histories* 3.53.4. In Greek, μὴ κακῷ κακὸν ἰῶ.

[23] The Latin is *locus communis*, a central aspect of Melanchthon's exegetical method, where he moves from the "species" of a text to the overarching "genus" or theme to which it belongs.

[24] 1 Thess. 5:16–18.

[25] Prov. 20:21.

awful punishments.26 Likewise, the sons of Ephraim entered the land of Canaan before Moses with carnal trust in the divine promise, since the offspring of Abraham had been promised the land of Canaan. However, because they acted without sufficient calling, they waged war only on the basis of a human conviction and were thus killed, making all of their plans useless (1 Chronicles 7). For the promise had been given according to the custom of *ius ad rem*, "a right to a thing," but not *ius in re*, "a real right."27 By way of contrast, even though David knew that the kingdom had been promised to him, nonetheless he by no means proclaimed himself king while Saul was alive. Neither did David seek to seize the kingdom from Saul nor kill him despite the fact that David had just cause to do so since Saul had murdered priests and had often armed himself with the purpose of seeking and killing David.28 Therefore, we must distinguish necessary from unnecessary things and not undertake anything without our vocation constraining us.

"It is shameful for a person to offer reproach to holy things and then afterward to make vows."29

In the Latin translation and version [of this text], there are errors that have given occasion to strange and bizarre interpretations, particularly when applied to monastic vows.30 Apart from this, the saying

---

26 The story of Absalom appears in 2 Sam. 13–15 and 17–18.

27 These terms first appear in the twelfth-century law text *Brachylogos* where they quickly became associated with Roman law. The *ius ad rem* is a right (in this case ownership) to a particular thing in particular circumstances, whereas the *ius in re* is a right (ownership) in any and all circumstances.

28 See 1 Sam. 16–31.

29 Prov. 20:25.

30 The *Glossa Ordinaria* and Nicholas of Lyra's commentary on the Bible talk about vows in general. Melanchthon probably had in mind the *Confutation*, a refutation of the Augsburg Confession at the 1530 imperial Diet of Augsburg, where, in rejecting article 27 of that Confession (on monastic vows), the authors cite Proverbs 20:25 (CR 27:169) to prove that monastic vows can be permanent. The Vulgate reads, "It is ruin for a person

of Solomon is clear. It reproaches the most common superstition held by most humans, who are already defiled by ungodliness, hatred of the Gospel, and other crimes against the conscience. As a result, they observe certain religious ceremonies out of anxiety, erroneously imagining that by doing so they are pleasing God; they puff themselves up over everyone else. For example, adulterous Spaniards and murderers approach Mass with great reverence, or they lacerate their backs on certain festivals during a public flagellation.[31]

In one of the sayings mentioned earlier about discerning right worship, it was stated, "The sacrifice of the wicked is an abomination to the Lord, but the prayers of the just please God."[32] Similarly, it is stated in Ecclesiastes 4, "Obedience is better than the sacrifice of fools who do not know what evil they do."[33]

---

to devour the saints and after [taking] vows to retract [them]." (*Ruina est homini devorare sanctos, et post vota retractare.*)

[31] The source of Melanchthon's description is unknown.

[32] Prov. 15:8.

[33] Eccl. 4:17 (Vulgate).

Chapter 21

"There is no wisdom, no insight, and no strategy against the Lord."

"The horse is prepared for the day of battle, but victory comes from God."[1]

There is a necessary rule in life to perform the duties of one's calling and to actively seek the Lord's assistance so that, with God's help, our efforts may be useful and salutary. However, any matters that we pursue unjustly—whether undertaken out of undue curiosity[2] or in the absence of trust in and prayer to God—will ultimately prove unsuccessful even though carried out with great cunning.

We must always keep in view commandments regarding Calling. As Paul said to the Thessalonians: "Endeavor to do this so that you may work on your own."[3] And to the Corinthians he said, "Into whatever calling one has been called, let him [or her] walk in it."[4] Furthermore, there are commandments about prayers to God and the promise of God's assistance in the Psalms: "Commend your way to God; put your hope in him and he will do it."[5] Likewise it is said to the Corinthians:

---

[1] Prov. 21:30–31.

[2] Here Melanchthon echoes a medieval worry over *vana curiositas*, "vain curiosity," especially among theologians.

[3] 1 Thess. 4:11.

[4] 1 Cor. 7:20.

[5] Ps. 37:5 (Vulgate 36:5).

"Your labor in the Lord will not be in vain."[6] And finally in John 15: "The one who remains in me, and I in him [or her], will produce abundant fruit."[7]

We must set these consolations in opposition to the difficulties we may encounter, which test our spirits and make us doubt whether our labor will prove useful. Indeed, our faith and our prayers must be awakened, and our labors must be diligently performed in the hope of divine assistance. For we must come to realize that during these challenging moments of life, God wants our faith, prayer, and hope to be put into practice, just as the psalm says: "Be subject to God and pray to him."[8]

Let us also realize that we censure trusting in our own powers, what the Greeks called "meddlesomeness" and "affectation."[9] As this text states, "There is no wisdom, no insight, and no strategy against the Lord." Likewise, "No one is able to receive something unless it is first given by God."[10] And the same is said here: "Unless the Lord builds the house, those who build it labor in vain."[11]

---

[6] 1 Cor. 15:58.

[7] John 15:5.

[8] Ps. 37:7 (Vulgate 36:7).

[9] In Greek, πολυπραγμοσύνη and κακοζηλία. "Meddlesomeness" is described in Plato, *Republic* 4.434b and 444b. "Affectation," or "rivalry," is discussed in Lucian, *The Dance* 82.

[10] John 3:27.

[11] Ps. 127:1 (Vulgate 126:1).

Chapter 22

"A good name is better than great riches."[1]

It has been rightly said, "It is necessary for me to have a good conscience before God and a good reputation before my neighbor."[2] It must be understood that a good reputation is a good thing. That is, a good reputation represents approval ordained by God and is something to be eagerly desired, since God wants the difference between right and wrong to be revealed by public testimonies, and God wants those who act rightly to be approved and preserved while those who do not act rightly are to be censured and destroyed. God wants these testimonies to be seen, so that we may learn the law, recognize God and God's nature, and understand that God is the avenger of evil deeds.

Therefore, a good reputation arises from divinely ordained testimonies of many people who judge matters rightly, approve upright things, and also act rightly. May those who act rightly be protected by such a testimony and let an honest place in the community be given to them, so that other people may learn and be induced to upright deeds.

When, therefore, a good reputation has been established as divinely ordained, and it has proven useful for life in many ways, it is evident that it is a good and highly desired thing. Therefore, Sirach 41 states,

---

[1] Prov. 22:1.

[2] Augustine, *Sermon* 355.1. Augustine preached this sermon around the year 425, while bishop of Hippo.

"Take care of a good name, for it is more durable than great treasures."[3] Accordingly, the following causes must be considered.

1. First, because God wants us to have regard for the judgment of honorable people, just as Sirach 6 says: "Stand in the company of elders, and cling to the one who is wise."[4] It is a form of arrogance and impudence to disregard the judgments of those who are sensible.
2. Second, God wants the honorable examples to be displayed to others. Therefore, it is said in 1 Corinthians 10: "Do all things to the glory of God, and do not give offense to the church."[5] Likewise in Philippians 4: "Take care to dwell on those things that are true, authentic, just, relating to friendship, praiseworthy, and those things which laud virtue and praise."[6]

Of these, let us first consider TRUTH,[7] which is the conservation of true doctrine as well as the preservation of the sayings and agreements of those who engage in honorable affairs. The conservation of true doctrine is, in fact, a virtue of the first table.[8] AUTHENTICITY is consistency of speech, which corresponds with a person's honorable actions. It is a part of modesty. PARTICULAR JUSTICE is causing harm to no one.[9] CHASTITY is the avoidance of prohibited sexual desires.

---

[3] Sir. 41:15 (Vulgate).

[4] Sir. 6:35 (Vulgate).

[5] 1 Cor. 10:31.

[6] Phil. 4:8.

[7] The terms in small caps appear in all caps in the original text.

[8] In the medieval and later Lutheran tradition, the first "table" of the law refers to one's relationship to God in the first three commandments of the Ten Commandments; the second "table" refers to one's relationship with others and includes the remaining seven, beginning with "Honor your father and mother."

[9] The distinction between "universal righteousness," *iustitia universalis*, justice in relations of citizens to the state, and "particular righteousness," *iustitia particularis*, justice in specific relations between human beings, goes back to Aristotle, *Nichomachean Ethics* 5.3.

Paul calls those things related to FRIENDSHIP "kindness," which is what the Greeks called "forbearance,"[10] without which harmony cannot be maintained. Paul also calls those things that are PRAISEWORTHY a virtue that diligently seeks to avoid scandals, which is named "love of honor" by the Greeks.[11] This is, effectively, a sincere desire for honor or for a good reputation. Finally, Paul also expressly lists both VIRTUE and PRAISE, so that he may designate that a good reputation must be preserved with deeds that are performed rightly without exhibiting empty ostentation.

In a similar way, Romans 14 says, "The one who serves Christ in these things pleases God and is approved by people."[12] Paul also wishes for us to regard and have respect for the judgments of honest people. Those who do not do so are arrogant and shameless. Therefore, it is rightly stated in the tragedy of Seneca, "He is fickle, and the honor of fame does not move him."[13]

The youth should also remember related sayings from other writings. For instance, we learn from the verses of Publilius Syrus: "An honorable report is like a second patrimony."[14] Likewise, Plautus, "If I keep an honorable reputation, I will be sufficiently rich."[15] Similarly, Hesiod commands us to avoid a bad reputation, adding that a public positive reputation is not entirely worthless: "A reputation is by no means fully lost if many people voice it; it is, in fact, divine."[16]

---

[10] In Greek, ἐπιείκεια.

[11] In Greek, φιλοτιμία.

[12] Rom. 14:18.

[13] Seneca the Younger, *Hercules on Oeta* 416.

[14] Publilius Syrus, *Maxims*. Publilius's *Maxims* have been reconstructed based on quotations; none of his own writings exist. By way of note, his praenomen, or given name, is also spelled Publius.

[15] Plautus, *The Haunted House* 1.3.

[16] In Greek, φήμη οὔ τις πάμπαν ἀπόλλυται, ἥν τινα πολλοὶ λαοὶ φημίξωσι· θεός νύ τίς ἐστι καὶ αὐτή. This statement comes from Hesiod, *Works and Days* 763–64.

"The rich and the poor are the same, and God has made both."[17]

Both the good fortune of the unrighteous and the calamities of the righteous upend our belief in God's providence, leading some to seek alternative causes for events, while others have recourse to physical causes or fate. Accordingly, we must recognize that God has set forth testimonies of providence both in ordinary and extraordinary works and in his expressed Word.

To begin with, ORDINARY works demonstrate God's presence. These include, for instance, the most beautiful order of the bodies of the universe, the changing of the seasons like winter and summer, the annual fruitfulness of the earth, the preservation of human society, punishment of evildoers like murderers, the law and the judgment of conscience in individuals, the begetting and earliest nourishment of offspring, and so forth.

Meanwhile, EXTRAORDINARY works appear more visibly. This is the way of all miracles, including, for instance, the exodus of the Israelites out of Egypt, the resurrection of the dead, and so forth.

And because these works testify that divine sayings are true, we must keep in mind all those maxims maintaining that neither favorable nor unfavorable events happen by chance, but rather they are governed by the counsel of God. May this faith shine in our hearts, asking for and expecting good outcomes from God.

Thus, Jeremiah says in Lamentations, "Who is the one who says, 'Shall not both good and evil come forth from the mouth of the Lord?'"[18] And in Zephaniah 1, "I will search Jerusalem with lamps, and I will visit the people who have been wallowing in their mire, who say in their hearts, 'The Lord will neither act favorably nor unfavorably.'"[19] Likewise, in Psalm 32, "The Lord has looked from heaven; he has seen all of humankind's children."[20] Similarly, in Matthew 10,

---

[17] Prov. 22:2.

[18] Lam. 3:37–38.

[19] Zeph. 1:12.

[20] Ps. 33:13 (Vulgate 32:13).

"None of these sparrows will fall to the ground outside of the will of the Father." Or, again, "And all the hairs on your head are numbered."[21]

By these and similar testimonies, we strengthen ourselves against the madness of the Epicureans. Let us give attention both to the commandments of God concerning praying for our bodily needs and to those promises that also testify to God's providence. Then let us recognize that, regarding the will of God, it must be judged by God's own Word, as it is said, "Your word is a lamp to my feet."[22] Therefore, it is necessary to obey the Word of God, even while the righteous are often harshly afflicted, because there are unwavering causes for why God wants to subject the church to the cross. Indeed, we must take to heart this saying, "The righteous face many troubles, but God delivers them from all of them."[23]

Therefore, even though Lazarus was poor, he did not for that reason cast aside his belief in God's providence.[24] Instead, he judged matters in the light of the Word of God, which affirms that divine providence exists, and that liberation would follow. Such things have been expressly handed down to us in the Word, and although Lazarus may have been poor and may not have possessed the empire of Tiberius, there is no need to look for alternative explanations. Rather, we must hold to the rule found in Sirach 3: "Consider carefully those things God has commanded for you, while not setting your curiosity upon those things God has hidden from you."[25] In this way, let what has been revealed be distinguished from what has not been revealed, and let each person be obedient to God in his [or her] own calling.

In sum, this saying teaches these things: "The rich and the poor are the same, and God has made both." Here is what it means: "Come to understand that providence and God's purposes—not blind chance—determine that some are rich while others are poor, and that each of

---

[21] Matt. 10:29–30.

[22] Ps. 119:105.

[23] Ps. 34:19.

[24] Cf. Luke 16:19–31.

[25] Sir. 3:22.

us must rightly come to serve God according to our place in society." This is in accordance with the saying, "Let each person walk in the way he [or she] has been called by the Lord."[26] The person who is poor must not grumble against God, but must defer to this saying: "Humble yourselves under the mighty hand of God,"[27] and take comfort in that. And also, "Blessed are the poor in spirit, for theirs is the kingdom of heaven."[28] Likewise, Proverbs 17, "The one who despises the poor also casts judgment on the one who made the poor."[29] Similarly, Proverbs 15, "It is better to have a little combined with the fear of God than great treasures and feelings of uneasiness."[30] Also, "Each day has enough trouble of its own."[31] And finally, "Pray without anger and doubting."[32]

"Do not surpass ancient boundaries that your fathers have set."[33]

"You shall not steal" pertains to this precept. It is a prohibition against new boundaries being formed and new borders being erected. As it is expressly stated in Deuteronomy 19, "You shall not move your neighbor's boundary marker."[34] And also in the twenty-seventh chapter of that book, "Cursed is the one who moves his neighbor's boundary marker."[35] Also in the *Pandects*, the chapter titled "About Moving a Boundary Marker" [*De termino moto*], there are laws of Julius, Nerva, and Hadrian about punishments for those who dig up boundaries.[36]

---

[26] 1 Cor. 7:17. Already with Melanchthon, this text was an important part of the Lutheran notion of vocation.

[27] 1 Peter 5:6.

[28] Matt. 5:3.

[29] Prov. 17:5.

[30] Prov. 15:16.

[31] Matt. 6:34.

[32] 1 Tim. 2:8.

[33] Prov. 22:28.

[34] Deut. 19:14.

[35] Deut. 27:17.

[36] *Pandectae* (*Digest*), lib. 47, tit. 21. Julius Caesar (ca. 100–44 BCE), Nerva (30–98), and Hadrian (76–138) were all Roman emperors.

Although this precept at hand is clear enough, it may be understood allegorically[37] to mean that ancient laws handed down by a formidable authority should not be changed unless absolutely necessary. For among precepts of a political nature, it has often been repeated that ancient laws should not be needlessly changed, as the following verse admonishes: "The Roman state survives by its ancient customs and powers."[38]

For this reason, it may be necessary to excerpt an entire passage from Demosthenes. It comes from a speech in *Against Timocrates* describing the Locrians,[39] who created the following law: If a new law were about to be proposed, the one proposing it would be forced to wear a noose around his neck; and if the proposed law was not pleasing to the people, the citizens would immediately strangle him with the noose.

Here are Demosthenes's own words:

> I would like, judges, to describe for you the example of the Locrians. For it will do you no harm to hear an example, especially from one of the city-states regulated by honorable laws. The people there are of the opinion that ancient laws are to be maintained and that the institutions of their fathers are to be fortified and preserved. New laws are not to be established for the sake of selfish desires or for the purpose of wrongdoing. As such, if anyone wishes to propose a new law, he must appear before the court with a noose strapped around his neck. If the people determine that the law would be honorable and useful, the one proposing the new law gets to depart alive and uninjured. If, however, the proposed law was not pleasing

---

[37] In Latin, *allegorice*. Unlike modern English usage, this word in Latin means taking one word or phrase as representative of a far broader set of circumstances. It is another example of how Melanchthon employed the *loci* method to interpret Scripture.

[38] Quintus Ennius, *Annals* 5. This epic poem was written by Ennius in the second century BCE.

[39] The Locrians, also called Locri or Locrenses, were an ancient Greek tribe that eventually became incorporated into mainstream ancient Greek society. Two of the most well-known Locrians were Ajax and Patroclus, the latter of whom was Achilles's best friend as portrayed in the *Iliad*.

to the people, the one proposing was immediately killed by tightening his noose. As such, no one dared propose new laws. Instead, the old laws were obeyed with the utmost care and seriousness. And after very many years, only one new law was passed. They passed the law there that if anyone plucked out his neighbor's eye, his own eye would likewise be plucked out; there was no option of punishment by a fine. Now, a certain man who had two eyes had an enemy with only one eye, and he threatened to pluck out the eye of the one-eyed man. The one-eyed man, terrified of this prospect, struck up enough courage to propose a new law, namely, that any person with two eyes who plucked out the eye of a one-eyed person would be punished by having both of his eyes plucked out. That, they say, is the only new law established for more than two hundred years.[40]

These are the words of Demosthenes.

If we were to have such severe laws in place today, we would not have as many new dogmatists and self-imposed legislators,[41] compliant and made of wax and similar properties, whose changing of laws is not necessary and brings about nothing useful. Some politicians prescribe some insignificant and inconvenient new measures lest, in moving the republic this way, as with a sick man, greater calamities befall the republic. In this way, we observe that Xenophon was not far from the truth when he wrote, "All changes in the government bring about death."[42] Thus this saying, too, is frequently repeated: "An evil which has been well hidden is not to be moved."[43]

---

[40] Demosthenes, *Against Timocrates* 24.139–41. Other sources also record Melanchthon's reference to this story. See CR 20:533, no. 50, and CR 17:877–80.

[41] Literally, "Lycurgus," which is the name of several kings in ancient Greece, particularly the famous lawgiver of Sparta.

[42] In Greek, πᾶσαι μεταβολαὶ πολιτειῶν θανατηφόροι. Xenophon, *Hellenica* 3.32. This ancient Greek work narrates the story of the Peloponnesian War.

[43] Erasmus, *Adages* 1.1.62. Melanchthon's proverb is a variant of the following, which means and can be translated the same way: *Malum bene conditum ne moveris*.

But on this point, it is necessary for a correction to be added.[44] When a teaching is ungodly, and corresponding laws support such ungodly opinions and idols, it is necessary for the following rules to take precedence: "Let anyone who teaches a different Gospel be considered anathema."[45] Similarly, "We must obey God more than human beings."[46] Likewise, "Blasphemy will not be forgiven in this age or in the one to come."[47] And also, when amendment is necessary, the "boundary markers of the fathers" are not so much moved about as they are to be restored, because the teaching handed down by God to our original fathers is being restored, as was stated by Tertullian: "That which is first is truest."[48] However, the true antiquity of something must be diligently investigated, and it is a great confirmation of faith in the process of knowing the progression of the church's various ages to harvest testimonies of those who retain the fundamentals.[49]

---

[44] Although Melanchthon expressed himself very carefully here, it would seem that he was touching on issues surrounding the adiaphoristic controversy, although here he stressed teaching (*doctrina*) and not practice. But he also was echoing some of Martin Luther's original arguments from the beginning of the Reformation, expressed, for example, in his letter to the emperor, written just after his departure from Worms and dated April 28, 1521 (LW 48:203–209).

[45] Gal. 1:8.

[46] Acts 5:29.

[47] Matt. 12:32.

[48] Tertullian, *Against Praxeas* 2.2.

[49] At this time, Melanchthon was lecturing on (and thereby expanding) the *Chronicon* of world and sacred history by Johannes Carion. He published two volumes from these lectures, bringing readers down to the time of Charlemagne. His son-in-law, Caspar Peucer, continued the lectures after Melanchthon's death, reaching Emperor Maximilian II.

Chapter 23

"When you sit and eat with a ruler, be careful, and put a knife to your throat so that you may preserve your life ..."[1]

This is an admonition for life at court. When your standing with a ruler is on shaky ground, be careful and vigilant when speaking, going so far as to imagine that a sword is moving closer to your neck, or you may accidentally say something that brings you to ruin. For example, Alexander [the Great] killed Clitus at a banquet after the latter openly contradicted him.[2] There are many similar admonitions about the dangers lurking in court life. Horace, for instance, writes as follows: "The cultivation of a friendship with a ruler appears sweet to the inexperienced, but the experienced tread in fear."[3] Likewise, Ovid composed an extended elegy on this subject:

> Live for yourself and stay as far as possible from glittering grandeur.
> It is a cruel lightning bolt that falls from the court of such glitter.
> For even though only the powerful can provide help,
> They would rather not; they are more likely to harm us.[4]

---

[1] Prov. 23:1–2.

[2] This story refers to the time when Alexander the Great killed one of his military officers, named Clitus (or Cleitus) the Black, in a moment of anger after an argument erupted between them. The story is told, among other places, in Plutarch, *Parallel Lives* 5.50–51.

[3] Horace, *Letter* 18.86–87.

[4] Ovid, *Sorrows* 3.4.4–7.

Similarly, Aesop wrote about Solon's interaction with Croesus.[5] When speaking with the king, this saying applies: "Interact with them as pleasantly as possible, or not at all."[6]

Political leaders and their ministers[7] are necessary, and God has so distinguished this class that he allowed them to participate in the very divine name. As the Scripture says, "I have said that you are gods,"[8] which means that those addressed possess a divine office. And those who are called to these offices are supposed to be faithful, prudent, and sensible. Regrettably, so few people in such a lofty position perform their office rightly. On the contrary, many are either lazy or ruthless. Indeed, it is astonishing that in that lofty seat of God, the devil advances his cause so horribly, as example after example in every age demonstrates. In fact, because many have abused that power, they have unleashed tragic punishments. As such, there are many complaints about the fickleness of fortune in court life. Consider the following verses from Seneca's *Agamemnon*:

> Not as the sea thus rages on Libyan shores,
> The waves wishing to roll wave after wave.
> Not the surge of the hospitable Black Sea swelling
>   from the lowest depths.
> [But] the waters rushing
> hard by the icy pole,
> Where, free in the black waves,
> [The constellation] Boötes turns his bright chariots.

---

[5] There is an account of Aesop being summoned by the wealthy Croesus, who praised Aesop but showed Solon, the lawgiver, no respect. See Plutarch, *Parallel Lives: The Life of Solon* 28.1–4. To Aesop's advice, Solon replied, "Either as rarely as possible or as beneficially as possible."

[6] These words appear in more than one place, for instance, Diogenes Laertius, *Lives and Opinions of Eminent Philosophers* 9.20. In Greek, ἢ ὡς ἥκιστα, ἢ ὡς ἥδιστα.

[7] Usually, Melanchthon uses this word to designate ministers of the gospel, but here it is used more broadly.

[8] Ps. 82:6. Luther wrote a "mirror of princes" based upon this psalm in 1530. See LW 13:39–72.

> Thus, the wheel of Fortune turns;
> The headlong fates of kings.[9]

Although it is true that there are many dangers lurking in princely courts, the commonly held evils of the human heart—Ambition and Arrogance—are there. Ambition strives for that which is exceedingly lofty. As Seneca alluded to above, human desires stretch upward because they are like fire. Arrogance among those who hold power is the squandering of one's position and to consume oneself in unrestrained license that subsequently results in punishments. Solomon, therefore, in an attempt to rebuke both Ambition and arrogance, has handed down this admonition through which he commands Moderation and circumspection.

However, these rules must be noted. Although it is just to petition for offices for which we are suitably equipped, our petition should neither impede the judgments of those doing the choosing, nor fight for offices using unjust means. Moreover, such a petition should prove itself in demonstrating a godly motivation, and offering itself to the society for the most difficult and dangerous kinds of work. Concerning such petition, the following saying applies: "The one who aspires to be a bishop desires an honorable thing."[10] Likewise, "God loves a cheerful giver."[11] Similarly, Paul's letter to Titus orders the teaching of honorable things so that we may be useful in governance.[12]

However, a morally defective ambition is one in which petitions are made in order selfishly to impede the judgments of those doing the choosing and to fight for [an office] using unjust means, or where we generally overstep the boundaries of our callings. Against such ambition, the following verses apply: "The one who exalts himself will be

---

[9] Seneca the Younger, *Agamemnon* Act I.64–72. Depictions of this wheel of fortune are found in many different forms, including on the outside of one of the rose windows of the Basel Cathedral.

[10] 1 Tim. 3:1.

[11] 2 Cor. 9:7.

[12] See especially Titus 3:1 and 3:14.

humbled."[13] Likewise, "All the prideful in heart are an abomination to the Lord."[14]

This morally defective ambition, which is called "unbridled aspiration" in Greek,[15] is manifested when exceedingly ambitious persons wish to be seen shunning that which they desperately seek. Aristotle, for his part, called those who exemplify this kind of ambition "wickedly deceitful."[16] Those infected with this kind of ambition eventually begin to abuse the power entrusted to them to fulfill their own private desires, as [King] David, along with many others, indulged them during his reign. Therefore, we must be mindful of the saying in Sirach 3: "The greater you are, the more you should humble yourself, thereby finding grace before God."[17] The saying of Plutarch must also be noted: "The ruler should imitate the sun, which, after rising in the northern sky and ascending to its greatest height, has the least motion. And by being slower, it ensures the safety of its course."[18]

"Do not strangle your soul to become rich. Do not lay aside your prudence."[19]

Previously, Solomon preached against Pride. Here he preaches against Greed. At the same time, however, this saying by no means prohibits the exercise of zeal, labor, or industriousness inasmuch as it falls within one's calling. On the contrary, Solomon very often and expressly enjoins industriousness and work, as in the illustration he provided

---

[13] Matt. 23:12.

[14] Prov. 16:5.

[15] In Greek, ἀκκισμὸς.

[16] In Greek, βαυκοπανούργος. See Aristotle, *Nichomachean Ethics* 4.7 (1127b, 15), which Melanchthon cites in Greek and Latin.

[17] Sir. 3:20.

[18] Plutarch, *To an Uneducated Ruler* 6. Melanchthon provides both this Latin translation and the Greek, μιμουμένου τὸν ἥλιον τοῦ ἄρχοντος, ὅς ὅταν ὕψωμα λάβῃ μέγιστον, ἐξαρθεὶς ἐν τοῖς βορείοις, ἐλάχιστα κινεῖται, τῷ σχολαιτέρῳ τὸν δρόμον εἰς ἀσφαλὲς καθιστάμενος.

[19] Prov. 23:4.

earlier about the ant.[20] A similar example appears in Ecclesiastes 9. Likewise, "Those who have charge of something should be industrious." And also, "Industriousness surpasses laziness."[21] Likewise, "It is necessary for us to be faithful."[22] What's more, the parable of the talents in Matthew 25 also applies to this precept.[23]

We must come to understand that our labors will be fruitful when they include God's assistance. As the saying from Psalms goes, "Unless the Lord builds the house, its builders labor in vain …"[24] As such, Solomon urges us to combine prayer to God with diligence in performing labors of our callings, in accordance with the following saying: "Commit your way to God; hope in God and God will do it."[25] But Solomon prohibits unrighteous showboating as well as what the Greeks called "meddlesomeness,"[26] which humankind seeks because it distrusts God and is tortured by such distrust. It is important to recognize, however, that Solomon reprimands only this distrust, not our diligence in performing the labor commanded. Therefore, Solomon says here that human judgment undertaken outside one's calling is both unrighteous and invalid, and that we should flee from riches like eagles swooping away in flight. Solomon thus calls us anew to the boundaries of our calling, to seeking God's help, and to diligence and prudence as a command given by God.

---

[20] See Prov. 6:6.

[21] Here, and above, Melanchthon is making very general allusions to biblical precepts, for instance, those discussed in Proverbs 6.

[22] 1 Cor. 4:2.

[23] Matt. 25:14–30.

[24] Ps. 127:1 (Vulgate 126:1).

[25] Ps. 37:5 (Vulgate 36:5).

[26] In Greek, πολυπραγμοσύνη. Melanchthon has referred to this concept before. See Plato, *Republic* 444b.

"Do not eat with a jealous person nor covet his food, for his soul is like an apparition ..."[27]

As Solomon said above, dangers lurk in the royal courts and in the company of the powerful. Then he warned us not to seek after power and riches that surpass our calling. Now Solomon advises us to flee from those who are jealous. Who are the jealous but those who are sad when others experience more goodness or favor by means of some gift or virtue or some other good things? For instance, Cain was irritated after his brother outshone him in glory since God had shown favor to his brother [Abel] in a public way. Such irritation is the cause of horrible evils in this life, as the examples of Cain, Esau, Marius, Pompey, and countless others demonstrate.[28]

The source of jealousy is Pride. For all of humankind wants to stand out and is, by nature, what the Greeks referred to as "ambitious,"[29] thereby personifying the devil's words to Eve: "You will be like God."[30] Likewise, Seneca says that human desires are like fire, and therefore, they stretch upward.[31] Indeed, many people lament when they see someone else surpass them, especially when it happens that they themselves were rejected. Therefore, it has been written in Sirach, "Pride is the beginning of all sin."[32] And, in this way, pride and jealousy are

---

[27] Prov. 23:6–7.

[28] For Cain, see Gen. 4; for Esau, see Gen. 27:41–45. "Marius" probably refers to Gaius Marius, to whom Plutarch devoted one of his *Parallel Lives* in which he contrasts devotion to the Greek Muses to Marius's savagery, ambition, and greed. See Plutarch, *Caius Marius* 2.3. Although Plutarch provided a very favorable view of Pompey (Gnaeus Pompeius Magnus), Pompey's contemporaries were not so kind, nicknaming him "the teenage butcher" for executing his political opponents.

[29] In Greek, φιλαρχικός. The noun is used in Plutarch's description of Marius, *Caius Marius* 2.3.

[30] Gen. 3:5.

[31] As quoted in the previous chapter, a poem illustrating these realities appears in Seneca the Younger, *Agamemnon* 64–72.

[32] Sir. 10:13.

CHAPTER 23

combined evils, as is evident in the following Greek verse: "All things of honor follow jealousy."[33] And in Cicero, "It is the fault and stain of this age to envy virtue."[34]

Thus, in this case, such irritation is unjust, because it does not give what is owed either to God or to human beings.[35] For example, Cain did not give thanks to God who provided testimony about his presence and about the gathering together of the church.[36] Nor did he want his brother to possess gifts from God, and so, in a rage, he proceeded to kill him.[37] So also, Saul did not give thanks to God for the many blessings that God gave through David and the testimonies of the church, and instead, Saul attributed the victories to his kingdom. Nor did Saul want David to have those God-given gifts. Burning with indignation, he plotted against his life.[38]

A similar vice is what ancient Greeks called "spitefulness,"[39] which describes the phenomenon of taking delight in the misfortune of those who are good or decent. The devil, for instance, is the consummate exemplar of "spitefulness." Such vices are condemned in this passage, however, and admonitions are provided urging us to flee the fellow-

---

[33] Melanchthon does not cite the exact source of this quote, but it seems to come from Dionysius. In Greek, ἀεὶ τὰ σεμνὰ πάντα ἕπεται φθόνος. See *Gnomai sive Thesaurus Sententiarum et Epophthegmatum ex Scriptoribus Graecis*, ed. T. O. Weigelius (Leipzig, 1889), 156. Melanchthon's translation seems to ignore the much more negative meaning of *semna* as "haughty," so that the Greek means that all haughtiness arises from jealousy.

[34] Cicero, *For Cornelius Balbo* 6.15.

[35] Here Melanchthon uses the Ciceronian/Aristotelian definition of justice, "give to each his or her own," to explain how such irritation at another's success is unjust.

[36] Melanchthon defined "church" as any assembly of believers in God throughout time, and thus referred to Old Testament believers as the "church."

[37] Gen. 4:1–16.

[38] 1 Sam. 16–31.

[39] In Greek, ἐπιχαιρεκακία. German has a better one-to-one correspondence with this word than English does: *Schadenfreude*. See Aristotle, *Nichomachean Ethics* 2.6.18 (1107a, 8).

ship of those who are envious and mistrustful. Indeed, true kindness of heart is to be commended in the undertaking of all our duties.

For example, the beginnings of the virtues of others arise from discernment, the will, and the heart. In this way, kindness ought to arise from the same sources. Therefore, it has been written, "God loves a cheerful giver."[40] And the following Greek saying is the sweetest: "The soul that shows kindness is the best."[41] And the saying of Fabius [Verrucosus] from Seneca also applies: "Kindness rudely doled out by a hard man is like bread made of stone."[42]

Therefore, in conferring benefits, let the will exist to encourage benefits, to encourage desire for helping, and to encourage the well-being of others. And when this occurs, then the knowledge of God, faith, love of communal welfare, and a will reflecting these offices back to the glory of God will shine forth in the heart. May such a virtue reflect the [true] worship of God.

However, against a jealous, malicious, and distrustful person, there remains a great confusion of the worst feelings. Therefore, Solomon says here, "In such a heart is an apparition." And, in fact, such a heart is the toilet of the devil. Therefore, it has been written in John: "Whoever does not love one's brother is a murderer."[43]

And it is extremely clear that many calamities arise from such things, when envy gives free rein to distrust and falsehoods are concocted, with the result that people defend themselves, attempting to destroy those whom they suspiciously mistrust. However, count it as good fortune to avoid such people, as the saying at hand says: "Do not eat

---

[40] 2 Cor. 9:7.

[41] Melanchthon does not identify this Greek saying of Lucius Annaeus Cornutus (20–65 CE), a Stoic philosopher during the reign of Emperor Nero. In Greek, χαρίτων δέτε θυμὸς ἄριστος. See Lucius Annaeus Cornutus, *Greek Theology: Fragments, and Testimonia*, trans. George Boys-Stones (Atlanta: SBL, 2018), 74.

[42] Seneca the Younger, *On Benefits* 2.7. The Latin word *beneficium* is capable of many possible English translations: "benefit," "kindness," "favor," or "service."

[43] 1 John 3:15.

your bread with a jealous person." And one must be very diligent in considering the desires of humankind, just as Christ said, "Be as innocent as doves,"[44] that is to say, do not act with malice but instead be "as prudent as snakes," who protect their own life, recognize their enemy in the crowd and attack him while leaving the others alone.

---

[44] Matt. 10:16.

Chapter 24

"Free those who are dragged to death and who hasten toward slaughter when you are able."[1]

The following precepts have already been noted: "Do not murder,"[2] and so on. Likewise, "Do not participate in another's sins."[3] God has commanded both government officials and private citizens not to kill the innocent. And God has also commanded us not to aid or abet unjust cruelty. Moreover, when and in what way a governmental official may remove the guilty has been explained in Deuteronomy 19 and elsewhere.[4] To be sure, a government official should protect the life of the innocent, as has been written in Romans 13: "The servant of God is an avenger for punishing the one who commits evil."[5] In addition, private persons, without being seditious and in line with their callings, can oppose unrighteous violence.

The following examples recounted below are worthy of consideration. For instance, Jonathan opposed his father and helped David not only in his testimony but also in his official capacities without being

---

[1] Prov. 24:11.
[2] Ex. 20:13.
[3] Eph. 5:7.
[4] Deut. 19:1–13.
[5] Rom. 13:4.

seditious.⁶ Also, Obadiah supplied food in secret to the prophets who were being slaughtered by Jezebel.⁷ The Eunuch freed Jeremiah from prison.⁸ Then, there is the example of the midwives in Egypt who saved the Israelite infant boys.⁹ Likewise, Rahab saved the Israelite spies.¹⁰ What is more, in the time of Diocletian, a noble man in the city of Nicomedia publicly tore to pieces a copy of the emperor's edict ordering the killing of Christians, disapproving of the unrighteous cruelty.¹¹

A completely opposite example is that of Doeg, who, carrying out the raging of Saul, cruelly killed innocent priests.¹² In the same way, many in our time encourage unrighteous fury, which is executed against our churches—either openly or by their silence. Let such people consider this saying of Solomon and similar ones and, being admonished by the harsh threat of Christ, emend their ways. For it has been written in Matthew 23, "Upon them will come all the righteous blood spilled upon the earth from the blood of Abel the righteous to Zechariah."¹³ There is also a worthy memory regarding the most honorable words of Trajan. While bestowing a sword upon his master of the cavalry, he

---

⁶ 1 Sam. 19:1–7 and 20:1–42.

⁷ 1 Kings 18:3–5.

⁸ Jer. 38:6–13, referring to King Zedekiah's Ethiopian eunuch, Ebed-melech.

⁹ Ex. 1:15–20.

¹⁰ Josh. 2.

¹¹ The Nicomedia mentioned here was a Greek city located along the southwestern part of the Black Sea in modern-day Turkey. It was the capital city of Bithynia under the Roman Empire. This city was the center of the Diocletian Persecution, which began in earnest in the year 303. Diocletian, who was the Roman emperor from 284 to 305, had authorized prosecution of Christians and destruction of their property. Many stories of martyrdom are narrated by Christians from this time period. The nobleman referred to here may be a reflection of the stories of St. Trophimus and St. Eucarpion, soldiers in Nicomedia who took part in the savagery but then converted and were themselves martyred.

¹² 1 Sam. 22:17–19.

¹³ Matt. 23:35.

said, "I am giving you this sword so that you may use it on my behalf when I act justly. And you may also use it against me if I act unjustly."[14]

"Do not lie in wait like a thief near the house of the righteous; for the righteous will fall seven times but will rise again ..."[15]

Here Solomon repeats the precept, "Do not kill," with an added admonishment spoken against what the Greeks called "spitefulness" and "mockery."[16] For when ungodly and savage people see the misfortune of the godly, their own vileness causes them to take delight in it, becoming even more hostile as, for instance, when Shimei cursed David.[17] When Solomon says "the righteous will fall seven times a day," he is primarily speaking about the evil of punishment, that is, about misfortunes. And, nevertheless, it also sometimes happens that the evil comes from guilt, which brings with it misfortunes. However, the righteous will always emerge from these misfortunes, as seen in the lives of David, Manasseh, and countless others.

"My son, fear the Lord and the king, and do not join with the seditious. For their destruction will come rapidly, and who knows the ruin of the seditious that will follow?"[18]

This saying, among the chief ones appearing in this book, must be observed, for it not only commands obedience but ordains it. It directs, first, obedience to God and, then, to the king, because it is the first office, especially of the political ruler, that such a one be the voice of the Ten Commandments, punishing the ones who violate them. And it is chiefly for this reason that God subjects the multitude to

---

[14] This story comes from Cassius Dio (ca. 155–235 CE), *Roman History* LXVIII.16.1/2. Trajan was the Roman emperor from 98 to 117 CE.

[15] Prov. 24:15–16.

[16] In Greek, ἐπιχαιρεκακία (*Schadenfreude* in German) and σαρκασμός respectively. As mentioned in a previous chapter, Aristotle's *Nichomachean Ethics* is the original source for Melanchthon's language.

[17] 2 Sam. 16:5–13.

[18] Prov. 24:21–22.

the civil authorities because God wants divine law to be heard clearly and understood, with the result that God is truly acknowledged. The second reason why the law exists is to protect human society from breaking apart into endless uprisings. God has decreed that we would obey the authorities for God's sake and that we would recognize that God punishes lawbreakers. God has also restricted the duties of rulers, lest they command anything contrary to divine laws. Therefore, this verse states first of all, "Fear God." We can then accordingly come to understand the rule of the apostles: "We must obey God rather than human beings."[19]

From this passage, the entire teaching concerning the reasons for political order and civil authorities must be understood, which Romans 13 and passages elsewhere amply discuss. Here, however, Solomon explicitly commands us to "avoid the seditious," where it is necessary during conflicts to judge which are seditious. Now, judgment concerning political matters is easier because over a long period of time the temporal powers have a place over the multitudes, as anyone can see.

Thus, it is obvious what the duties of the temporal powers are, namely, to state publicly the message of the Ten Commandments and to punish the disobedient. Likewise, the temporal powers are to establish appropriate laws that do not conflict with the Ten Commandments, punish the disobedient, execute judgment, and pass sentences in accordance with the law. And when it comes to dubious matters of the law, sentences are valid based not only on probable cause but also upon the authority bestowed upon government officials from God. Indeed, God wants us to obey these officials in civil affairs and for us to be obedient even in uncertain matters. And because God gives more peacemaking and calming authority to some while giving less to others, God also wants us to bear some heavier burdens, as long as they are tolerable, are not heinous or notorious wrongdoings, and do not cause us to sin through obedience.

Concerning these matters, the following rule of Paul must be upheld: "It is necessary to submit to the authorities, not only for the sake of

---

[19] Acts 5:29.

wrath but also for the sake of conscience."[20] In this way, the disobedient sin when they do not wish to obey the legitimate authorities. Moreover, the seditious—that is, those who are insolent toward government officials in word, or those who attempt to overthrow the government by force using splinter groups or arms—sin even more. Here Solomon threatens a punishment against such people in this passage, just as the Lord does in the following saying: "The one who takes up the sword will die by the sword,"[21] that is, whoever unlawfully takes up arms will perish just like Absalom,[22] Sheba,[23] Adonijah,[24] Joab,[25] Cassius, Brutus,[26] and countless others.

But against heinous and notorious wrongdoings, concession has been made for defense. For example, there was a law, written in the *Pandects*,[27] permitting the killing of a consul who had been caught in adultery by the husband of the adulterous wife.[28] And Marius[29]

---

[20] Rom. 13:5.

[21] Matt. 26:52.

[22] 2 Sam. 15–16.

[23] See 2 Sam. 20.

[24] 1 Kings 1.

[25] 1 Kings 2:29–34.

[26] Brutus (85–42 BCE) and his brother-in-law, Cassius (before 85 to 42 BCE), were part of the plot to assassinate Julius Caesar. They died at the Battle of Philippi under the forces of Octavian and Marc Antony in 42 BCE.

[27] The *Pandectae* or *Digestum* was a compendium of fifty books of Roman civil law made by order of Emperor Justinian in the sixth century CE.

[28] The Julian law on adulteries was passed in 18 BCE. The original text of the laws no longer exists, and scholars refer to them in various ways. Because the original text no longer exists, the exact wording can only be inferred from Roman writers and later Roman laws. For one famous Roman jurist's explanation of the Julian law on adulteries, see Julius Paulus Prudentissimus, *Opinions* 2.26. He confirms Melanchthon's statement.

[29] The name Melanchthon uses is simply "Marius," which was a common Roman name. Most likely, Melanchthon was referring to Gaius Marius, a prominent Roman general who lived from 157 to 86 BCE. He held the office

absolved an adolescent who killed a military tribune in defense of his virtue.[30] Similarly, Victorinus, who was the Roman ruler of Cologne in Germany, was killed by a scribe whose wife the former had seduced,[31] even though elsewhere Victorinus's virtue was praised, as was similarly the case of [the Roman emperors] Nerva and Trajan.[32]

The Gospel, however, concedes that political laws are to be used when they correspond with human reason. In fact, if such a defense were not conceded, the Gospel would have been transformed into mere political teaching, and it would have established an unending tyranny. But about such a disputation, enough has been said elsewhere.[33]

However, concerning the refutation of error in the church, we must come to recognize that those resisting those princes and bishops who promote [theological] errors by no means commit sin against them.[34] On the contrary, it is necessary to obey God in the confes-

---

of consul a record number of times, and he was a leading general during both the Jugurthine wars and the Roman civil war. For a less favorable use of his example, see Melanchthon's comments in chapter 23.

[30] Cicero refers to this story in his speech *For Milo* 9. In the speech, delivered in 52 BCE, Cicero was seeking to make a case for his friend Milo, who was a military officer on trial for murdering an officer of a higher rank. Milo claimed self-defense, and the facts of the case are not materially different from the point Melanchthon is seeking to make here.

[31] This story refers to Marcus Piavonius Victorinus, a ruler of the Gallic provinces from ca. 268 to 271 CE. The Roman colony of Colonia Claudia Ara Agrippinensium is the origin of the modern Germany city of Cologne. This was the capital of the brief-lived Gallic Empire, a breakaway part of the Roman Empire that lasted from 260 to 274 CE.

[32] Nerva was briefly emperor before Trajan. Both were considered good emperors, more favorably disposed toward Christians than others.

[33] See, for example, Melanchthon's comments in his *Scholia* on Colossians 2:23 (editions from 1527, 1528, and 1534), in the various editions of the *Loci communes*, and in his 1539 *De officio principum*.

[34] Melanchthon, like his colleague Martin Luther, had been using this and similar arguments and these scriptural passages since the very beginning of the Reformation, distinguishing obedience to governmental authorities from resistance to ecclesiastical ones that did not promote the Gospel.

sion of truth, just as the apostles have said: "We ought to obey God rather than human beings."[35] Likewise, "If anyone will deny me before human beings, I will deny him [or her] before my heavenly Father."[36] Similarly, "If anyone should speak blasphemy against the Holy Spirit, his [or her] sin will not be forgiven."[37] Likewise, "If anyone should teach a different Gospel, let this person be anathema."[38] Backed by these commands from God, let us stand strong against the clamoring of kings and bishops who cry out that we are seditious because, through our teaching and through our confessing, we continue to condemn [theological] errors and idols, just as God has commanded us to do.[39] Let us recognize, then, that ministers of the Gospel are not to bear arms and that whenever those who wield temporal powers commit heinous sins, their wrongdoings are to be endured in accordance with these sayings. For instance, 2 Corinthians 10 says, "Our weapons are not physical ones."[40] Likewise, "As my Father has sent me, so I send you."[41] And finally, "My kingdom is not of this world."[42]

---

[35] Acts 5:29.

[36] Matt. 10:33.

[37] Matt. 12:31.

[38] Gal. 1:8.

[39] Twice during 1548, in the immediate aftermath of the Schmalkaldic War, Melanchthon was threatened by the imperial court with banishment as a *persona non grata*. He is here also referring to the experiences of others during the same time until the 1555 Peace of Augsburg gave Evangelicals certain rights in the Holy Roman Empire.

[40] 2 Cor. 10:4.

[41] John 20:21.

[42] John 18:36.

Chapter 25

"It is the glory of God to conceal the Word and the glory of kings to search it out."[1]

Teaching proper to the church of God naturally differs from human wisdom, and it is especially the case that powerful people often make errors in the governing of society by giving preference to political wisdom over the Word of God. For instance, Nebuchadnezzar established his own form of worship, imagining that uniformity of ceremonies would contribute to peace in his kingdom. In the same way, heretics today turn from Gospel and cleave to their own imaginations.[2] As a result, Solomon[3] admonishes us here that the Word of God is like hidden wisdom and must be discerned through serious study. That is to say, God wants us to be disciples of God's message, but God does not want us to give preference to our human thoughts or to fashion new dogmas or new rites.

On the contrary, it is the honor of kings, that is, of all who have power, to inquire after hidden wisdom by listening and by not being unsettled by sophistries. But as Paul commanded, "May the wisdom of God live in you."[4] That is to say, "May the sources be wisely searched,

---

[1] Prov. 25:2.

[2] In addition to unnamed heretics, Melanchthon also may have had in mind his Roman Catholic opponents, who insisted upon uniformity in ceremonies.

[3] Following the CR. The original has "Hezekiah."

[4] Melanchthon is probably generally referring to Paul's words in 1 Cor. 2.

may the testimonies be brought forward, and may we remember that we are to be disciples of the divine message," just as Solomon said, "The wise who listen will become wiser."[5] Indeed, the human wisdom residing in David urged him to kill Saul, but the Holy Spirit in David did not allow him to offer such an example to the people of God.[6]

"Like vinegar upon soda ash, so is the one who sings songs to a depraved heart."[7]

The properties of salt and soda ash are similar. Both, for instance, aggravate and burn the skin. And the singular ability of soda ash is in expelling [poisons], and when mixed with lime and vinegar it irritates them. As Pliny said, "Apply soda ash to snake wounds along with lime and vinegar."[8]

As a result, the metaphor used in this saying refers to those who become even more obstinate when admonished, nearly becoming rabid, just as soda ash infused with a lot of vinegar burns more vigorously and is more forcibly diffused and expelled on account of what the Greeks called a [chemical] "imbalance."[9] For example, Saul became even more ruthless when he was admonished.[10] There are many such examples of ungodly people among whom bouts of madness erupt when admonished.

However, this saying does not prohibit the teaching of true doctrine but instead is describing the facts or outcome, and it illustrates how hearers respond in different ways. While some are teachable, others are obstinate and do not wish to be taught. Such people are exempli-

---

[5] Prov. 1:5.

[6] 1 Sam. 24.

[7] Prov. 25:20. *Nitrum*, sodium carbonate, functions like lye. The original Hebrew text probably referred to pouring vinegar on a wound.

[8] Pliny the Elder, *Natural History* 31.46.

[9] In Greek, ἀντιπερίστασις. Part of Aristotle's theory of motion is the theory that opposites repel and thus become stronger. For example, exposure to cold could make a body warmer.

[10] See, for example, 1 Sam. 18:6–16; 19:1–10; 22:6–19; 28:1–25.

fied in Romans 11 when Paul speaks about blasphemies: "Their eyes are blinded so that they do not see."[11]

Although I said above that this saying does not prohibit the teaching of true doctrine, it nonetheless means that different kinds of hearers need to be distinguished. The teachable of heart carry themselves in a godly and attentive way as Paul said, "Bear the one who is weak in faith."[12] Concerning others who blaspheme, the following saying applies: "Do not give what is holy to dogs."[13] Likewise, Proverbs 23, "Do not speak in the ears of fools because they will despise the wisdom of your advice."[14] And, nonetheless, before you can distinguish among the hearers, doctrine must be propounded to all. It is only afterward that we may follow this rule from Paul: "Avoid a heretic after the first and second admonishment."[15]

"The righteous yielding to the ungodly is like a polluted fountain or poisoned well."[16]

It is most evident that the minds of all the wise are greatly disturbed by the disfigurement of the church when they see that the ungodly possess ruling authority, power, and wisdom [on earth]. Meanwhile, in fact, the church is feeble, abject, and scant, not possessing a particular ruling authority scattered among different nations. Likewise, innocent people have been killed by the most wretched of rulers—for instance, Israelite boys by Pharaoh, John the Baptist by Herod, and Paul by Nero. Such astonishing spectacles move the wise to think that God does not care for these wretched people.

But the divine message teaches two things. First, it teaches that the true church exists where God has revealed himself: in the proclaimed promise and illustrious testimonies, in the resurrection of the dead,

---

[11] Rom. 11:10.

[12] Rom. 14:1.

[13] Matt. 7:6.

[14] Prov. 23:9. The original has Prov. 13.

[15] Titus 3:10.

[16] Prov. 25:26.

and in many other signs. Second, it teaches that God cares for the church, hears its prayers, and protects it, and that the church is also the inheritor of eternal glory from God—and all this despite being feeble and subject to the cross for many reasons.[17]

By these divine testimonies, let us come to strengthen ourselves against these public spectacles, which are described in the phrase "the scandal of the cross," and let us be mindful of the following sayings. Matthew 11 says, "You have hidden these things from the wise and revealed them to little children."[18] Likewise, in 1 Corinthians 1, "Not many are wise according to human standards, not many powerful ..."[19] Indeed, the entire Pauline teaching in Romans 9 applies here,[20] and many psalms speak similarly. For example, "Do not copy evildoers."[21] And, finally, it says in Psalm 73, "My feet had almost slipped."[22]

So it happens in private lives. For example, when [King] David was driven into exile, the ungodly took delight in his calamity, and many ridiculed him with public derision. These judgments are ably described in the above analogy: "The righteous before the wicked is like a polluted fountain."[23] But the godly should take real comfort in this and should come to recognize the nature of the church's true identity and the reasons it is subject to the cross. On this basis, they may pray for unshakeable consolations.

---

[17] This is an example of what might be called Melanchthon's "ecclesiology of the cross," where God is revealed among the weak.

[18] Matt. 11:25.

[19] 1 Cor. 1:26.

[20] Starting in his commentary on Romans from 1532, Melanchthon applied Romans 9–11 and its discussion of predestination to the whole church rather than to individual souls. See, for example, his *Commentary on Romans*, trans. Fred Kramer (St. Louis: Concordia, 1992), 185–94.

[21] Ps. 37:1 (Vulgate 36:1).

[22] Ps. 73:2. Melanchthon, of course, using the Vulgate, refers to this as Ps. 72.

[23] Prov. 25:26.

1. God wants sin to be acknowledged, for it still abides in this human nature.
2. The church often includes those who have publicly lapsed [in their faith], so God wants us to be brought to repentance.
3. God wants to be invoked in prayer, and God wants to show his presence during times of great need, for such needs are not able to be met through human counsel.
4. God wants the murder of the saints to witness to their teaching and to the future judgment.

Chapter 26

"Like night in summer and rain in harvest, glory is not fitting for a fool."[1]

This is talking about the outcome, as does this saying: "Fate makes a fool out of the one she favors."[2] For it describes people who are prodigal with their resources who have not yet been corrected or chastised, and where restraints have been loosened by various wanton desires. For example, Alexander [the Great] was initially very modest and very meek, but he later made himself out to be like a god and became cruel. For when people are not reined in, they become self-satisfied, they no longer seek help from God, they become drunk with success, and they think much of themselves and their own plans. Indeed, the disasters befalling otherwise illustrious men are numerous and sad, as seen in the examples of Hercules, Nebuchadnezzar, Julius Caesar, Pompey, and countless others.

Although the verse at hand speaks only about the outcome pertaining to the rule about communal occurrences, it also implicitly includes an admonition or precept about Modesty. As Sirach explains in chapter 3, "The greater you are, the more you should humble yourself, so that you may receive grace before God."[3] Likewise, "God resists the

---

[1] Prov. 26:1.

[2] Publilius Syrus, *Sentences* 271.

[3] Sir. 3:20.

proud but gives grace to the humble."[4] Also, as I recorded above from a saying of Plutarch, "Rulers should imitate the sun, which, after rising in the northern sky and ascending to its greatest height, has the least motion. And by being slower, it ensures the safety of its course."[5]

"Like a bird flying and a swallow fleeing, a curse said in vain will not last."[6]

This rule of life must be upheld: "*Fight the good fight, clinging to faith and a good conscience.*"[7] By holding on to these things, we will also have the approval of many honorable people. Indeed, as Sirach said in chapter 41, there is one thing in particular to be desired: "Take care of a good name."[8] Nonetheless, the envious of this world are legion, and they disparage those whom they attempt to emulate. As Cicero says, "It is the fault and stain of this age to envy [even] virtue."[9] Indeed, many people are venomous by nature, taking delight in reviling others. They complain about many people, as Plautus says, "This here is the treasure lodged in the tongue of a fool—to think it proper to speak wickedly to their superiors."[10] And I have already noted the verses from Menander:

---

[4] James 4:6; 1 Peter 5:5.

[5] Plutarch, *To an Uneducated Ruler* 6. In chapter 23, Melanchthon had quoted the Greek version of this; in this chapter, however, he gives only the Latin. See p. 148, n. 18.

[6] Prov. 26:2.

[7] 1 Tim. 1:18–19, printed in all capital letters.

[8] Sir. 41:15 (Vulgate).

[9] Cicero, *For Cornelius Balbo* 6.15.

[10] Titus Maccius Plautus, *Poenulus* 3.3.12–13. This comedy, also known as *The Little Carthaginian*, was written by the Latin author in the late second century BCE.

> They say that life is greatly alluring to the perverse
> And that the flatterer prospers best of all,
> Followed second by the sycophant
> And third by the wicked.[11]

Moreover, stories from all of history show that many noteworthy people have been crushed by false accusations, for example, Joseph, Palamedes, Aristides, Theramenes, Socrates, and countless others.[12] And in Ecclesiastes it says, "False accusations unsettle the wise and break the strength of their hearts."[13] As experience shows, good men are often impeded by false accusations.

Therefore, a consolation has been handed down here against false accusations. Namely, false reviling, although lasting for a while, is eventually uncovered as empty and blameworthy, as it is said, "The truth may struggle for a while, but it cannot be extinguished."[14] The following psalm also offers a very sweet consolation: "While they curse you, may you bless them."[15] And David, in the face of Shimei's public censure of him, said, "God will give me some good in exchange for [Shimei's] curses."[16]

---

[11] Menander originally recorded these words, but most of his writings only survive in fragments. Portions of this saying appear in Euripides, *Hippolytus* 426. In Greek, ὁ βίος μάλιστα τοῖς πονηροῖς ἥδεταί πράττει δ' ὁ κόλαξ ἄριστα πάντων δεύτερος ὁ συκοφάντης ὁ κακοήθης τρίτατος. Melanchthon provided a Latin translation of the first line, used here.

[12] For more on Joseph, see Gen. 39. Palamedes, a figure depicted in Greek legends as an excellent warrior, was hated by Odysseus for involving him in the Trojan War. Aristides (530–468 BCE) was an Athenian statesman, known for his just behavior, who was ostracized by Themistocles. Theramenes (d. 404 BCE) was another Athenian statesman who was attacked after his death by the orator Lysias.

[13] Eccl. 7:8 (Vulgate).

[14] Livy, *History of Rome* 22.39.19.

[15] Ps. 109:28 (Vulgate 108:28).

[16] 2 Sam. 16:12.

Let us take to heart these consolations, but let us do so simply by preserving the integrity of our conscience, as it is so often commanded, "This is our boast, namely, the testimony of our conscience."[17] And Paul writes to the Galatians, "Let each person prove his own work and, in this way, he will have glory in himself and not in others."[18] Here is what Paul means here: Act rightly, namely, in such a way that your conscience does not condemn you; and when your conscience is no longer stricken, you will have glory, namely, not because you depend upon the foolish applause of others but, instead, you will gain the true approval of your conscience in believing that this is a truly necessary, God-pleasing work.

We must acknowledge these precepts and these consolations as being given by God. For a false accusation is no trivial matter, even though Truth, once revealed, will ultimately refute such a charge. For example, when Socrates was killed, it was later depicted as a tragedy in the play *Palamedes*, from which the following verses appear: "You have killed, you have killed the best of the Greeks, the nightingale, who has done no wrong."[19] And after this tragedy, the city expelled Socrates's accusers from Athens.

What follows below are additional sayings pertaining to that which has been previously discussed. In short, these sayings offer a wise admonition about how to make judgments, namely, determining when a false accusation should be refuted and when it should not be refuted.

---

[17] 2 Cor. 1:12.

[18] Gal. 6:4.

[19] Euripides's tragedy *Palamedes* has not survived intact. The verses cited appear only in part as *Fragment* 588. The person killed is Socrates. In Greek, from a sixteenth-century version combining Isocrates and Plato, ἐκάνετε ἐκάνετε τὸν ἄριστον ἑλλήνων, μηδένα βλάψασαν ἀηδόνα.

Chapter 26

"Do not answer a fool according to his foolishness lest you become like him. [Answer a fool according to his foolishness lest he imagine himself to be wise.]"[20]

These twin, contrary sayings are put here, which contrast to each other because revilings are sometimes to be refuted, and sometimes it is not necessary to refute them. It must be prudently decided which response is required.[21] However, it is still relatively easy for pastors to determine the right response when teaching in their public office. They always have a diverse audience: the godly, the strong, the weak, and the teachable, as well as those who are obstinate and incurable adversaries. But it is necessary for pastors to serve the better contingent of people so that the uncorrupted doctrinal message may refute adversaries. Let the pastors also determine the nature of the revilings: some mutilate doctrine, while others disfigure the character of the teacher.

However, it has been mandated that doctrine is to be illuminated and defended. First, it says in 2 Timothy 1: "I have preserved the trustworthy deposit through the Holy Spirit living in us."[22] And then in Titus 1, "It is necessary to silence the mouth of those [subverting the truth]."[23] And, finally, in Titus 2, "Speak authoritatively with every power,"[24] which is to say that we are to instruct with earnestness so that detractors will come to accept the Word.

Indeed, let pastors contend on behalf of necessary matters, and let them endeavor to strengthen those who are weak in faith. As Paul said, let them endeavor to bring them back [to the truth],[25] not getting

---

[20] Prov. 26:4–5. The bracketed material is implied in the text by "etc." and by Melanchthon's exposition.

[21] This entire section may be viewed on the backdrop of Melanchthon's various approaches to his opponents, especially the fellow Lutheran Matthias Flacius, whom he alternately ignored or attacked.

[22] 2 Tim. 1:14.

[23] Titus 1:11.

[24] Melanchthon is paraphrasing the whole chapter, but the passage is most similar to Titus 2:1 and 2:15.

[25] Gal. 6:1.

entangled in inextricable disputes, nor separating from the congregation in bitterness. However, pastors should either refute personal insults in gentleness or ignore them altogether, as it is said in Psalms: "They were disparaging me, but I was praying."[26]

In other private meetings, however, teachers and others should consider the different kind of listeners present. If those present are [theologically] curable, let them be taught correctly. But if someone should come upon a group of people that is incurable, let that person follow the example of the apostle John. For when in a [public] bathhouse he happened upon a faction [of heretics] led by Cerinthus, he, in order to demonstrate confession [of faith] in this situation, instantly fled lest he appear to be in collusion with Cerinthus [and his heretical followers], were that possible.[27] All this was in line with the saying, "Reject a heretic after a first and second warning,"[28] as John did, who immediately left the bathhouse. As it is also said, "Do not give what is holy to dogs."[29]

But it is also sometimes appropriate to offer either no refutation when confronted with a personal reviling or to offer only a few words [in defense]. For example, as alluded to above, David remained quiet when Shimei cursed him.[30] In fact, there are many examples of famous rulers who elected to ignore revilings, such as Pericles, Fabius, Scipio,

---

[26] Ps. 109:4 (Vulgate 108:4).

[27] Cerinthus was a Gnostic Christian whose teachings and writings were opposed by several early Christians. According to tradition, and the story that Melanchthon tells, Cerinthus and the apostle John knew each other, though John was convinced that Cerinthus was an unrepentant heretic. John reportedly fled a Roman bathhouse in Ephesus upon learning that the heretic Cerinthus was inside, afraid that God's wrath would be kindled by the presence of the heretic and therefore destroy the walls. See Irenaeus, *Against Heresies* 3.3.4.

[28] Titus 3:10.

[29] Matt. 7:6.

[30] 2 Sam. 16:12.

and many others.[31] For instance, the Spartans, provoked by [the Persian commander] Mardonius,[32] taught this. According to Herodotus, Mardonius became more enraged by the silence of the Spartans and became overconfident through this "cold victory."[33] Also in Herodotus's *Histories*, the story is told of a Spartan envoy who responded haughtily to a Gelonian.[34] The Gelonian said to him, "Shameful words of a person usually kindle anger. Although you hurl reproach upon my words, this will not persuade me to respond disgracefully with equal insults."[35]

Most of the time, people are incited to anger in the face of insults against them. Indeed, it is foolish to enter into a dispute with someone who has become angry, as stated elegantly in the following Greek verses: "When two people are saying angry things to each other, the one who does not become contentious with his words is the wiser."[36]

Finally, when it comes to personal offenses, let us be mindful of Peter's saying in 1 Peter 3: "Do not repay insult with insult."[37] We should also remember this truth: When refuting an offense, it is not only the

---

[31] These are three very famous statesmen and generals. Pericles, of course, was an Athenian (Greek), and he lived in the fifth century BCE. Quintus Fabius Maximus Verrucosus (280–203 BCE) and Publius Cornelius Scipio Africanus (236–183 BCE) were important Roman public and military officials.

[32] Mardonius (d. 479 BCE) was a Persian military commander who fought against the Greeks during the Persian Wars, and he was also a fighter in the famous Battle of Thermopylae in 480.

[33] See Herodotus, *Histories* 9.49. In the Greek phrase Melanchthon cites, which is "cold victory," the word "cold" refers figuratively to "imaginary," for Mardonius was ultimately defeated on account of his arrogance.

[34] The Gelonians were a people of mixed Scythian and Greek heritage. The capital of the Gelonians (or Geloni) was called Gelonos

[35] Herodotus, *Histories* 7.160.1.

[36] In addition to the Latin translation, Melanchthon provides the Greek, δυοῖν λεγόντοιν θατέρου θυμουμένου ὁ μὴ ἀντιτείνων τοῖς λόγοις σοφώτερος. This saying was compiled by Johannes Stobaeus, and possibly coined by Euripides. It appears in *Anthologium*, vol. 1, section 18, ed. Thomas Gaisford (Oxford: Clarendon, 1822), 146.

[37] 1 Peter 3:9.

other person's offense that must be corrected but essential teaching must also be made clear in all earnestness, because it is not sufficient to contradict others using the customs of the Academy. One must also demonstrate what is [truly] to be thought, just as Demosthenes warns, "You rebuke everyone, but you do not offer any advice to anyone."[38]

"Whoever does business through a foolish messenger is like someone who walks with lame feet."[39]

This saying has a parallel in Homer, which Pindar praises: "A noble messenger brings great honor to every endeavor."[40]

"An artisan crafts a product. But by employing a fool, it becomes worthless."[41]

The lawyer says, "The quality of a product varies greatly from artisan to artisan."[42] Indeed, there are many sayings about distinguishing the work of an artisan from that of deceivers and impostors who sell products as works of art when they are not. For example, there are many charlatans who parade around as doctors, and there are also plenty of uneducated preachers who are praised by commoners or the powerful.

Therefore, this admonition here, which pertains to prudence, is handed down so that a person may choose appropriately in any field whatsoever. At the same time, it has also been commanded for those who profess to be skilled, lest they are tempted to become deceivers

---

[38] This quote from Demosthenes could not be identified. In Greek, ἐπιτιμᾶν παντός ἐστι, συμβουλεύειν δ' οὐ παντός.

[39] Prov. 26:6.

[40] Pindar, *Pythian* 4.277; Homer, *Iliad* 15.207. In Greek, ἐσθλὸν καὶ τὸ τέτυκται ὅτ' ἄγγελος αἴσιμα εἰδῇ.

[41] Prov. 26:10, with a very different reading of the Hebrew, also shared with the Luther Bible.

[42] *Pandectae seu Digestorum Iuris Caesarei Tomus Tertius* [=*Digestum Novum*], bk. 46, tit. III: "De solutionibus & liberationibus," law 31.

and impostors. However, as Paul says, may they be faithful,[43] meaning that they may know exactly the skills they are professing and may always demonstrate faithfulness and diligence. Such a virtue, which is called EARNESTNESS, is defined as understanding and faithfully undertaking the works of our own office or calling.[44]

The following sayings drive home the point being made: "A person should practice whatever craft he [or she] knows best."[45] Likewise, "One cannot teach what one does not know."[46] Also, "One wears a crown, another plays a lute."[47] Likewise, "Although a carpenter, you are not doing carpentry."[48] And Phocylides says, "For you should never allow ignorant people the ability to judge."[49] Similarly, "The one who has learned to row should take the oar."[50] Likewise in this saying of Sulla, "First be a rower before you can pilot the boat."[51] And, finally, to a large extent, the ignorant become even more rash, in accordance with the saying, "Ignorance leads to rashness."[52]

---

[43] Titus 1:6.

[44] This definition reflects an understanding of daily life as God's calling held in common by Luther and Melanchthon.

[45] Cicero, *Tusculan Disputations* 1.41. Cicero attributes the original quote to Aristotle.

[46] Ovid, *Sorrows* 2.348.

[47] This common proverb rhymes and has great symmetry in Latin: *Aliud est sceptrum, aliud est plectrum*. The point of the proverb is that each person has different roles to play.

[48] Euripides, *Fragments* 988. In Greek, τέκτων γὰρ ὢν ἔπραττες οὐ χυλουργικὰ.

[49] Phocylides, *Poem of Admonition* (Andover, MA: Warren F. Draper, 1879), 15.

[50] Erasmus, *Adages* 1.2.76.

[51] Aristophanes, *Knights* 541.

[52] Thucydides, *Funeral Oration of Pericles* 2.40.3. Melanchthon is paraphrasing the Greek quote as follows: ἀμαθ[ε]ία θράσος ἀπεργάζεται.

"Like a dog returning to his vomit, such is the fool who repeats his foolishness."[53]

Regarding the causes of punishments in this life, it has been frequently stated elsewhere[54] that there are four clear causes.

1. God is righteous and destroys that which is contrary to that nature.
2. God wishes to be known—particularly to be known as righteous—and, therefore, God wants people to learn the difference between righteous and unrighteous things.
3. God wants the destructive parts of us to be taken away.[55]
4. God wants our own punishments—as well as those of others—to serve as warnings that deter us from sinning, just as was discussed above in chapter 19, where it is stated, "When the mocker is struck down, the fool will become more attentive."[56] Also, Paul says in 1 Corinthians 10: "The punishments of the people of Israel were written as examples."[57] And the Lord said to Abraham that he was to remember the example of the punishment of Sodom so that his descendants would be warned about God's judgment.[58] What is more, there are additional examples of those later cured who became more attentive to God after initially being punished. Consider the following sayings, for instance: "Once bit, twice shy."[59] Like-

---

[53] Prov. 26:11.

[54] See above comments on Prov. 19:25.

[55] The word for "parts" here is *membra* in Latin, which could refer either to parts of society or, more literally, to parts of the body, as in Matt. 5:29–30.

[56] Prov. 19:25.

[57] 1 Cor. 10:11.

[58] Gen. 18:16–33. The destruction of Sodom is recounted in the next chapter of Genesis.

[59] This old Latin proverb is similar to the English "Once burned, twice wary," meaning that an initial bite, sting, or burn—though it hurts—will make the person more cautious in the long run. In Latin, *ictus sapit*.

wise, "We learn through suffering."[60] Also, "Foolish is the person who trips over the same stone twice."[61] And, finally, about other examples, it is said, "I have learned by watching the bad behavior of others."[62]

Nevertheless, many people are stubborn and inflexible, unwilling to mend their ways when they themselves or others are punished. Indeed, many get carried away and become even more violent when punished. And there are also some who show some measure of restraint for a short period of time, like Saul briefly did, before quickly relapsing into the same vices.[63] The saying at hand is referring to such people who relapse, just as God warns very frequently in other places, lest, by relapsing, we suffer even greater punishments. As it is said in Amos 1, "I have spared three sins, but I will not spare a fourth."[64] And both Christ and Peter said, "The final punishment for such people will be worse than the first."[65] And, here, Solomon is saying the same thing, namely, that those who relapse are like dogs. This is much sadder still, because the Lord said that the devil would return with seven spirits worse than the first.[66]

There are many horrible public and private examples that should be considered here. For instance, madness grew within Pharaoh, Saul,

---

[60] This Greek phrase, coming from Aesop's *Fables* 233, rhymes in Greek, which is part of its allure: παθήματα μαθήματα, which could be rhymed "a burn makes us learn."

[61] This well-known proverb literally means, "Foolish is the person who kicks his foot against the same stone twice." It has a Greek genesis: Δὶς πρὸς τὸν αὐτὸν αἴσχρὸν προσκὺνειν λίθον.

[62] Menander, *Paidion* 377, given in both Greek and Latin.

[63] See 1 Sam. 9–31, *passim*.

[64] Paraphrasing Amos 1:3.

[65] Compare Matt. 12:43–45; Matt. 27:64; 2 Peter 2:20.

[66] Matt. 12:45.

Absalom, and Ahab.[67] What is more, the citizens of Sodom, even after seeing that they had been spared by God after Abraham overcame the army of their enemies, nevertheless quickly forgot about their earlier punishments and liberation and ran headlong into even more appalling crimes.[68] Also, when their brothers, the Maccabeans, had been killed after many ups and downs, the Jews brazenly mutilated doctrine by separating themselves into different factions, namely, into Pharisees and Sadducees. They also wrecked the kingdom through various civil wars.[69]

In that history, we also see now an image of Germany. Even after teaching has been corrected, many still return to their former errors—thereafter becoming godless. Indeed many obliterate the light of true teaching with new errors and incite rebellions. And many teachers, having abandoned the search for [true] doctrine, instruct the people using pleasing words. And the people, delighting in their wantonness, relax any restraints through their own evil desires. By doing so, we only attract more punishments. Despite this, however, God will preserve some remnants of the true church. If we wish to be members of this church, we must turn genuinely toward God, beg to be converted, governed, and strengthened by the Son of God, lest we relapse. We ourselves must be diligent to avoid those temptations and occasions that lead us to sin, just as Paul commanded, "Be careful that you do not receive God's grace in vain."[70] Likewise, "Walk carefully, not as fools do ..."[71] Consider also the following saying: "To avoid sin means

---

[67] See, e.g., Ex. 8 on the hardening of Pharaoh's heart; 1 Sam. 16:14 on Saul being possessed by an evil spirit; 2 Sam. 17:14 on Absalom's rejection of Ahithophel's counsel; and 1 Kings 21:25–26 on Ahab's abominations.

[68] See, e.g., Gen. 14 and 19.

[69] Melanchthon is probably depending upon Josephus as well as 1 and 2 Maccabees.

[70] 2 Cor. 6:1.

[71] Eph. 5:15.

avoiding opportunities to sin."[72] And, finally, Sirach says, "Whoever loves danger will be destroyed by it."[73]

---

[72] This Latin proverb was common. The German equivalent, "Nimmer tun ist höchter Buß" (Not to do something is the highest form of penitence), was used by Luther and became part of the struggle between Johann Agricola and Philip Melanchthon in their 1527 fight over the role of the law in penance. See Timothy J. Wengert, *Law and Gospel: Philip Melanchthon's Debate with John Agricola of Eisleben over "Poenitentia"* (Grand Rapids: Baker, 1997), 30–32.

[73] Sir. 3:26.

Chapter 27

"Do not boast about tomorrow, for you do not know what tomorrow will bring."[1]

This proverb parallels a Roman saying: "You do not know what the evening may bring."[2] Likewise, "The divine powers play with human affairs, and we can scarcely have faith in the present hour."[3] And also, "All human things hang by a slender thread; and the one who used to be strong falls into ruin through sudden misfortune."[4] Likewise, "The rich king becomes a beggar in an instant."[5] In short, book after book is filled with such admonitions concerning the fickleness of fortune. As such, these things are set forth to admonish us about Moderation and to prohibit these two very serious vices: trust in ourselves and the rashness of being distracted by inconsequential things through foolish hope. These two things get between us and our goals, keeping us from performing those duties necessary to our calling, just as Paul said, "Do

---

[1] Prov. 27:1.

[2] Aulus Gellius, *Attic Nights* 1.22.4. In this line, Gellius is quoting Marcus Varro, *Fragment* 340, whose works have not survived intact.

[3] Ovid, *Letters from the Black Sea* 4.3.49–50.

[4] Ovid, *Letters from the Black Sea* 4.3.35.

[5] Ovid, *Sorrows* 3.7.42. Literally, "The one who was like Croesus is suddenly Irus." Croesus was the king of Lydia renowned for his wealth, and Irus was the beggar in the house of Odysseus in Ithaca who became synonymous with a poor person.

everything in a proper way."6 Indeed, in the recognition of our own weaknesses, let us bind ourselves in prayer to God according to the saying, "Be subject to God and pray to him."7 Likewise, "Without me, you can do nothing."8 And Jeremiah says, "I know, Lord, that the way" (that is, the callings) "of human beings is not in their own power."9 For this passage does not say that human beings do nothing, but rather that without God's help, human plans and actions cannot be successful.

Therefore, we must always observe the rule that necessary and present things must be properly done, things demanded by reason of our office. And we must request help from God, lest we trust our own powers or out of foolish hope we undertake unnecessary things, such as when Pericles waged an unnecessary war for the flimsiest of reasons when he could have overlooked the matter, with many afterward condemning his decision.10 Similarly, Alcibiades invaded Sicily without cause,11 and Hannibal entered into war against the Romans also without cause.12 What is more, Pompey, if he had wanted, could

---

6 1 Cor. 14:40.

7 Job 22:21.

8 John 15:5.

9 Jer. 10:23. By adding this gloss, Melanchthon avoids connecting this passage to predestination. By contrast, see John Calvin, *Institutes of the Christian Religion* (1559), I.xvi.6, already in the second edition of 1539.

10 Melanchthon is probably referring to Pericles's declaration of war against Sparta to his fellow Athenians in 431 BCE. Despite Pericles's confidence, the Spartans proved more resilient than he thought.

11 Alcibiades, whom Melanchthon has mentioned in other chapters, was a younger contemporary of Pericles. This reference alludes to the so-called Sicilian Expedition, from 415 to 413 BCE, when Athenians, originally under the military guidance of Alcibiades, suffered great casualties.

12 Hannibal was the great Carthaginian general who fought against the Romans, most notably in the so-called Second Punic War, which lasted from 218 to 201 BCE and resulted in the deaths of countless Roman and Carthaginian soldiers.

have brokered peace.¹³ All of these wars proved extremely destructive for their states. And Charles, Duke of Burgundy, entered into war against the Duchy of Lorraine and the Swiss without cause, in which he was unfortunately killed in battle.¹⁴ Thus, the unfortunate are properly called "meddlesome"¹⁵ in Greek, which is to do unnecessary things in foolish hope. As the following Greek saying goes: "Vain people do vain things due to evil desires."¹⁶

It is very useful to in mind keep these admonitions, which relate well to this saying of Christ: "Do not worry about tomorrow, for it will worry about itself. Each day has enough trouble of its own."¹⁷ We may interpret Christ's saying as follows: "Do what is necessary in the present moment, things that have enough troubles of their own. So, do not pile up vain troubles today with worry or concern over future things."

"Stone is heavy and sand is weighty, but the anger of a fool is heavier than both."¹⁸

Distinctions among sayings must often be kept in mind. Some sayings expressly command or prohibit something, others are divine promises or threats, while still others describe the consequences. At the same time, the latter also offer a subtle warning about how hearts may be protected against these very consequences. The saying at hand

---

¹³ Melanchthon is probably referring to Pompey's ability to come to peace terms with Julius Caesar in the first century BCE, when Rome was in the midst of a civil war.

¹⁴ Charles, who had many epithets—including Charles the Bold and Charles the Reckless—was Duke of Burgundy from 1467 to 1477. The Duchy of Lorraine was a medieval kingdom that succeeded the Carolingian and Ottonian Empires. René, Duke of Lorraine, defeated Charles with an army of Swiss mercenaries at the Battle of Nancy in 1477. Charles had invaded Nancy, the capital of the Duchy of Lorraine, which led to his demise.

¹⁵ In Greek, πολυπραγμοσύνη. Melanchthon's argument echoes that of Plato, *Republic* 4.444b.

¹⁶ In Greek, μάταιοι μάταια λογίζονται δι ἐπιθυμίας.

¹⁷ Matt. 6:34.

¹⁸ Prov. 27:3.

describes an outcome that is a common vice of many who are prone to anger and are less likely to be placated. For the most part, such angry people are very hardened and ignorant; they neither recognize the weakness of the human condition nor think that the many errors of others are to be gently endured and corrected. Therefore, it has been said, "There is nothing more unreasonable than an ignorant person."[19] However, goodness stands out as a prominent attribute in God, and God himself also endures the many weaknesses of his own people, commanding, "Forgive, and it will be forgiven you."[20] As such, the wise more ably bend their hearts toward goodness and are mindful of the common weakness, theirs and others'; they take to heart the divine precept just mentioned: "Forgive, and it will be forgiven you." Indeed, the image of the merciless and foolish cannot be portrayed more clearly than the image of the cruel servant in the Gospel who owed sixty barrels of gold [to his master].[21]

Now, although this saying in Solomon's book is a description of the outcome, it nevertheless offers many warnings. It commands us to consider human weakness, to temper our anger, and to be mindful of the precept called "forbearance"[22] in ancient Greek. It likewise warns us to avoid foolish people who know neither what to take offense at nor what to overlook. Many sayings relate to this. For instance, "The greater the person, the more restrained his anger; an honorable mind is capable of kind impulses."[23] And Seneca says, "Nothing is great that

---

[19] Terence, *Brothers* 1.2.18.

[20] Matt. 6:14.

[21] Matt. 18:21–35. In something of an exception, Melanchthon may be using a common German term, *Tonne*, for a large barrel. Similar terms are found in Old French, English, and Scandinavian languages. There is also a medieval Latin term, *tonna* (related to the medieval *tolnetum*) for an exorbitant amount of money.

[22] In Greek, ἐπιείκεια. Used before by Melanchthon, this category is critical in the ethical considerations of all early Lutheran thinkers. It comes from Aristotle via Cicero, who also calls it *aequitas*.

[23] Ovid, *Sorrows* 3.5.31–32.

is not also peaceful."²⁴ What is more, the following verses of Homer in book 7 of the *Odyssey* are the sweetest:

> Stranger, you may not reckon my heart to be in such a state as
> To be burning so much in wrath without cause.
> It is a virtue most beautiful to be moderate in all things.²⁵

Similarly, Pliny says, "Whoever hates vices, hates humanity."²⁶ However, such a saying must be understood very carefully. For Pliny is not speaking about the unusualness of committing vices, nor of approving them; instead, he is speaking about extending some level of tolerance toward those who have gone astray yet not committed a crime. Other commands handed down from God about the moderation of anger may be found in Matthew 5 and 8, Romans 12, and elsewhere.²⁷

"Like a bird wandering from its nest, such is the man wandering from his place."²⁸

There is no kind of life or existence that one can lead that is free of annoyances and dangers. Therefore, in every station of life, unpleasurable things overwhelm us. As the following saying indicates, "The lazy ox envies the horse's saddle, but the packhorse envies the ox's plow."²⁹ This verse warns us, therefore, lest when crushed by loathsome duties, we abandon our station in life to which we have been rightly called.

---

²⁴ Seneca, *On Anger* 1.21.4.

²⁵ Homer, *Odyssey* 7.308–310, where Alcinous is speaking to Odysseus. Given in Latin and Greek, ξεῖν οὐ τοιοῦτον ἐνὶ στήθεσσι φίλον κῆρ μαψιδίως κεχολῶσθαὶ Ἀμείνω δ' αἴσιμα πάντα.

²⁶ Pliny the Younger, *Epistle* 8.22. According to Pliny, he was quoting a saying from Publius Clodius Thrasea Paetus, a Roman who died in 66 CE. See also similar thoughts in Seneca, *On Anger* 1.14.2.

²⁷ See Matt. 5:21–26; 7:1–5; and Rom. 12:14–21. The reference to Matt. 8 may be the result of a printer's error.

²⁸ Prov. 27:8.

²⁹ Horace, *Epistle* 1.14.43.

As Paul said, "Let each person remain in the condition in which he [or she] was called."[30]

Many sayings that have been handed down against Fickleness found in an ephemeral life pertain to this precept, since such a life changes its purpose repeatedly. As stated elsewhere, "A rolling stone gathers no moss."[31] Likewise, "A frequently transplanted plant cannot take root."[32] Also, "If you be a donkey, a bitter lot follows every kind of donkey whatever; the one who bears this burden calmly is wise."[33] Finally, "Why do you wish to be called a bad poet instead of a good physician?"[34]

"Just as iron is sharpened by iron, so a person sharpens the countenance of a friend."[35]

Let us recognize our own weakness, and let us understand that all people ignore their own faults, erring and stumbling frequently, as Solomon says, "The number of fools is infinite."[36] Likewise, "There is a way that appears right, but it ultimately leads to death."[37] This kind of lament looms large among the writings of many. For instance,

---

[30] 1 Cor. 7:24. This text, cited many times before by Melanchthon, was considered the locus classicus for the Lutheran understanding of vocation.

[31] This well-known saying has a lengthy history and is found in Greek, Latin, German, and English sources, among others.

[32] Seneca, *Epistle* 2.3

[33] Johann Stigel (1515–1562) was a former student of Melanchthon who taught Latin. Melanchthon is referring to one of his epigrams, the same one he mentioned in chapter 20.

[34] Plutarch, *Morals*. The person being addressed here is Periander. This saying appears in the section titled "Of Archidamus the Son of Agesilaus," in *Plutarch's Essays* (Boston: Little, Brown, 1883), 448.

[35] Prov. 27:17, mirroring the Vulgate's rendering.

[36] Eccl. 1:15 (Vulgate).

[37] Prov. 16:25.

Euripides said, "Nobody sees everything."³⁸ And also Theognis, "Not a single human being is wise in all things."³⁹

It is for that reason that God has chiefly fashioned us for communicating with words, so that some would teach others, and others would govern through the counsel of others. Therefore, Paul has said, "Teach and admonish one another."⁴⁰ And Sirach 6 says, "If you should see a wise person, go to him in the morning and let your feet wear a path to that one's door."⁴¹

Additionally, there are many sayings that command us to listen to the counsels and judgments of those with experience, and to discuss our thoughts with others. Daily experience also confirms how dangerous it is, as the Greeks say, "to take counsel with oneself."⁴² And regarding craftsmen, it is said, "The worst teacher is oneself."⁴³ And Euripides writes sweetly, "Conversation has spawned the arts,"⁴⁴ which is to say, when many people compare their thoughts and others call to mind the judgments or examples of others.

Indeed, this very thing shows that doctrines are corrupted by those who do not listen to others, but instead, hiding or even fleeing from the light, they fashion their own newfangled opinions, recoiling from the acceptable form of teachings. There are many such people today who boast about themselves being "self-taught."⁴⁵ They admire their own dreams and refuse to listen to the judgments of more sensible

---

³⁸ Euripides, *The Phoenician Women* 752. Melanchthon provides both the Latin and the Greek. In Greek, εἷς ἀνὴρ οὐ πάντα ὁρᾷ.

³⁹ Theognis, *Elegiac Poems* 901–2. Melanchthon cites only the Greek here: οὐδεὶς ἀνθρώπων ἐστὶν ἅπαντα σοφός.

⁴⁰ Col. 3:16.

⁴¹ Sir. 6:36.

⁴² In Greek, ἰδιοβουλεύειν. See for example Herodotus, *Histories* 7.8D.

⁴³ This is a common Latin saying; however, the source is unknown.

⁴⁴ The source of this quote from Euripides is not known, although a few later sources attribute it to his Andromache. Here in Latin and in Greek, ὁμιλία ἔτεκε τέχνας.

⁴⁵ In Greek, αὐτοδιδάκτους.

people. Instead, let us obey the commandments that order us to listen to those with experience, and let us compare our thoughts with others, as Paul said, "Teach and admonish one another."⁴⁶

The proverb at hand also speaks about such comparing judgments and counsels [with each other]: "Just as iron is sharpened by iron, so a craftsman sharpens another craftsman."⁴⁷ This diligence in sharpening is, first of all, a part of Modesty, which considers one's own weakness. Next comes prudence, the practice of learning what you do not know. And, in this same chapter, Solomon, praising trustworthy counsel, says, "Just as pleasant smells are fragrant to the heart, so a friend who gives counsel to the soul is sweet."⁴⁸ For example, Synesius writes that [the painter] Apelles was in the habit of seeking the judgment of [the sculptor] Lysippos when it came to his paintings, just as Lysippos invited Apelles to offer judgment on his statues.⁴⁹ And, believe it or not, many things can also be learned through the testimonies of one's enemies. Therefore, this verse of Sophocles is to be praised: "The wise learn many things from their enemies."⁵⁰

"Like a face [reflected] in the water, so is the heart of a person toward another."⁵¹

Just as the faces appearing in water seem fleeting and disappear, so hearts are fickle and deceitful. Similar laments concerning the

---

⁴⁶ Col. 3:16.

⁴⁷ This is Melanchthon's own paraphrase of Prov. 27:17.

⁴⁸ Prov. 27:9.

⁴⁹ Synesius of Cyrene (ca. 370–ca. 413 CE) was the bishop of Ptolemais in Northern Africa. Apelles of Kos was known in the classical world for his extraordinary painting abilities, just as Lysippos was known for his expert sculpting. Synesius mentions the story of Apelles and Lysippos judging each other's art in *Letter 1: The Eulogy of Baldness*.

⁵⁰ Aristophanes, *The Birds* 375. This quotation comes from Aristophanes rather than Sophocles. In Greek, ἀπ' ἐχθρῶν πολλὰ μανθάνουσι οἱ σοφοί. Luther says much the same thing in his preface to his German works (LW 34:287).

⁵¹ Prov. 27:19. Both the text and the interpretation vary greatly from the Vulgate and medieval commentators.

inconstancy of the human heart are found everywhere. For instance, "Nowhere is faithfulness secure."[52] Likewise, "Faithfulness stands or falls with fortune."[53]

And when the fickleness of the human heart is condemned, we are admonished not to easily fall prey to putting our trust in humankind. Therefore, this admonition has been repeated frequently, as, for instance, when Cicero warned, "Keep this saying from Epicharmus in mind: 'Remember to exercise skepticism, for such are the sinews and limbs of wisdom.'"[54] Likewise, "Flee those you believe to be faithful, and you will be secure."[55] And in Jeremiah, "Cursed is the one who trusts in a human being."[56]

These sayings offer warnings primarily about doctrine, lest we esteem dogmas about God to be inspired by human authority alone. On the contrary, when it comes to teaching, let us strive to always draw from those sources coming from God.[57] If we do so, we will not become confident in human defenses, which only stir us to pursue unnecessary things. For human desires are always changing. For instance, Octavius

---

[52] Virgil, *Aeneid* 4.373. In chapter 6, Melanchthon quotes this same excerpt along with several others also cited here, demonstrating how *loci communes* functioned in his thought. Since the text touches on inconstancy, all of these authors share this common theme.

[53] Ovid, *Letter from the Black Sea* 2.3.10.

[54] Cicero, *Letter* 12.9.34. Epicharmus of Kos was a sixth-century BCE Greek dramatist whose writings only endure in fragments. The Greek original from Epicharmus reads, μέμνησο ἀπιστεῖν. Melanchthon quotes a fuller version of this saying in chapter 6. Here he conflates Greek and Latin, whereas he cites only the Greek in chapter 6.

[55] Ovid, *Art of Love* 1.752.

[56] Jer. 17:5.

[57] This statement is a fine example of how Melanchthon's evangelical view of Scripture's authority matches the humanist cry of *ad fontes*, "to the sources."

abandoned Cicero, Dion killed his friend Heraclides, and Dion, in turn, was killed by his very good friend Calippus.[58]

---

[58] Cicero was killed in 43 BCE as part of the proscription in Rome, in which those connected to Caesar's death were avenged. Parts of Cicero's body were publicly displayed in Rome. Dion, Heraclides, and Calippus were Greeks who lived during the fourth century BCE. Dion ruled in Syracuse and quarreled with Heraclides, later killing him. Calippus, a former student of Plato, was a close friend of Dion, but he had been bribed by a man named Dionysius to kill Dion, which he did. Calippus ruled over Syracuse for thirteen months before being exiled and eventually killed by the same sword that was used to kill Dion.

Chapter 28

"Because of the sins of the land, rulers quickly follow in succession. But because of a prudent and understanding person, political rule is more enduring."[1]

It is common for there to be complaints about the negligence of rulers, their pilfering of resources, as well as their negligence in making judgments and in defense. To be sure, the populace routinely makes accusations against both rulers and courts, as the following verse states, "Whatever wrongs kings commit, the Achaeans suffer."[2] However, the divine message makes accusations against both rulers and people. It is said in Hosea 4, for instance, "Like priest, like people."[3] And it is often foretold that respectable rulers will not be established due to the sins of the people, as mentioned in Isaiah 3: "The Lord of Hosts will take away warrior, judge and prophet."[4]

Thus, it says here, "Because of the sins of the land," namely, the sins of the rulers and the people, "many rulers will arise," which means that none of the rulers rule for very long or that many conflicts will

---

[1] Prov. 28:2.

[2] Horace, *Epistle* 1.2.14. The Achaeans were the Greeks who fought against the Trojans.

[3] Hos. 4:9.

[4] Isa. 3:1.

rule the day, with one ruler driving out the one before, as when John ruled in Hungary for a while, then Ferdinand, and now the Turks.[5]

These changes [from one ruler to another] did not come about without great calamities, as Xenophon most truly asserts: "All changes in government are attended by loss of life."[6] And when it comes to rebellion, Thucydides says it this way: "In rebellion, every notion of evil unites as one."[7] Likewise, "In a time of civil strife, even an absolutely evil person receives honor."[8] As such, let us come to recognize that the causes of public disasters are attributable to the sins of many people and that for the sake of public weal let individuals restrain these violent impulses.

However, the antithesis of this has been added here, which contains an important and necessary reminder for both rulers and people. Solomon says that "the rule lasts longer because of a prudent and understanding person." What he means is that a wise ruler may yield his legal right at some point and suffer some kind of misfortune in order to avoid more significant misfortunes later on. For instance, the [Roman] dictator Fabius deigned to place himself equal to the master of the horse. For Fabius did not put rumors [of the master's attacks]

---

[5] In the Kingdom of Hungary, John I (1490–1540) and his son John Sigismund Zápolya (1540–1571) ruled over parts of the country. Ferdinand I (1503–1564), who became the Holy Roman emperor after the abdication of his brother, Charles V, in 1556, was named king of another part of Hungary in 1527. With the conquest of Buda by the Turks in 1541, the kingdom (larger than today's Hungary) was divided into three parts.

[6] Xenophon, *Hellenica* 2.3.32. Melanchthon provides both the Greek and a Latin translation.

[7] Thucydides, *Peloponnesian War*, paraphrasing 3.83: ἐν θάσει πᾶσα ἰδέα κακῶ ἔνι.

[8] Zenobius, 3.77. In Greek, ἐν δὲ δυχοστασίῃ καὶ πάγκακος ἔμμορε τιμῆς. Zenobius was a Greek teacher active in the second century CE.

above the health [of Rome].⁹ Similarly, Cicero withdrew from the province for Lucius Antonius so that he would gain a fellow colleague.¹⁰

Thus, let those who give counsel to the people give advice so that they do not urge greater evil through seditious counsel. For instance, there is no doubt that in Judea there were many seditious men shouting to expel the Romans with arms, just as their fathers had expelled Antiochus [Epiphanes].¹¹ But Zechariah and Simeon discerned these to be different cases and different times, and so they advised against wars. For they knew that that was the end of Jewish political rule and that God had mitigated their servitude in exceptional moderation. For

---

⁹ Quintus Fabius Maximus Verrucosus (ca. 280–203 BCE) was a Roman statesman and general. He served as dictator of the Roman Republic from 221 to 217. He was instrumental in the Second Punic War against Hannibal, where he earned the epithet *Cunctator*, "Delayer," for his delaying tactics against the famous general Hannibal, who led Carthage's army in Rome. Melanchthon is probably referring to a story from Plutarch about the Master of Horse. In *Parallel Lives* 3.5.4, Plutarch tells the story of Fabius's master of the horse, an officer named Minucius, who disagreed with Fabius's delaying tactics and openly ridiculed him. The office of master of horse, *magister equitum*, was an important one in the Roman Republic who held *imperium*, or "ruling authority," but only through appointment by the Roman dictator—in this case, Fabius.

¹⁰ Lucius Antonius was the younger brother of the more famous Roman general and statesman Marc Antony. Lucius lived in the first century BCE and was a contemporary of Cicero, Caesar, and many other important Roman leaders at this time. He later rebelled against Octavian along with Marc Antony's wife Fulvia. Cicero paints a very negative portrait of Lucius in his *Philippics* 6.

¹¹ Antiochus IV Epiphanes ruled the Seleucid Empire from 175 to 164 BCE. His reign in the Middle East was narrated in certain books in the Old Testament Apocrypha, particularly 1 and 2 Maccabees. He is remembered in the Jewish tradition as a great villain who attempted to Hellenize the Jewish people. It is possible that the connection to Zechariah alludes to texts in that biblical book prophesying the reign of Antiochus, and the Simeon mentioned is probably referring to Simon Thassi, one of the sons of Matthias and a leader in the Maccabean Revolt against the Hellenistic rule of Antiochus.

the Jews enjoyed freedom[12] in worship matters, and they had observed that their own rulers were wanting. Antiochus [Epiphanes], however, had not granted the Jews freedom in worship matters, and the learned ones knew that it was not yet the end of Jewish political rule.

Thus, astute rulers carefully consider what is worth fighting over and what is not worth fighting over. For example, Isaiah advised against surrender while, on the other side, Jeremiah was an advocate of [Judah] surrendering during his lifetime. In this way, it is apparent that we must take into consideration different situations and different cases, and we must also wisely bear servitude when it is to be endured as well as solicit counsel and protection from God with heartfelt lamentation, just as these very prophets did. Isaiah, for example, exclaimed, "We are your clay, [Lord], do not be too angry with us."[13] Likewise in Jeremiah, "Do not reduce us to nothing."[14] And Psalm 7 says, "Rise up, Lord, for the precept that you have commanded so that a congregation of the peoples will surround you,"[15] which is to say, "Preserve both your Law and your church, lest universal destruction come, as is also said in these verses: 'May the church always remain in safety in you, Christ, and may your right hand cover all those found within.'"[16]

"Whoever hides his sins will not be prosperous. But the Lord will be gracious to the ones who confess and forsake their sin."[17]

There are some who knowingly persist in horrible sins through a manifest stubbornness. Such people undoubtedly rush into punish-

---

[12] In Greek, ἀυτονομίαν.

[13] Isa. 64:8–9.

[14] Jer. 10:24.

[15] Ps. 7:7–8 (Vulgate).

[16] These verses, written by Melanchthon himself, appear in his correspondence as well, MBW 6804 (CR 8:74), a letter to Johannes Mathesius dated April 23, 1553, by MBW. On March 1, 1554, in a letter to Simon Haliaeus, MBW 7097 (CR 8:23), Melanchthon mentions that this was the daily prayer recited by boarders at table. See also CR 10:617.

[17] Prov. 28:13.

ments in accordance with the saying, "Because of these sins, the anger of God comes."[18] But here Solomon makes a comment about those who seek to conceal their sins, that is, those who cleverly exonerate themselves as, for example, those who establish ungodly worship and endorse false teachings through spurious rationalizations. Solomon threatens these people with punishments. For even though they may not be held in check by human beings, they will eventually be held in check by God, in accordance with the saying, "Every plant that my Father has not planted will be uprooted."[19] The Jewish leaders, for instance, did not want to be supplanted by the apostles; nevertheless, the total destruction of Jewish political rule served as a testimony of divine judgment against them.[20] In the same way, the Manichaeans, Arians, and similar [heretical groups] have been destroyed.

For in every conversion, there must first be contrition, that is, an acknowledgment of one's error and sin as well as an accompanying sorrow and change of will. Thus, confession is required here—and, in fact, the kind of confession in which actual correction occurs, just as Paul first confessed that he had erred when he was an enemy of the church and only thereafter became a witness and propagator of the Gospel.[21]

In this way, it is eloquently stated here, "But the Lord will be gracious to the ones who confess and forsake their sin." For in conversion, it is necessary for evil intentions to be cast out, for there is no conversion or repentance as long as a person remains steadfast in evil intentions. However, both the remission of eternal punishment and the lessening of temporal punishment have been promised on account of the

---

[18] Col. 3:6.

[19] Matt. 15:13.

[20] Here Melanchthon follows the medieval tradition that blamed the lack of a Jewish nation on the rejection of Jesus and the apostles. For Melanchthon's view of the Jews, see Timothy J. Wengert, "Philip Melanchthon and the Jews: A Reappraisal," in *Jews, Judaism, and the Reformation in Sixteenth-Century Germany*, ed. Dean Philip Bell and Stephen G. Burnett (Leiden: Brill, 2006), 105–35.

[21] See 1 Cor. 15:9; Gal. 1:13; and 1 Tim. 1:15–16.

Mediator,[22] just as it has been said, "As surely as I live, declares the Lord, I do not wish the death of the sinner, but rather that he would turn from his ways and live."[23] Likewise in Zechariah 1, "Return to me, and I will return to you."[24] Similarly in Isaiah 1, "Though your sins are like deep scarlet, you will be as white as snow."[25] And finally, "It is due to the Lord's mercy that we have not been consumed."[26]

"Blessed is the one who is always fearful, but a hardened heart will fall into ruin."[27]

This saying corresponds to the one above [in verse 13]. For it exhorts humankind to practice repentance, ordering us to maintain fear [of the Lord], acknowledging the judgment and wrath of God against sins, with the result that we would be diligent in avoiding evil thoughts and falling [into sin], as Paul said, "Work out your salvation with fear and trembling,"[28] which is to say, "Hold on to the purity of doctrine, being diligent to examine its sources with great care; likewise with great concern, be diligent to avoid falling [into sin] against your conscience."

This teaching does not contradict the saying about faith, the consolation of consciences, and the joy of having a Mediator, for both of them command sorrow in one's heart that deplores our stubbornness, uncleanness, and doubts, as well as the many evils clinging to us. But let faith direct our fear and sorrow, for it establishes that we, though

---

[22] This comment and the one in the next verse reflect Melanchthon's deep commitment to Evangelical theology, as in Article IV of the Augsburg Confession, which states that justification occurs by grace through faith on account of Christ and not because of any works.

[23] Ezek. 33:11. For the importance of this verse, see Melanchthon's comments on Prov. 15:1.

[24] Zech. 1:3, where the verb is the root of the word *conversio*.

[25] Isa. 1:18, following Melanchthon's own rendering.

[26] Lam. 3:22 (Vulgate).

[27] Prov. 28:14.

[28] Phil. 2:12.

unworthy and wretched, nevertheless please God on account of the Mediator.29

Therefore, this saying offers a reprimand against carnal security and overweening confidence in one's own wisdom, righteousness, and power—such that gives no concern for the judgment of God. Many examples demonstrate this. For instance, Pharaoh rushed headlong toward destruction because of his confidence in his own power.30 Likewise, Bellerophontes, full of confidence, wanted to be flown through the heavens by Pegasus, but was thrown off.31 Also, Antiochus [Epiphanes] was overconfident in his own power as he tried to destroy God's Law.32 Therefore, these admonitions about the fear of God and the purposes of our vocation must always be kept in mind. As this verse states, "Blessed is the one who is always fearful." Likewise, "Where will the Lord dwell? In a contrite and lowly spirit and trembling at my words."33

---

29 Melanchthon was aware that texts like this one were used by his opponents to insist that one could not trust the absolution in the sacrament of penance but must continue to doubt the promise as a sign of true humility before God.

30 See Ex. 5–14.

31 For this Greek myth, see p. 75, n. 77.

32 As mentioned previously in this chapter, Antiochus IV Epiphanes attempted to Hellenize the Jewish people in the second century BCE.

33 Isa. 57:15.

Chapter 29

"A ruler who loves dishonesty will have a government full of ungodly officials."[1]

For the most part, people are governed by examples. That is because people naturally recognize imitation and, in fact, learn through imitation. Many exceptional personalities stand out as the examples of rulers and teachers. Therefore, the admonition is often repeated: that rulers should offer honorable examples and that the populace should observe these honorable examples and thereby avoid moral turpitude. The following verses have been noted:

> The examples of those ruling remain among the people.
> Every subject is patterned after the example of the king.
> The soldier follows not only a leader's standard, but also his character.[2]

And, to some extent, these examples stand out in each part. Terrible contagions, for instance, spread more quickly, especially among those who live in the same house or are friends. As the Greeks have most charmingly said, "As are the ladies, so are [their] lapdogs."[3] And it is said

---

[1] Prov. 29:12.

[2] Claudian, *On Stilicho's Consulship* 1.68–69. Melanchthon previously cites many verses from Claudian, but not in this section.

[3] Melanchthon only provides the Latin to this proverb, not the Greek. See Erasmus, *Adages* 2.6.13, where he cites Plato, *Republic* 8.563c, who calls this saying a proverb.

in the following common proverb, "When, in a moment of madness, an abbot first casts the dice, the monks think that playing is allowed."[4]

It is in this vein that Solomon says, "A ruler who loves dishonesty will have a government full of ungodly officials." Conversely, an exceptional virtue in the administration of government is Truth and Truthfulness, which fights against falsehood, treachery, trickery, suspicion, and sophistry. That is, on the contrary, ruinous evil exists in every government, for the love of dishonesty and many a vice comprise that evil, given that there are many kinds of dishonesty.

The first, obvious kind of dishonesty is Falsehood or Treachery in relation to keeping one's promises and contracts. For instance, Alcibiades's treachery was censured.[5] And Virgil said about Mettius Fufetius, "Tullus was dragging the entrails of that lying man."[6]

A second kind of dishonesty is the love of Trickery, which is extremely common in the [princely] courts. For many take delight in disparagement of others, possessing ears that itch for such fables. About such people, the verses of Menander have previously been noted:

> They say that life is greatly alluring to the perverse,
> And that the flatterer prospers best of all,
> Followed second by the sycophant
> And third by the wicked.[7]

---

[4] Melanchthon offers both the Greek and the Latin. This proverb circulated widely in both languages. See Augusto Arthaber, *Dizionario Comparato di Proverbi e Modi Proverbiali in Sette Lingue* (Milan: Hoepli, 1972), 876. In Greek, Ὅτταν πρῶτα κύβους βάλλῃ πότε μάργος ὁ ἄββας, παίζειν οἴονται οἱ μοναχοὶ νόμιμον.

[5] Alcibiades is mentioned previously by Melanchthon. Alcibiades was a fifth-century BCE Athenian statesman and general and was a polarizing figure in Greek society.

[6] Virgil, *Aeneid* 8.642. Mettius Fufetius is narrated as a contemporary of the legendary founders of Rome, Romulus and Remus. Mettius was a dictator of Alba Longa who betrayed the Romans in battle. His punishment, decreed by Tullus, the third king of Rome, was being torn limb from limb by chariots, as described here by Virgil.

[7] Menander originally recorded these words, but most of his writings only survive in fragments. Portions of this saying appear in Euripides, *Hip-*

CHAPTER 29

And in Plautus's [play] *Pseudolos*, it is said, "Those who listen to whatever criminal accusation is spread against someone, if it were up to me, they should all be hanged—those bearing false testimony by their tongues and those heeding [their lies] by the ears."[8]

The third kind of dishonesty is Suspicions, which those of an unfaithful nature and a propensity to disparage grow out of their own heads, and which very often give occasion for great evils. For instance, tyrants get rid of many people simply on the basis of suspicions. Take Alexander [the Great], for example: He found Parmenion worthy of blame [even though he was innocent].[9] And because those of a suspicious nature naturally and eagerly listen to disparaging comments, those exemplifying this kind of dishonesty occupy many courts.

The fourth kind of dishonesty is Sophistry, which defends false opinions and evil causes under the preposterous pretext of duty to rulers. It is this kind of dishonesty which is praised in the courts as the highest form of wisdom, just as the papal courts currently praise to the hilt the writings of those who defend false worship with sophistic sleight-of-hand, which is really nothing other than the supposed wisdom hidden in the Sphinx.[10]

---

polytus, 426. In Greek, ὁ βίος μάλιστα τοῖς πονηροῖς ἥδεταί πράττει δ' ὁ κόλαξ ἄριστα πάντων δεύτερος ὁ συκοφάντης ὁ κακοήθης τρίτατος. As Melanchthon himself notes, he cites this set of verses on more than one occasion in his commentary on Proverbs.

[8] Plautus, *Pseudolos* act 1, scene 5. Titus Maccius Plautus was one of the earliest Latin playwrights. His play *Pseudolos* was first put on in 191 BCE.

[9] Parmenion was Alexander the Great's most trusted and senior general, as well as of Alexander's father, Philip II of Macedon. When one of Parmenion's sons, Philotas, was found to be rebellious in the army ranks, Alexander killed Philotas and his father, Parmenion—the former for rebellion and the latter for fear of retaliation since there was no evidence that Parmenion was part of the conspiracy.

[10] It was common in the Middle Ages for theologians to employ *sophismata*, which were puzzling sentences in Latin that challenged the intellect. The student would have to offer a logical response to the puzzle presented. The riddle of the Sphinx was especially connected to the stories of Oedipus. Melanchthon often derided his Roman Catholic opponents as sophists.

Since so many horrible evils may arise from all these kinds of dishonesty, Solomon advises us to be cautious and to flee such courts, just as Odysseus was commanded to pass by Scylla and Charybdis.[11]

"When prophecy ceases, the people are scattered; but the one who keeps the law will be blessed."[12]

Prophecy, that is, prophetic rule, includes when God delivers fruitful counsel and prosperous outcomes through some wholesome leader. But here Solomon says that such kingdoms flourish only when there are such leaders. For instance, roughly seventy years after Elijah, Elisha attempted to guide the plans of kings amid great calamities. Samaria was delivered from a siege in which a famine was rampant, where the head of a donkey was being sold for eighty pieces of silver, that is, eighty didrachmas, and a sixth part of the dung of doves was worth five pieces of silver.[13] But after the death of Elisha, the kingdom did not last much more than a hundred years, having been embroiled in constant rebellions.

In the same way, the leadership of Isaiah avoided many calamities for around eighty years.[14] Afterward, destruction followed, except that at the time a part of the populace was preserved thanks to the counsel of Jeremiah.[15] It is out of such examples that one is able to understand why Solomon says, "Once prophecy ceases, the populace is scattered," because with the cessation of stable leaders comes nothing in kingdoms but battles fueled by ambition, rebellions, and, finally, dissolution, as

---

[11] This story is narrated in *Odyssey* 12. Scylla and Charybdis were mythical sea monsters that Odysseus and his men had to sail by on their way back to Ithaca. Proverbially, to pass between Scylla and Charybdis became a phrase indicating how to navigate between two difficulties, and Erasmus referred to this story in his *Adages* 1.5.4.

[12] Prov. 29:18.

[13] See 2 Kings 6:24–33.

[14] See 2 Kings 19:1–37.

[15] For Jeremiah's various interactions with Judah's final king and other leaders, see Jer. 32–44.

it is said in the following verse, "For pride, extravagance, vice, and venom have destroyed many kingdoms."[16]

But Solomon explains the nature of prophetic leadership when he adds, "Blessed is the one who keeps the law." It is as if Solomon were saying that prophetic leadership encompasses the following: preserving true doctrine and true worship, offering counsel congruent to the Word of God, and not seeking protection contrary to the Word of God, just as in the story of [King] Ahaz, who, against the commandments of Isaiah, sought to establish treaties with the surrounding kings as well as the worship of their gods.[17] Likewise, the Greek and Hungarian empires were destroyed as a result of their treaties with the Turks.[18]

The second part of this saying also offers this admonishment: "The one who keeps the law will be blessed." In the midst of this very destruction a remnant will survive—those who maintain possession of divine teaching, as it is said in Amos: "Behold, the anger of the Lord is upon a sinful kingdom," that is, a guilty kingdom, since it has been appointed [by God] to punishment, "but I will gather a remnant, I will preserve and sift the grain."[19]

As such, let both rulers and the populace, who accept admonishment from both this saying and similar ones, consider that a stable government is the work of God, and both rulers and the populace should ask God for such a government, lest sins amass, forcing God to take away salutary leaders.[20]

---

[16] Claudian (also known as Claudius Claudianus), *On Stilicho's Consulship* 3.160–61. Melanchthon quotes this verse several times in his commentary.

[17] See 2 Kings 16, where Ahaz seeks to establish a treaty with the king of Assyria.

[18] The Ottoman-Hungarian Wars refer to a series of battles between the Ottoman (Turkish) Empire and the Kingdom of Hungary throughout the late 1300s and early 1500s.

[19] Amos 9:8–9.

[20] Melanchthon here is doubtless reflecting upon a decade of unrest from the beginnings of the Schmalkaldic War in 1547 through the Rebellion of the Princes to the brink of the Peace of Augsburg in 1555.

Chapter 30

["The Words of the Gatherer..."][1]

When it comes to collections of written maxims, there is typically one author for most of them. However, it is also often the case that certain similar sayings are inserted. For example, it has been said that oracles from the sibyls were inserted into the poems of Phocylides.[2] In this way, it is completely plausible that the sayings of others were added into this collection of maxims from Solomon. This explains the addition of a new title here in the thirtieth chapter: "The Words of the Gatherer," that is, the collection of other sayings from the son of Jakeh. To be sure, this name, as well as those of others that follow, ought to be understood as epithets for prophets.[3]

---

[1] Prov. 30:1.

[2] Phocylides was a Greek poet from Miletus who was active in the sixth century BCE. However, Melanchthon is probably referring to the *Sentences* of what is now known to be Pseudo-Phocylides (active between 100 BCE and 100 CE), a popular text during the Reformation. The sibyls were female oracles in ancient Greece who spoke in poetic verse. Some of Phocylides's maxims may be found in book 2 of *Sibylline Oracles*.

[3] Melanchthon's literary method takes seriously the title to this chapter and does not seem bothered that someone other than Solomon wrote it—except to number this author among the prophets.

Now, the first saying in this chapter reads as follows: "I am the most foolish of people."[4] This constitutes a confession of human ignorance, and it laments the dullness of this miserable human nature. Indeed, not only the examples of pagans demonstrate the horrible darkness of the human mind regarding God; rather, all people sense that they are sometimes unsettled by various waves of doubts.

For instance, Simonides was asked by Hieron about God's nature. Simonides then requested three days to think it over, but eventually responded to him that the longer he thought about the matter, the less he discovered that he could affirm.[5] However, Simonides is wrong here. For the knowledge of God's laws shines in the minds of all people in one way or another, and this knowledge helps distinguish God from evil things. It is from this that Plato's description is derived: "God is eternal mind, the cause of all good in nature."[6] Nevertheless, despite this glimmer that exists in human minds, the will to assent is weak. Instead, humankind falls into all kinds of doubts, which happens when they observe things that run contrary to this order (namely, that the good are often overcome by the evil). Because they do not know the cause of this, they doubt Providence.

To begin with, therefore, this human ignorance is deplored here—an ignorance that all people ought to acknowledge and then lament with groanings, just as the prophets lamented, "Everyone is a liar."[7] Likewise, "The heart of humankind is crooked and wretched."[8] There even

---

[4] Prov. 30:3.

[5] Simonides of Ceos was a Greek poet active in the sixth and fifth centuries BCE. Hieron I of Syracuse was a contemporary ruler on the island of Syracuse. This story is told, among other places, in Cicero, *On the Nature of the Gods* 1.22.

[6] Melanchthon seems to be summarizing parts of Plato's writings, specifically *Timaeus* 28a and following where Socrates and Timaeus discuss the nature of God. For a full discussion of Melanchthon's use of a Platonic concept of God, see Günter Frank, *Die theologische Philosophie Philipp Melanchthons (1497–1560)* (Leipzig: Benno, 1995), 212–25.

[7] Ps. 116:11; Rom. 3:4.

[8] Jer. 17:9.

exist among pagans the saddest lamentations about human nature, which are recited in order to bring humankind back to Moderation. Pindar wrote in Ode 8 of his book *Pythian*, "What is someone? What is no one? The human race is the dream of a shadow."[9] It is useful to always keep these sayings in view.

But the wisdom of humankind has no knowledge of any remedies against ignorance and infirmity. In the church, by contrast, we know the divine revelations, through which both the causes of this calamity and its remedies are demonstrated. Therefore, even in this text we are led to the teaching handed down by God, where it is commanded that we should listen to and embrace it, be motivated by its threats, assent to its consolations, and not add corruptions to it.

These kinds of precepts have been repeated frequently in Scripture. For instance, "This is my beloved Son; listen to him."[10] Likewise, "I am the way, the life, and the truth."[11] Also, "Your word is a lamp to my feet."[12] From Isaiah, "To the law and to the testimony."[13] And, finally, it says in Numbers, "Do not follow your own thoughts."[14]

["Every word of God is pure; it is a shield to the one trusting in God."][15]

In a similar way, it is said in this passage, "Every word of God is pure," that is, free of corruptions. And "it is a shield to the one trusting in God," that is, God has sent the Son and revealed himself by means

---

[9] Pindar, *Pythian* 8.95. The genre of Pindar's work is known as a "victory ode." In Greek, τὶ δε τις; τὶ δε οὔτις; σκιᾶς ὄναρ ἄνθροποι.

[10] Matt. 17:5.

[11] John 14:6.

[12] Ps. 119:105.

[13] Isa. 8:20, where the Latin Vulgate turns a rebuke by the people of Isaiah— "Should not a people consult their gods ... for teaching and instruction"—into a positive statement: "Do the people require from God himself a vision for life or death? [No], but rather for law and testimony."

[14] Num. 15:39.

[15] Prov. 30:5.

of his message and immense goodness, so that you[16] do not err, but instead so that you would hear and embrace the Son's message. In accord with this message, you may make judgments about the essence and will of God, the Law and the Gospel, and God's wrath and grace. May you acknowledge and pray to this true God, who revealed himself by means of the Son he sent, and brought his message into the world through the Son, as he himself said, "This is eternal life—that they would come to acknowledge you as the true God, and recognize that you sent Jesus to be the Messiah."[17] If you correctly acknowledge and pray to God, you will sense how efficacious God is, and, in this way, you will also come to acknowledge that the eternal church is being gathered together in this way and not in any other.

Indeed, consider the image used in this verse: "The word of God is a shield to those who trust in God" according to the Word. Paul also called it "the shield of faith,"[18] since it is certain that God is so effective that we may sustain ourselves by faith using the Word of God and prayer, as Paul said, "that we may have faith through the comfort of the Scriptures."[19] Likewise, "The Gospel is the power of God for salvation to all who believe."[20] And also, "My soul has endured in his Word; my soul has hoped in the Lord."[21] These sweetest of sayings must be opposed to the Pagans, to other ungodly conjectures, and to Anabaptist and Schwenkfeldian blasphemies, which reject the outward message of teaching.[22]

---

[16] "You" is singular throughout this paragraph.

[17] John 17:3.

[18] Eph. 6:16. Prov. 30 uses the word *clypeum*, the round, brazen shield of Roman soldiers, and Eph. 6 *scutum*, an oblong shield made of boards and covered with leather.

[19] Rom. 15:4.

[20] Rom. 1:16.

[21] Ps. 130:5.

[22] By "Anabaptists," Melanchthon had in mind all of those who practiced believers' baptism. Early Lutherans often equated them with people who neglected or denied the external Word of God and the church's teaching.

At the same time, it is commanded here to preserve the purity of the divine Word. Such purity may be understood in two ways. The first refers to the very Word of God being properly understood, free of carnal imaginations. For example, the Sadducees did, indeed, retain "the word"[23] found in [the books of] Moses, but understood the promises only in a carnal way about the present life. In the same way, monks understand the Law in terms of external works, and faith in terms of historical knowledge, and the like.

The second form of purity occurs by refusing to add any corruptions, as the Pope has added prayers for the dead, fees for Masses, false adoration [of the Eucharistic elements], the prohibition of [clerical] marriage, and many other ungodly traditions. Concerning both meanings of purity, Psalm 12 speaks: "The words of the Lord are pure words, like silver refined in a crucible, like silver refined seven times."[24] That is to say, first, the Word of God must be understood rightly, which is learned by means of the true exercise of repentance and in the cross. For it is through these that our minds are refined, with the result that the Word of God may be understood, first and foremost, free of carnal conjectures. Such occurred when Paul denounced unrighteous behaviors, teaching instead that the prophets spoke about the eternal reign of Christ, not about a political reign. For example, Paul wrote, "A 'carnal person' does not perceive those things from the Spirit."[25] Second, the Word of God must be pure, with absolutely no added traditions about new worship practices. The falsity of such practices

---

Caspar Schwenkfeld (ca. 1490–1561), was a Silesian nobleman who, over against Luther, Melanchthon, and others of the Wittenberg circle, rejected infant baptism, understood Christ's presence in the Lord's Supper spiritually, and insisted that Christ's resurrected body was different from a human body. As here, Wittenberg theologians often labeled these groups *Schwärmer*, "ravers," who gave authority to their own ideas rather than to God's Word.

[23] In Greek, τὸ ῥητον, that is, the words and phrases.

[24] Ps. 12:6.

[25] 1 Cor. 2:14, where Melanchthon keeps the Greek word, ψυχικὸς.

is taken away in true repentance and in the cross, just as Paul said, "The straw of one's doctrine will be consumed in fire."[26]

In conclusion, Solomon is essentially saying that the refined Word of God must be understood here in regard to its prior purity, that is to say, "the word"[27] must be rightly understood; and only then are new traditions to be expressly prohibited, just as it is stated elsewhere quite frequently. Indeed, the Lord cites the verse in Isaiah as saying, "They worship me in vain in the form of human commandments."[28]

"I have asked two things from you: Keep falsehood far from me and give me neither poverty nor wealth."[29]

The first and highest good is the true knowledge of God, just as the Lord has said, "Seek first the kingdom of God."[30] Solomon, too, in his prayer placed Wisdom above other good things, just as he said, "The fear of the Lord is the beginning of wisdom."[31] Likewise, "Humankind does not live by bread alone."[32] Second, to be of moderate means is safer than living in affluence or in scarcity. Therefore, these two requests are recounted in this order here so that they may serve as a light and rule of life for us. Let us first seek the kingdom of God,[33] and let us also be mindful of this saying: "Those who fear the Lord lack no good

---

[26] 1 Cor. 3:13. Melanchthon is, of course, referring to Paul's famous discourse on the different kinds of foundations in 1 Cor. 3:10–15, about which his colleague Martin Luther also wrote by comparing the book of James to straw. For more about Luther's discussion of this topic, see Timothy J. Wengert, *Reading the Bible with Martin Luther: An Introductory Guide* (Grand Rapids: Baker, 2013), 1–21; and Derek Cooper, *Thomas Manton: A Guided Tour of the Life and Thought of a Puritan Pastor* (Phillipsburg, NJ: P&R, 2011), 101–20.

[27] Again, in Greek, τὸ ῥητὸν.

[28] Isa. 29:13; Matt. 15:9.

[29] Prov. 30:7–8.

[30] Matt. 6:33.

[31] Prov. 1:7. See also 1 Kings 3:1–28.

[32] Deut. 8:3; Matt. 4:4.

[33] Cf. Matt. 6:33.

thing."³⁴ Such is Jesus's parable in the Gospel, ordering us to sell all the good things we possess in order to buy the pearl.³⁵

Second, we are to know that it is the will of God that each of us perform the honest labors of our calling, from which we may have nourishment, just as Paul said, "Do things appropriate to your calling."³⁶ Indeed, we are to be content with a moderate station in life, just as it has been said elsewhere, "The proud in heart are an abomination to God."³⁷ Similarly, Sirach says in chapter 3: "Do not foolishly seek things that are too difficult for you: Instead, think righteously about those things that have been commanded for you."³⁸

In fact, even the pagans have garnered through their own experiences the knowledge that it is prudent to occupy a moderate station in life. For instance, the following verse says, "Many things are best for those in the middle, and in the middle is where I want to be in society."³⁹ Indeed, many who had either power or wealth abused it, which resulted in destructive vices having their way with them, in accordance with the saying, "Feelings run wild amid prosperity, and to endure such with evenness of mind is not easy."⁴⁰

---

34 Ps. 34:10.

35 Matt. 13:45–46.

36 1 Cor. 14:40. Melanchthon often used this text to support Wittenberg's arguments about callings in this world.

37 Prov. 16:5.

38 Sir. 3:22.

39 Aristotle, *Politics* 4.11. In Greek, πολλὰ μέσοισιν ἄριστα μέσος θέλω ἐν πόλει εἶναι. Here, Aristotle is actually quoting Phocylides, which comes from a line found in fragment 10 in Ernst Diehl, *Anthologia Lyrica Graecae*, 2 vols. (Leipzig, 1925), translating the Greek word *polis* (πόλις), classically rendered as "city" or "commonwealth," as "society."

40 Ovid, *Art of Love* 2.437.

"This generation throws scorn upon the father." [41]

The sayings that follow are complaints about various vices, that is, they are proverbs illustrating what might happen and warning us to be more vigilant and firmer in avoiding such vices, as well as warning us to flee from fellowship with wicked people and their contagions, as Horace says, "The one who attacks an absent friend or who does not come to his defense when he is attacked by another and not present—such a person is in darkness, and you, Romans, must guard against him."[42]

Thus their vices are described here like doctors describing the symptoms of poisoning. This is a similar description or complaint: "Three things unsettle the earth: a slave who has obtained ruling authority and a fool who has become rich and powerful ..."[43] About the former it is said, "There is nothing harsher than a lowly person elevated to a high position."[44] And about the latter it is said, "No one is more insolent than a fool bestowed with fortune."[45] Lastly, Theognis said, "Insolence surely leads to pride when wealth comes to the evil person."[46]

"There are four things [on earth] that are small, and they are wiser than the wise." [47]

This charming collection is about small creatures that, [the author] says, surpass the so-called wise people. Solomon warns, though, that the great misery inherent in human nature, which fights against itself, must be acknowledged. Such a nature acknowledges God and the Law

---

[41] Prov. 30:11.

[42] Horace, *Satires* 1.7.

[43] Prov. 30:21–22. Melanchthon is paraphrasing this passage, and he omits the third item that unsettles the earth, which is described in 30:23 and relates in the Vulgate to an unflattering woman and a maidservant.

[44] Claudian, *Against Eutropius* 1.181.

[45] Cicero, *On Friendship* 15.

[46] Theognis, *Elegiac Poems* 153. In Greek, τίκτει τοι κόρος ὕβριν ὅταν κακῷ ὄλβος ἔπηται.

[47] Prov. 30:24.

yet refuses to obey and, in fact, knowingly rebels against God and against natural judgment, thereby summoning upon itself innumerable calamities, as it has been said in the verses of Menander: "More people are evil by choice than by nature."[48]

And, in fact, virtue is not more lasting in eminent people's lives, as seen in the examples of David, Nebuchadnezzar, Hercules, Themistocles, Alexander [the Great], and so on.[49] Animals, on the other hand, conform to their natures, and they do not deviate from what they are designed to be. Therefore, this weakness of our human nature must be acknowledged, and the remedy offered in the Son of God must be sought. Regarding the passage at hand, the ant is described because it admonishes [human beings] about work and zeal. The rabbit, by contrast, is the seeker-out of hiding places and offers a warning to the weak lest greater things attack [them] by force. The locust, which loves to be in groups, is neither seditious nor a disruptor of order or peace. The spider, meanwhile, surpasses others by its stealth.

So, then, the lazy are contrasted to ants because they lack energy and, as such, are called Slothful. The rabbits are contrasted to what the Greeks call the boastful. These braggarts,[50] though always claiming much, are unable to sustain anything. Such people lack Fortitude.

---

[48] Here Melanchthon mixes Latin with Greek words, thereby obscuring the exact location of Menander's quote.

[49] For more on David, see 2 Sam. 11–12. For more on Nebuchadnezzar, see Dan. 1–4. Hercules is the godlike hero often referred to in Renaissance writing and art. Themistocles (d. 459 BCE) was an Athenian general who aroused the ire of the Spartans with the refortification of Athens and of the Athenians through his arrogant behavior. Alexander the Great (356–323 BCE) was the famous founder and ruler of the Greek Empire. Plutarch attributes to him a fiery personality. For Melanchthon, and in line with other Renaissance thinkers, these were examples of "heroes" who all exhibited certain character flaws in addition to their virtues.

[50] "Boastful" in the previous sentence translates Melanchthon's word θρασύδελοι, and "braggarts" translates *Thrasones*. The word *Thrasones* is the plural form of *Thrasos*, a spirit personified as arrogance or recklessness in ancient Greek mythology. See for example Aeschylus, *Agamemnon* 763ff.

Next, locusts are contrasted to the rebellious, who are disturbers of order and peace. Such people lack Justice, which regards a situation of debt with geometric proportion,[51] and does not disturb the communal order. And spiders are contrasted to fools, who put their faith in their own powers and [thereby] disregard the counsel of others. Such people lack Prudence.

***"If you have become foolishly carried away with pride, put your hand over your mouth."*[52]**

Here the author issues a command about repentance and correction of errors. When you have fallen, do not defend your errors but instead, having been admonished and recognizing your error, grieve for your mistakes, embrace the truth, and by an open confession show what you really feel, lest your error is confirmed in others, as when Paul confessed that he had erred when he was an enemy of the Gospel.[53] Solomon has already spoken about such things: "The righteous person makes accusations against himself from the beginning."[54] And in Zechariah, "Correcting error, I have received these wounds in the house of those who love me."[55]

If anyone stubbornly defends his [or her] error after being admonished, Paul orders such a person to be forsaken, going so far as to call such people "self-condemned,"[56] that is, ones who have been condemned by their own judgment, because the ones being convicted know that they are fighting against their own conscience. And should they commit blasphemy, they fall into ruin without end in eternal death. About such things, it has been said, "To err is human, but to

---

[51] Legal theory of the time identified two kinds of justice, that of arithmetic proportion, as in "to each his own," and that of geometric proportion, for example, reducing the debt of someone in bankruptcy.

[52] Prov. 30:32.

[53] Gal. 1:13.

[54] Prov. 18:17 (Vulgate).

[55] Melanchthon is referring loosely to Zech. 13:6.

[56] Titus 3:10, citing the Greek word αὐτοκατάκριτος.

persevere in error is diabolical."⁵⁷ Nonetheless, many continue to fall, as it is said, "A friend will frequently lend gold, wealth, and dishes; but the one who agrees to forfeit creativity is rare."⁵⁸

And here mention is made of Pride, which is confidence in one's own wisdom or power against God. Carried away by this confidence, many people either give birth to new dogmas or establish new religious practices, and, afterward, impressed with themselves, they arrogantly defend their erroneous opinions, as it is said, "Opinion constrains the truth."⁵⁹ And it is even sadder that many people defend errors, cleverly seeking out sleights-of-hand and adding lies upon lies. We must both ponder and then flee from such horrible sins.

---

⁵⁷ This well-known saying is often attributed to Seneca, but none of his existing works attest to this. Instead, there are sayings that are somewhat comparable, but by no means exact, in a variety of classical figures, ranging from Cicero (*cuiusvis hominis est errare, nullius nisi insipientis in errore perseverare*; "it is characteristic of humanity to err, but no one, unless he is a fool, will persist in error," in *Philippics* 12.2.5), to Jerome (*errasse humanum est, et confiteri errorem, prudentis*; "it is human to have erred and wise to confess one's error," in *Epistle* 57.12), to Augustine of Hippo (*humanum fuit errare, diabolicum est per animositatem in errore manere. Melius quidem erat si nunquam erraremus*; "it was human to err, but diabolical to remain in error due to stubbornness. Indeed, it would have been better if we had not erred," in *Sermons* 164.14). For more, see Ingride Edlund-Berry, "*Experientia Docet*: What Experience Can Teach according to Lucretius, Tacitus, and Buster Brown," in *Rome and Her Monuments: Essays on the City and Literature of Rome in Honor of Katherine A. Geffcken*, ed. Judith Dickinson and Judith Hallett (Wauconda, IL: Bolchazy-Carducci, 2000), 512–13.

⁵⁸ Martial, *Epigram* 8.18. This poem was written to Cirinius. Martial paid a compliment to Cirinius for not publishing his own epigrams so that they would not compete with Martial's.

⁵⁹ Simonides, *Fragments* 598. Melanchthon has cited this verse before, but here he cites both the Greek and a Latin translation.

> *"The one who presses forth milk brings out butter. And the one who blows his nose too often draws out blood. Likewise, whoever provokes anger brings about strife."*[60]

The first of these sayings means that ruling authority should be exercised in moderation. As Plato said, "There are two optimal goods: moderate freedom and moderate servitude, just as there are two utter evils: immoderate freedom and immoderate servitude."[61] And in the verses of Solon, there is the following saying: "Let the people submit to their governors, neither being exceedingly unrestrained nor [exceedingly] restricted."[62]

Here, "the mean" has been established by the Ten Commandments. As John the Baptist said, "Don't extort money and don't make false accusations. And also, be content with your wages."[63] Likewise, it is written in Sirach: "Fodder, a rod, and a burden are for the donkey; while bread, discipline, and work are for the servant."[64] To this saying in Proverbs was added a sentence reprimanding anger so that public discord would not arise, which afterward brings about untold ruin and is always provoked by minor causes that should have been resolved and repaired by means of a little moderation.

---

[60] Prov. 30:33.

[61] Plato, *Letter* 8. It is important to keep in mind that "moderate servitude" in Plato refers to "being the slave of God" while "immoderate servitude" refers to "being the slave of human beings." See especially section 354e of Plato's letter.

[62] Solon's sayings were quoted by many people. See Aristotle's *Constitution of the Athenians* 12. In Greek, δῆμος ἅμα ἡγεμόνεσσιν ἕποιτό μήτε λίαν ἀνεθεὶς μήτε πιεζόμενος.

[63] Luke 3:14.

[64] Sir. 33:25.

Chapter 31

The addition of this last chapter[1] features three general sayings. The first contains a prohibition against Drunkenness. The second includes a commandment about Confession, which is spoken against those who suppress the innocent, as now in the royal courts many recognize true doctrine, but they do not demonstrate what they approve when they take advantage of the innocent who plead for mercy. Here, therefore, the author commands those who understand true doctrine by their own confession [of faith] to protect the innocent, lest rank injustice be established by means of their silence or collusion. For instance, Jonathan openly protected David from his father, Saul.[2] Doeg and his men, by contrast, kindled the rage of the king.[3] Then there is the story of when Callisthenes and Clitus openly scolded the insolence of Alexander [the Great], while many others were in agreement [with

---

[1] By King Lemuel. See Melanchthon's comments at the beginning of chapter 30. In Hebrew, verses 10–31 are written as an acrostic poem.

[2] See 1 Sam. 19:1–7.

[3] Doeg was King Saul's herdsman, who informed the king of Ahimelech the priest's protection of David. Eventually, Doeg killed Ahimelech and his priests (eighty-five total) at the command of Saul. See 1 Sam. 22.

Alexander].[4] For, indeed, many are evil, and the following Greek saying is true:

> They say that life is greatly alluring to the perverse
> And that the flatterer prospers best of all,
> Followed second by the sycophant
> [And third by the wicked.][5]

Finally, the third section to this last chapter contains a hymn about the virtues of the woman of a household. Just as the Ten Commandments should serve as a rule of life for all people, so in this song of praise the virtues found in the Ten Commandments are apportioned out here. Now, the first table of the law corresponds to this saying: "The woman who fears God will be praised."[6]

In this saying, FEAR should be understood as complete and true worship, true knowledge of God, Fear, Faith, Prayer, and love for God, as well as other corresponding virtues, just as the prophets make use of the phrase "fear of God" most wisely to refer to all true worship that is pleasing to God. And, as a result, it has been said earlier, "The fear of the Lord is the beginning of wisdom."[7] And likewise, "Blessed is the one who fears the Lord."[8]

---

[4] Clitus the Black was one of Alexander the Great's military officers, and Callisthenes was a philosopher who was also a great uncle to Aristotle. Alexander killed Clitus in a fit of rage, while Callisthenes died in prison on charges of conspiring against Alexander. Both were reported to have criticized Alexander. See Plutarch, *Parallel Lives* 5.50–54.

[5] Menander originally uttered these words, but most of his writings only survive in fragments. Portions of this saying appear in Euripides, *Hippolytus* 426. Hippolytus was the illegitimate son of King Theseus of Athens and Queen Hippolyta of the Amazons. In Greek, ὁ βίος μάλιστα τοῖς πονηροῖς ἥδεταί πράττει δ' ὁ κόλαξ ἄριστα πάντων δεύτερος ὁ συκοφάντης. Melanchthon has cited this passage several times before.

[6] Prov. 31:30.

[7] Prov. 9:10.

[8] Ps. 112:1.

Other virtues are likewise recounted in this section: marital chastity, love of one's spouse without fretfulness, attentiveness in all of one's household labors, thrift, frugality and gentleness within the governance of one's household, diligence in educating one's children, perseverance in one's home, and generosity toward the poor. The explanation of all of these virtues has already been noted, and it should be considered to which part of the Ten Commandments each of these virtues corresponds.

However, this entire account must be understood without allegory, in a plain way as a mirror of an honorable woman.[9] As Simonides says, "Happy is the man who marries a woman who is like a bee."[10] But this entire teaching is most sweetly embraced in the saying of Paul to Timothy, "The woman will be saved through childbearing, if they remain in faith, love, holiness, and modesty,"[11] where the particular

---

[9] The "mirror," *speculum* in Latin, was a genre of literature beloved in the Renaissance in which authors often wrote "mirrors" to guide the behavior of princes and others or, as here, of female heads of households. The allegorical interpretations of this passage are outlined in Nicholas of Lyra's *Postilla super Bibliam*, ad loc., where he notes that "our teachers" interpret the poem as describing the relation of the church and Christ, where the children are individual believers. However, Rabbi Solomon (Schlomo Itzhaki), that is, Rashi, the rabbinic source upon which Lyra often relies, interprets the passage to be describing the reading of Scripture. Lyra follows this latter approach.

[10] Quoting Semonides of Amorgos (seventh century BCE), *Types of Women*, sometimes called *Semonides 7*, a poem of 118 lines first printed in 1535 by Vittore Trincavelli (1498–1588) in Venice as part of an anthology of Johannes Stobaeus (fifth century AD).

[11] 1 Tim. 2:15. This passage was an important one for Wittenberg exegetes, who had to demonstrate that it does not mean that women are saved by works, but instead that their vocation of childbearing is a good one, as opposed to the curse of Eve. For example in 1540, Caspar Cruciger Sr. (1504–1548) published a commentary on 1 Timothy. In 1538, George Spalatin (1484–1545) had already excerpted a section of Cruciger's original lectures on this verse and published a German translation as *Herrn Doctor Caspar Creutzigers auslegung uber Sanct Paulus spruch zum Thimotheo, wie die Eheweiber selig werden* (Erfurt: Golthammer, 1538). Spalatin dedicated this volume to his

virtues and duties of her calling are recounted. Paul eloquently denotes Faith (namely, true knowledge of God and trust in the Son of God), which should outshine all virtues. And when by such faith the remission of sins, reconciliation, and the inheritance of eternal life are received, at the same time new light in one's heart, life, and righteousness are kindled. As the saying goes, "We are being transformed into his image, as by the Spirit of the Lord."[12] Therefore, when God is acknowledged by faith and when the mercy of God, on account of the promised Mediator, is exhibited, love of God and true prayer are simultaneously kindled in our hearts, as for instance when with the light of the sun, warmth is spread at the same time. For the Son of God is called the "Sun of righteousness"[13] because he brings forth light, that is, he brings about true knowledge of mercy and reveals the true God. And the love of God, true prayer, and other virtues always accompany true knowledge of God's mercy. David, upon hearing the message "the Lord has taken away your sin"[14] revived, knew God, and subjected himself to God, loving and calling upon God. In a similar way, Paul also wants faith, that is, true knowledge of God and trust in God's mercy, to shine forth in the female head of a household.

In addition to these qualities, the author also adds other virtues: love of God and love of one's neighbor on account of God, as well as love of one's husband and children. He also identifies the wife's holiness as a virtue, which is oftentimes referred to as chastity. Now Chastity, which is described at more length in the passage at hand, is a virtue that avoids all commingling or unsanctioned sexual relations that are prohibited by God, for, in a marriage, conjugal rights must be maintained. Also, in this text, Temperance refers to moderation in eating and drinking that is in agreement with the nature of the body.

---

own wife, Catherine. Melanchthon's own commentary on 1 and 2 Timothy, based upon lectures from 1550 to 1551, did not appear until 1561, a year after his death. See CR 15:1323–31, which contains the kind of lengthy study of women's calling that he decided not to include in this commentary (see below).

[12] 2 Cor. 3:18.

[13] Mal. 4:2.

[14] 2 Sam. 12:13.

Chapter 31

Therefore, Paul hands down the sweetest consolation that opposes the hypocrisy of monks, since Paul expressly affirms that the married woman of a household, who maintains faith and a good conscience, will be saved.[15] It is necessary that we put emphasis on this teaching against fanatics who condemn marriage.

Another disparagement of marriage among such people must also be refuted, for they abuse this passage from Paul to defend the monastic conjectures[16] that imagine that good works are meritorious and deserving of eternal life by citing this saying: "The woman will be saved through childbearing."[17] On the contrary, by no means does Paul say that the duties of a woman are meritorious or deserving of eternal life; rather, he immediately mentions faith. For instance, when Paul says, "if they remain in faith," he is referring to acknowledgment of God and a woman's trust in the Mediator; this excludes any notion of meritorious works.

But Paul states here what has been very frequently repeated in the preaching of Christ, the prophets, and the apostles, namely, that it is necessary that faith and the righteousness of a good conscience are present in the reborn, as he says, "Fight the good fight... holding on to faith and a good conscience."[18] Likewise, "Do not be deceived: The sexually immoral, adulterers, and murderers will not be inheritors of eternal life."[19] Now, in the enumeration of virtues, mention must be made about works, which are appropriate to the vocation of each person, as John [the Baptist] says to the soldiers, "Do not extort money and don't make false accusations. And be content with your wages."[20] Just as it is necessary, therefore, to offer admonishment for

---

[15] 1 Tim. 2:15. See also 1 Tim. 5:14.

[16] Melanchthon often uses the term "monks" to designate medieval scholastic theologians, many of whom were mendicant friars.

[17] 1 Tim. 2:15.

[18] Melanchthon has combined two similar passages. The first part comes from 1 Tim. 6:12 and the second from 1 Tim. 1:19.

[19] 1 Cor. 6:9.

[20] Luke 3:14.

everyone to fulfill the duties of one's calling, so Paul here preaches about the [nonmeritorious] mother's labors in bearing children, nursing them, and educating them. Yet, nevertheless, this firm position remains: that a person is freely received and pleases [God] by faith through the Mediator, not through that person's own worth,[21] as it is said in Psalms: "For in your sight no living person will be justified."[22] Likewise, Romans 3 says, "All have fallen short of the glory of God, but we are justified freely by faith on account of the Son ..."[23] Here, let the learned call to mind this pure teaching concerning faith and works, as is recounted in the confession of our churches.[24]

Concerning the duties of a married woman, many things have been most sweetly written in the writings of others.[25] As such, in the explication of this passage, my explanation could be more greatly expanded, but I do not wish to be longer than necessary.

---

[21] Similar summaries of justification by faith are found throughout Melanchthon's works.

[22] Ps. 143:2.

[23] Rom. 3:23–24.

[24] Here Melanchthon is referring to the Augsburg Confession, article IV, presented to the Emperor Charles V in 1530, especially since, beginning in 1555, it legally and theologically defined the Evangelical churches.

[25] Melanchthon may have been thinking not only of comments in the Evangelical catechisms but also of Evangelical tracts on marriage and women. See for example, Heidi Lauterer-Pirner, "Vom 'Frauenspiegel' zu Luthers Schrift 'Vom ehelichen Leben': Das Bild der Ehefrau im Spiegel eineger Zeugnisse des 15. und 16. Jahrhunderts," in *Frauen in der Geschichte*, vol. 3, ed. Annette Kuhn and Jorge Rüsen (Düsseldorf: Schwann, 1983), 63–85, and more recently, Heidi Wunder, *He Is the Sun, She Is the Moon: Women in Early Modern Germany*, trans. Thomas Dunlap (Cambridge, MA: Harvard University Press, 1998).

I pray that the Son of God, our Lord Jesus Christ, the one who was crucified for us and raised, the protector of his church, may mercifully govern and preserve our Churches, Governments, and Households.[26] Amen.

Praise God!

---

[26] Based upon medieval interpretations of Aristotle, the Wittenberg reformers defined these three "walks of life" (Latin: *genera vitae*; German: *Stände*) as overarching all of the various Christian or human callings in life: government, household, and church.

Scripture Index

OLD TESTAMENT

Genesis
2:24	47
3	123
3:5	150
3:15	123
3:17	73
4:1–16	82, 151
4:4–5	82
10:1–4	7
14	180
18:16–33	178
19	180
19:1–29	124
27:41–45	150
39	171

Exodus
1:15–20	156
5–14	199
8	180
19:4	74
20:3	113
20:7	113
20:13	40, 91, 155
20:14–15	45
20:15	48, 77
20:16	113
23:2	49–50
32:6	78, 121

Leviticus
17	69
18	120
18:1–30	120
19:18	69

Numbers
15:39	209

Deuteronomy
4:2	52
4:6	90
4:24	124
8:3	74, 212
8:14	74
19:1–13	155
19:14	140
19:19	67
19:21	67
27:17	140
30:20	74

Joshua
2	156
9:1–27	124

1 Samuel
9–31	179
16–31	131, 151

Scripture Index

16:14	180	23:28–29	89
18:1–5	79, 104	24:18–20	101
18:6–16	164	25:1–7	101
19:1–7	156, 219		
19:1–10	164	**1 Chronicles**	
20:1–42	156	7	131
21:1–6	67		
22	219	**2 Chronicles**	
22:6–19	164	17–20	11
22:17–19	156	20:12	100
24	164	24:20–24	28
28:1–25	164	35:20–27	99
2 Samuel		**Job**	
11	45, 122	22:21	184
11–12	215		
11:1–12:23	64	**Psalms**	
12:13	222	1:1	35
13–15	131	2:12a	24
13–17	31	2:12b	24
15–16	159	4:5	97
15–17	31	7:7–8	196
16:5–13	157	12:6	211
16:12	171, 174	33:13	103, 138
17	53	33:17	72
17–18	131	34:9	73
17:14	180	34:10	64, 213
20	159	34:10b	37
		34:19	139
1 Kings		37:1	41, 166
1	159	37:5	54, 62, 65, 73, 74, 90, 100, 127, 133, 149
2:29–34	159		
3:1–28	212	37:7	73, 134
3:16–28	107	49	95
12:6–11	122	50	96
18:3–5	156	50:13	95
21:25–26	180	55:22	73
		58:11	32
2 Kings		60:10–11	72
6:24–33	204	62:12	32, 103
16	205	73:2	166
19	127	82:6	146
19:1–37	204	91:14	73
21:1–18	64	109:4	92, 174

Scripture Index

109:28	171	5:14	49
112:1	220	5:15	21, **48–49**
116:11	89, 208	5:16	21, **49**
119:1	39	5:17	48, **49**
119:105	50, 90, 139, 209	5:18	**25**, 45
127:1	54, 72, 100, 127, 134, 149	5:19	21, 47
128:1	29	6	149
128:2	73	6:6	149
130:5	210	6:12	**56–58**
143:2	224	6:32	45
146:3	52	8	60
		8:1	59
Proverbs		8:3	59
1:1–4	27	8:4	13
1:1–8	**27**	8:14	**62**
1:5	**29–30, 164**	8:15	**61**
1:5–6	27	8:22	**60**
1:7	10, 22–23, 27–28	8:23	13, **60–61**
1:8	**30–31**	8:30–31	**61**
1:9	31	8:31–32	13
1:10	**32**	9:10	220
1:17	**32–33**	10:1–3	77
1:28	32	10:3	**63–64**
2:4–5	43	10:4	**65**, 73
3:3	**37–38**	10:12	**66–69**
3:5	10, **24**	10:14	**70–71**
3:5a	37	10:22	**71–73**
3:5b	38	11:1	**77–78**
3:5–6	23	11:2	**78–79**
3:6	55, 62	11:15	9
3:9	**38–39**	11:31	**80–82**
3:11	**39**	12:22	**83**, 87
3:12	23	13	165
3:13	**39–40**	13:10	**85–87**
3:27	**40**	13:23	**87–88**
3:28	**40**	14:12	**89–90**
3:29	**40**	14:32	23
3:30	**41**	15:1	**91–95**, 198
3:31	**41**	15:8	**95–97**, 104
3:34	78	15:16	140
3:35b	**41**	16:1	**99–101**
4:7	43	16:3	**74, 101**
5	77	16:4	**101–3**
5:9	**48**	16:5	**104**, 148, 213

229

Scripture Index

16:6	**104–5**	27:9	190
16:9	73, 99	27:17	**188–90**
16:10–11	**105–7**	27:19	**190–92**
16:11	**78**	28:2	**193–96**
16:25	188	28:13	**196–98**
17:5	140	28:14	**198–99**
17:7	11	29:12	**201–4**
17:9–12	**109–13**	29:18	**204–5**
18:17	**115–18**, 216	30:1	**207**
18:22	**118–20**	30:3	**208**
19:10	**121–23**	30:5	**209–12**
19:14	118	30:7–8	**212–13**
19:25	**123–25**, 178	30:11	217
20:12	73–74, 107, **127–28**	30:20	35
20:14	**128–30**	30:21–22	**214**
20:21	**130–31**	30:24	**214–16**
20:25	**131–32**	30:32	**216–17**
20:28	**105**	30:33	**218**
21:30–31	**133–34**	31	xxiii, 25
21:31	73	31:30	220
22:1	**135–37**		
22:2	**138–40**	**Ecclesiastes**	
22:26	9	1:15	89, 188
22:28	**140–43**	4:17	95, 132
23:1–2	**145–48**	7:1	57
23:4	**148–49**	7:8	171
23:6–7	**150–53**	7:20	117
23:9	165	9	149
24:11	**155–57**	9:10	54, 72
24:15–16	**157**	9:11	72
24:21–22	**157–61**		
25:2	**163–64**	**Song of Songs**	
25:20	**164–65**	4:5	21
25:26	**165–67**	7:5	21
26:1	**169–70**		
26:2	**170–72**	**Isaiah**	
26:4–5	**173–76**	1:16	111
26:6	**176**	1:18	32, 198
26:10	**176–77**	3:1	193
26:11	**178–81**	8:20	209
27:1	**183–85**	29:13	212
27:3	**185–87**	33:1	77
27:8	**187–88**	40:11	65, 74

46:4	74	**Daniel**	
51:7	50	1–4	215
57:1	14	2:21	54, 73, 105–6, 128
57:15	199	3:1–30	119
64:8–9	196	4:30	71
66:1–2	79		
66:3	95	**Hosea**	
		4:9	193
Jeremiah		6:6	95, 104–5
7:22	95		
10:23	54, 72, 100, 127, 184	**Amos**	
10:24	196	1:3	179
17:5	52, 191	9:8–9	205
17:9	208		
27–28	28	**Habakkuk**	
32–44	204	2:3	97
37–39	127		
38:6–13	156	**Zephaniah**	
52:2–3	101	1:8	5
		1:12	138
Lamentations			
3:22	69, 198	**Zechariah**	
3:37–38	138	1:3	43, 198
		8:19	112
Ezekiel		13:6	216
33:11	91, 198		
36:27	38	**Malachi**	
		4:2	222

DEUTEROCANONICAL BOOKS

Wisdom of Solomon		3:26	181
6:12	43	6:35	136
6:12–13	36	6:36	189
		10:13	104, 150
Sirach		33:25	122, 218
3:20	148, 169	33:29	121
3:22	139, 213	41:15	135–36, 170

Scripture Index

NEW TESTAMENT

Matthew
4:4	212
5:3	140
5:9	91
5:16	11
5:21–26	187
5:29–30	178
6:14	68, 186
6:33	35, 212
6:34	129, 140, 185
7:1–5	187
7:3–5	116
7:6	165, 174
7:7	29, 36, 54, 100
10:16	153
10:29–30	138–39
10:33	161
10:42	38
11:25	166
11:29	70, 79, 86
12:1–8	67
12:31	161
12:32	113, 143
12:43–45	179
12:45	179
13:45–46	213
15:9	212
15:13	197
17:5	209
18:15	109
18:21–35	186
23:12	148
23:35	156
25:14–30	149
25:29	29
26:52	77, 103, 159
27:64	179

Mark
1:15	111

Luke
1:52	78
3:14	40, 218, 223
9:35	31
11:13	29, 36, 43, 54
11:41	49
16:15	104
16:19–31	139
17:1	57
22:3	89

John
1:1	60
1:3	61
1:4	123
3:27	72, 100, 134
4:24	95
6:44	44
14:6	97, 209
14:23	31
15:5	72, 100, 134, 184
15:16	97
16:23	97
17:3	210
18:36	161
20:21	161

Acts
5:29	143, 158, 161

Romans
1:16	210
3:4	89, 208
3:21	xxiii
3:23–24	224
5:12	103
6	xxii
8:13	120
9	166
9–11	166
9:22	31

Scripture Index

9:23	14, 31	**Galatians**	
11:10	165	1:8	143, 161
12	xxii, 187	1:13	197, 216
12–13	54	6:1	173
12:14–21	187	6:4	57, 117, 172
12:18	91		
13	xxii, 106, 158	**Ephesians**	
13:4	155	5:7	155
13:5	159	5:15	120, 180
14–15	xxii	6:4	30
14:1	165	6:16	210
14:18	137		
15:4	210	**Philippians**	
		2:5–11	79
1 Corinthians		2:12	198
1:26	166	2:13	62
2	163	4:8	136
2:14	211		
3:10–15	212	**Colossians**	
3:13	212	3:6	197
4:2	149		
6:9	48, 120, 223	**1 Thessalonians**	
7:17	54, 140	2:7	xii
7:20	133	4:10–11	54
7:24	188	4:11	72–73, 133
10:7	78, 121	5:16–18	130
10:10	129	5:22	120
10:11	178		
10:31	136	**1 Timothy**	
10:32	57	1:15–16	197
12	54	1:18–19	170
13:7	53	1:19	105, 223
14:40	184, 213	2:8	140
15:9	197	2:15	xxiii, 221, 223
15:58	134	3:1	147
		5:14	223
2 Corinthians		6:9	88
1:12	57, 172	6:12	105, 223
3:18	222		
6:1	180	**2 Timothy**	
9:7	147, 152	1:14	173
10:4	161	4:2	94

233

Scripture Index

Titus
1:6	177
1:11	173
2:1	173
2:15	173
3:1	147
3:9–11	112
3:10	165, 174, 216
3:14	147

Hebrews
1:3	61
5:7	120
8:6	120
12:29	63, 124
13:2	64
13:4	120

James
1:5	43–44
4:6	78, 170

1 Peter
3:9	175
3:15	95
4:17–18	80
5:5	79, 104, 170
5:6	129, 140

2 Peter
2:20	179

1 John
3:15	152

Subject Index

Abel, 82
Abraham, 131, 178, 180
Absalom, 31, 130, 180
adiaphora controversy, 95n19, 110n4, 143n44
admonishment, 109–10, 111–12
adultery, 45, 47–48, 159–60
Aesop, 128, 146, 179n60
Agricola, Rudolf, xxii, 181n72
Agrippa, Cornelius, 110n6
Ahaz, king, 55, 205
Ahithophel, 31, 53, 180
Albert I, Johann, 5, 13
Alciati, Andrea, x
Alexander the Great, 11, 71, 122, 145, 169, 203, 215, 219–20
allegorical reading, 141
ambition, 56–57, 147–48, 150
Anabaptists, 48, 78, 210
anger, 86, 145n2, 186–87, 218
   responses to, 94, 175
animals, 214–16
Antiochus IV Epiphanes, 195–96, 199
aphorisms. *See* maxims, aphorisms
Aquinas, Thomas, xi
Arians, Arianism, 60, 111n6, 197
Aristides, 11, 12, 171

Aristotle, xxiii, xxivn40, xxv, 80n23, 88, 164n9, 225n26
   Cicero and, xviin26, xxvin40, 22n26, 66n16, 177n45, 186n22
   commentaries on, xviin26, xxivn40
   ethics, xxv, 148, 157n16
   justice, 22n26, 66n16, 136n9
Arnold, Gottfried, ix–x
arrogance, 79, 122, 136–37, 147, 169, 215, 217
Athens, Athenians, 55n28, 59n1, 68n24, 92n9, 171–72
   Sparta and, 110n4, 184n10, 215n49
Augsburg Confession, xviii, 15, 131n30
   Article IV, justification by faith, 198n22, 224
   Charles V, emperor, 15, 224n24
Augsburg, Peace of, 161n39, 205n20
Augustine of Hippo, 135n2, 217n57
authenticity, 136

blasphemy, 113, 143, 165, 210, 216–17
boundary markers, 140–41

235

Subject Index

Cain, 82, 150, 151
callings, 19, 40, 79, 187–88
  Evangelicals and, 53n14, 54n17, 140n26, 188n30
  God enabling, 73–75, 99–101, 133–34
  labor, work, 53–56, 65, 148–49, 213, 223–24
  obedience, 72–73, 139–40
  Paul on, 133–34, 172, 177, 183–84, 187–88, 213
  prayer and, 133–34
  waiting for, 130–31
Calvin, John, ix–x, 91n3, 101n16
  Melanchthon and, xviii, 101
candor, 53, 70, 109–10
Carion, Johannes, xx, 143n49
Cato the Younger, 121
Charles V, emperor, xv, 15, 194n5, 224n24
chastity, 47, 120, 124, 136, 222
childbearing, salvation and, xxiii, 221–24
Christ, Jesus. *See* Jesus Christ
church, the, 209
  external blessings, 63–65
  giving, 38
  Israel as, 10–11, 30–31
  pastors, 173–74
  philosophy, Western and, 6–9, 22–23, 39
  refuting error, 160–61
  religious ceremonies, 96–97, 132
  Son speaking to, 59–62
  teaching, 12–14, 24, 30–31, 188–90
  traditions, 211–12
  true, 166–67, 180, 210
  tyrants and, 81–82, 156, 165
  wisdom, 60–61
  See also doctrine

Cicero, Marcus Tullius, 67, 92, 102n18, 107n41, 195, 217n57
  Aristotle and, xviin26, xxvin40, 22n26, 66n16, 151n35, 177, 186n22
  commentaries on, xviin26, xxivn40
  death of, 191–92
  justice, 22n26, 66n16, 151n35
  love of self, 115–16
  Milo and, 160n30
  jealousy, envy, 151, 170
Cicero, Quintus Tullius, 46–47
Claudian, Claudius Claudianus, 41, 56, 79, 86, 205n16
conscience, 117, 172
  conviction, sin, 112, 132, 216
  good, 57, 135, 170, 198, 223
conversion, 197–98
creation, 102–3, 138
Cyril of Alexandria, xxiv, 7, 23

David, 24, 55, 67, 92, 122, 215, 222
  Ahithophel and, 53
  exile, 157, 166, 171, 174
  Jonathan and, 37, 53, 79, 104–5, 155–56, 219
  Saul and, 131, 151, 164, 219
  sin and repentance, 33, 45, 64, 80, 122, 148, 222
death, 103, 123
Decalogue. *See* Ten Commandments, Decalogue
deliberation, 28, 86–87, 89
Demosthenes, 92, 112, 117, 141–42, 176
  wars, 55, 62, 100
devil, the, 97, 146, 151–52, 194
  disorder, 77, 106
  sin and, xxiv, 89, 120–21, 150
  wickedness, 66, 179

236

Dionysius, 80n24, 151n33
doctrine, 6, 17, 97, 180
    corrupt, 180, 189, 212
    defending, 173–74, 205
    from God, 52, 97, 105–6, 191
    true, 136, 164–65, 198, 219

Elisha, 204
Empedocles, 111
envy, jealousy, 41, 151, 170
Epicharmus of Kos, 18, 52, 191
Epicureans, 29, 35, 102, 139
Erasmus of Rotterdam, ix, xi–xii, xviii, xxvi
    loci interpretation method, xxi–xxii, xxv
eternal, xxiv, 65
    punishment, 32–33, 63, 82
    rewards, 63–64, 81–82
Euripides, 8, 94, 172n19, 175n36, 189
Evangelicals (Lutherans), xiii–xiv, xv, xvi–xvii, xxii, 161, 224n25
    adiaphora, 95n19
    Anabaptists, 210n22
    Augsburg Confession, 198n22, 224
    callings, 53n14, 54n17, 140n26, 188n30
    ethics, 186n22
    Melanchthon and, xviii, xxii, 93n12, 110n4, 191, 198n22
    Ten Commandments, 9n17, 136n8
evil, 32, 40–41, 157

faith, 37–38, 198–99, 219–20
    justification by, xxii, 12n27, 198n22, 222–24
    prayer and, 65, 97, 210
    wisdom and, xxiii, xxiv–xxv, 25

faithfulness, 105, 191
false accusations, 170–72, 202–3
faults, 115–17, 128
fear of God, 10–11, 28, 53, 78–79, 105, 198–99, 220
    wisdom and, 29–30
fickleness, 57, 128, 137, 188, 190–91
    of fortune, 146–47, 183
foolish hope, 183–85
fools, foolishness, 94–95
forbearance, 66–70, 111, 137, 186–87
forgiveness, 66–70, 97, 186

generosity, 48–49
gentleness, 86–87, 93
Germany, German, x–xi, 5, 49n22, 68, 160, 180
    Luther Bible, xiv
    Wittenberg, University of, xii–xviii, xix–xx, xxiii
glory, 57, 86
God, 91
    assistance, enabling, 73–75, 99–101, 127–28
    doctrine from, 52, 97, 105–6, 191
    fear of, 10–11, 28, 29–30, 53, 78–79, 105, 198–99, 220
    judgment, 80–82, 197–99
    justice, order of, 80–82, 123–24
    knowledge of, 7–8, 10–11, 30, 37–38, 208–10, 212–13
    mercy of, 37, 104–5, 222
    protection, 119–20
    providence, 63, 80–81, 102–4, 138–40, 208
    twofold righteousness of, xxiii–xxv, 8n14
    voice, 12–13
    See also Word of God
Gospel, 8–9, 39
    law and, 8–10, 23–24, 59, 61

Subject Index

government, xxiii, 20–21, 61, 105–7, 122, 127
  dishonesty, 202–4
  examples, 201–2
  officials, 145–48, 155–61, 193–96, 219–20
  sedition, 158–60, 194–95
  wisdom, 163–64
greed, 48, 148–49
Greek mythology, 74–75
Gregory of Nazianzus, 56, 118

happiness, 71, 88n16, 118
heretics, heretical, 89, 93, 112, 163, 165, 174, 217
Herodotus, 124–25, 175
Hesiod, 7–8, 88n15, 137
Hezekiah, king, 14, 31, 127, 163n3
Holy Spirit, 10–12, 29, 164
Homer, 7–8, 11, 51, 176, 187
Horace, 116, 128n9, 145, 214
human, humans, 214–15
  faults, 115–17, 128
  judgment, 89–90, 99–101
  strength, 71–72, 74–75, 184–85
  trust in, 183, 184–85, 191, 199
  weakness, 79, 89–90, 100, 186, 188–89
  will, 52–53, 99–100, 123
  wisdom, 39, 61–62, 208–9
humanism, x, xii, xiv, xix, xxiii–xxiv, 52
humility, 78–79, 86, 148, 169–70, 190
hypocrites, 116, 118

idleness, 121–23
ignorance, 6, 8–9, 123–24, 177, 186, 208–9
imitation, 49–50, 201–2
inheritance, 49, 130–31

instruction, 17–18, 28, 30–31. *See also* teaching
insults, 174–76
Isaiah, 127, 196, 204–5
Isocrates, 23n34, 172n19
Israel, 10–11, 30–31, 131

jealousy, envy, 150–54, 170–71
Jehoshaphat, king, 11–12
Jeremiah, 28, 100, 127, 138, 191, 196, 204
Jesus Christ, 179, 185
  Messiah, 24–25, 123n14
  Son of God, 12, 14, 209–10, 222
Jews, 6n5, 180, 197
  Antiochus IV Epiphanes and, 195–96, 199
  Sadducees, 180, 211
John, apostle, 174
John the Baptist, 40, 218, 223
Jonathan, 37, 53, 79, 104–5, 155–56, 219
Josiah, king, 89, 99–100
Judas Iscariot, 33, 66, 89
judgment, 28, 109–10, 178
  faults, 115–17
  of God, 80–82, 197–99
  human, 89–90, 99–101
  perverse, 117–18
Julian the Apostate, xxiv, 6–9, 23–24
Julius Caesar, 66–67, 86, 93, 159n26, 192n58
  Pompey and, 66n18, 184–85
justice, 66–68, 77–78, 130, 216
  God's, order of, 80–82, 123–24
  particular, 48n14, 66, 77, 136
  protecting the innocent, 155–57
  self-defense, 68, 92
justification by faith, xxii, 12n27, 198n22, 222–24
Juvenal, 20, 56, 81, 86

Subject Index

knowledge, 28–29, 35–36
  fear of the Lord and, 29–30
  of God, 7–8, 10–11, 30, 37–38, 208–10, 212–13
  law, 7–8

labor, work, 121–22, 176–77
  callings, 53–56, 65, 148–49, 213, 223–24
  diligence, 55–56
  God aided, 72–75, 148–49
  human strength, 71–72, 74–75, 184–85
Lactantius, 7–8, 92n8
law, Law, 91
  ancient, 140–43
  Gospel and, 8–10, 23–24, 59, 61
  knowledge of, 7–8
  obedience to, 157–59
  prophecy and, 106–7, 204–5
  Roman, 131n27, 140–41, 159–60
Lazarus, 139
loci interpretation method, xxi–xxiii, xxv, xxvii
Locrians, 141–42
Lucan, 66n18, 93
Lutherans. *See* Evangelicals (Lutherans)
Luther, Martin, xxiii, 69, 143n44
  callings, 40n16, 53n14, 177n44
  ethics, 66n15
  forbearance, 66n15
  interpretations, 82n27
  Melanchthon and, x, xii–xiii, 69n31, 71n41, 93n11, 110n6, 160n34
  Ten Commandments, 20n21
  theology, xxii, xxiii, xxv, 211n22, 212n26
  two kingdoms, governments, xxiii–xxiv, xxv

work, xiii–xiv, xix

Magnus III, prince, 13–15
Major, Georg, xix–xx
Manichaeans, 78, 197
marriage, 21, 25, 38, 45–47, 118–20, 222–23
maxims, aphorisms, xxi, 9–10, 12, 17–20, 207
  classification of, 20–22, 185–86
  Messiah and, 24–25
  philosophy, Western and, 22–23
meddlesomeness, 55–56, 134, 149, 184–85
Melanchthon, Philip, 15
  Augsburg Confession, xviii, 131n30, 198n22, 224n24
  commentaries, xiii–xv, xx–xxi
  early life, x–xi
  education, xi–xii
  exegetical method, xviii–xxv
  God, twofold righteousness of, xxiii–xxv
  humanism, x, xii, xiv, xix, xxiii–xxiv, 52
  interpretation, ix–x, xxii–xxiii
  loci interpretation method, xxi–xxiii, xxv, xxvii
  Luther, Martin and, ix–x, xxi, xviii, xxiii, 71n41, 93n11, 107n44, 143n44
  Proverbs translations, commentaries, xiv–xvi, xix–xxi, xix, xxv–xxvi
  publications, xvii–xviii
  rhetorical analysis, xx–xxi
  teaching, xii–xiv
  Wittenberg, University of, xii–xviii, xix–xx, xxiii
Menander, 170–71, 202, 215, 220
mercy, 37, 104–5, 118

Subject Index

miracles, 138
mocking, 125, 157
moderation, 87–88, 92–93, 129, 147, 183, 187, 209, 218
   of life station, 212–13
monks, monasticism, 48, 96, 202, 211, 223
mothers, 31
murder, 155–56, 157

Nebuchadnezzar, king, 71, 163, 169, 215
Nicolas of Lyra, 105n37, 131n30, 221n9
Nicolaus Gallus, 44n7
Nicolaus the Sophist, 18n5

obedience, 157–59
   callings, 72–73, 139–40
   Ten Commandments, 157–58
obstinance, 164–65, 179–80, 196–97
Oppian, 46
Osiander, Andreas, xvi–xvii, 6n4, 111n6
Ovid, 51–52, 145

parents, 30–31
patience, 129–31, 187–88
Paul, apostle, 88, 103, 137, 147, 165, 197–98
   calling, 133–34, 172, 177, 183–84, 187–88, 213
   faith, 210, 211–12, 221–24
   marriage, 47–48
   obedience, 158–59
   punishment, 178, 179
   Romans, letter to the, xxii
   teaching, 189
   truth, 173–74
peace, 91–92, 93
Pericles, 55, 59, 62, 110n4, 175, 184
Persius, 116

Peter, apostle, 79, 80, 175–76
Peter Lombard, xxii
philosophy, Western, 22–23
   church and, 6–9, 22–23, 39
Phocylides, xxiv, 17, 88, 213n39
   maxims, 117, 207
   Solomon and, 6–7, 22–24
   wrath of God, 22
Pindar, 8, 129–30, 176, 209
Plato, 71, 96, 110n5, 192n58, 208, 218
Plautus, 137, 170, 203
pledging, 51–53
Pliny the Elder, 164
Pliny the Younger, 187
Plutarch, 148, 150n28, 170, 195n9, 215n49
political, 61
   order, 77–78, 105–8
   sayings, 9–12, 20–21, 69
Pompey, 86, 89, 99, 150
   Julius Caesar and, 66n18, 93n12, 184–85
poor, the, 139–40
prayer, 30
   calling and, 133–34
   faith and, 65, 97, 210
   labor and, 54–55, 184
   for purity, 119–20
pride, 78–79, 85–87, 94, 104, 115–18, 150–54, 216–17
   arrogance, 79, 122, 136–37, 147, 169, 215, 217
prophecy, 106–7, 204–5
prosperity, 78–79, 121
proverbs, 18–20
Proverbs, book of
   ancient wisdom and, 9–10
   aphorisms, maxims, xxi, 9–10, 12, 17–20
   as collection, 207–8, 219
   history, xix–xx, xxi

structure, xxi, 11, 17–18
theological intention, xxi, 10–11
voice of God, 12–13
providence, 63, 80–81, 102–4, 138–40, 208
prudence, 28, 148–49, 173, 176, 190
punishment, 32–33, 45, 62
    causes of, 124–25, 178–80
    eternal, 32–33, 63, 82
    levels of, 66–68, 80–81
    providence and, 103–4
    rewards and, 63–64
    of wanton pleasures, 47–48
Pythagoras, 94n16, 129

Quintilian, Marcus Fabius, xxiin38, 79

Rashi, Schlomo Itzhaki, 221n9
Rehoboam, king, 122
religious ceremonies, 96–97, 132
repentance, 32–33, 45, 63, 80, 197–98, 211–12, 216
    relapsing, 179–81
reputation, good name, 135–37, 170–72
Reuchlin, Johannes, xi, xii
righteous, the, 116–17
    suffering, 138–39, 157
righteousness, 28, 48, 105
    of God, twofold righteousness of, xxiii–xxv
unrighteousness and, 63–64, 67, 166–67
Ripensis, Johannes Franciscus, 118n26
Roman Catholic Church, Roman Catholics, 38, 111, 163n2, 203, 211
    mass, 96, 132, 211
    monks, 48, 96, 202, 211, 223
Roman law, 131n27, 140–41, 159–60

sacrifices, 95–96, 105–6, 132
Saul, king, 63, 80, 156
    David and, 131, 151, 164, 219
    repentance, 31, 33, 179–80
Schmalkaldic War, xv, 81n25, 161n39, 205n20
sedition, 158–60, 194–95
self-defense, 68, 92
self, love of, 115–18
    trust in, 183, 184–85, 191, 199
Seneca the Younger, 57, 137, 146–47, 150, 152, 186–87, 217n57
Septuagint, 21n25, 83n2, 117
Simonides of Ceos, 48n14, 90, 208, 221
sin, 103, 123–24, 196–97
    conviction of, 112, 132, 216
    relapsing, 179–81
    repentance, 32–33, 45, 63, 80, 197–98, 211–12, 216
    of rulers, 193–96
slander, 111–12, 202–3
sloth, 55, 56, 215
Socrates, 18n8, 87n11, 172, 208n6
Sodom, 124, 178, 180
Solomon, xxi, xxiv–xxv, xxvi–xxvii
    theological intention, xxi, 10–11, 24, 27–28
    Western wisdom and, 5–7, 8–10, 22–23, 23–24, 39
Solon, 7, 8, 146, 218
Sophocles, 8, 128, 190
Spain, Spanish, 107, 132
Sparta, Spartans, 19n16, 38, 110n4, 175, 184n10, 215n49
spitefulness, 151–52, 157
stealing, 45, 48, 77–78, 140
Stigel, Johann, xvin23, 129, 188n33
Stobaeus, Johannes, 93–94, 175n36, 221n10
Stoics, 29n8, 101, 152n41
strife, love of, 93–95, 110–12

Subject Index

Strobel, Georg Theodore, ix
Suetonius, 19, 46n7
Sulla, 66, 86, 177
Synesius of Cyrene, 190

teaching, 12–14, 24, 30–31, 188–90
  instruction, 17–18, 28, 30–31
teachable, being, 164–65
temperance, 222–23
Ten Commandments, Decalogue, 39, 59, 218
  adultery, 45, 47–48, 159–60
  Evangelicals, 9n17, 136n8
  first table, 9, 20–21, 22–23, 112–13, 136
  murder, 155–56, 157
  obedience to, 157–58
  prophecy, 106–7
  second table, 20–22, 66
  stealing, 45, 48, 77–78, 140
  virtues and, 220–21
Terence, xin6, 128–29
Tertullian, 143
testimonies, 135–36, 166
Thales of Miletus, 7, 9n16, 23–24
Theognis of Megara, xxiv, 7, xxiv, 7, 8, 17, 22–24, 189
Thrasybulus, 67–68
Thucydides, 110n4, 129, 194
Tiberius, emperor, 46, 80, 139
Trajan, emperor, 156–57, 160
truth, 70, 83, 87, 105, 136, 173–74
  false accusations, 170–72
  heresy and, 109–10, 112–13
Tübingen, University of, xi–xii
tyrants, 81–82, 156, 165

vices, xxiii, xxvi, 49–50, 121–22, 183, 213
  ambition, 56–57, 147–48, 150

animal examples, 214–16
arrogance, 79, 122, 136–37, 147, 169, 215, 217
fickleness, 57, 128, 137, 188, 190–91
greed, 48, 148–49
jealousy, envy, 150–54, 170–71
loathing present good, 128–30
meddlesomeness, 55–56, 134, 149, 184–85
mocking, 125, 157
pride, 78–79, 85–87, 94, 104, 115–18, 150–54, 216–17
shamelessness, 57
slander, 111–12, 202–3
sloth, 55, 56, 215
spitefulness, 151–52, 157
strife, love of, 93–95, 110–12
  of tongue, 70–71, 83
trust in self, humans, 183, 184–85, 191, 199
See also anger
Virgil, 21n23, 51–52, 88n15
virtue, virtues, 137, 152, 215–16
  biblical, Christian, 12, 22–23
  candor, 53, 70, 109–10
  diligence, 55–56
  forbearance, 66–70, 111, 137, 186–87
  gentleness, 86–87, 93
  humility, 78–79, 86, 148, 169–70, 190
  instruction in, 6–7, 20
  kindness, 152
  patience, 129–31, 187–88
  temperance, 222–23
  of women, 220–24
  vices and, xxiii, xxvi
Vulgate, xix, 21n25, 83n2, 95n22, 209n13

weakness, human, 79, 89–90
   acknowledging, 100, 186, 188–89
wisdom, 9–10, 28, 212
   adulterous woman and, 35, 45
   church, 60–61
   faith and, xxiii, xxiv–xxv, 25
   fear of the Lord, 29–30
   Gospel, 8–9
   government, 163–64
   hidden, 163–64
   human, 39, 61–62, 208–9
   learning, 43–44, 178–79, 188–90
   Western, 5–7, 8–10, 22–23, 23–24, 39
Wisdom personified, 36, 60–61
women, 220–24
   salvation and childbirth, xxiii, 221–24
Word of God, 39, 52, 61–62, 90
   cut off, 123–24
   human judgment and, 99–101
   knowledge of God, 209–10
   obeying, 139
   purity, 209–10, 211–12
   wisdom, hidden, 163–64
work. *See* labor, work

Xenophon, 142, 194

Zedekiah, king, 101, 127
Zenobius, 194

Index of Authors and Works before 1600

Aeschylus: *Agamemnon*, 215n50
Aesop: *Fables*, 128, 146, 179n60
Agricola, Rudolf, 181n72
   Rodolphi Agricole Phrisii [the Frisian] *de inventione dialectica libri tres*, xxii
Agrippa, Cornelius: *De occulta philosophia libri tres*; *Of the Vanity and Uncertainty of Arts and Sciences*, 110n6
Aristides, 11, 12, 171n12
Aristophanes:
   The Birds, 190
   Knights, 177
   Plutus, 19
Aristotle:
   Constitution of the Athenians, 218n62
   Nicomachean Ethics, xxv, 136n9, 148, 151n39, 157n16
   Politics, 88, 213n39
   Topics, 80n23
Augustine of Hippo: *Sermons*, 135n2, 217n57

Brachylogos Totius Juris Civilis, 131

Calvin, John, ix–x, xviii, 91n3, 101
   The Bondage and Liberation of the Will, 101n16
   Institutes of the Christian Religion, 184n9
Carion, Johannes: *Chronica Ioannis Carionis (Chronicon)*, xx, 143n49
Cato, Dionysius: *Distichs of Cato*, 116n14
Cato the Younger, 121
Catullus: *Songs*, 20, 116
Chrysostom, John: *Homilies*, 44
Cicero, xxvi, 46, 67n19, 92, 100, 106n41, 192n58, 195
   Aristotle and, xviin26, xxvin40, 22n26, 66n16, 151n35, 177n45, 186n22
   Atticus, Letters to, 19n16, 115–16, 191
   For Cornelius Balbo, 151, 170
   De Fato, 102n18
   De officiis, 106n41
   On Friendship, 214
   For Milo, 160n30
   On the Nature of the Gods, 115n6, 208n5

Index of Authors and Works before 1600

Philippics, 195n10, 217n57
Tusculan Disputations, 177n45
Claudian (Claudius Claudianus), 41, 56, 79, 86, 205n16
  Against Eutropius, 214
  Against Rufinus, 79, 125
  On Stilicho's Consulship, 41, 86, 201, 205
Cornutus, Lucius Annaeus: *Greek Theology*, 152n41
Corpus Juris Civilis:
  Codex (Code), 92n7, 159
  Digesta (Digest), 140n36, 159n27, 176n42
Cyril of Alexandria, xxiv, 7, 23
  Against Julian, 7n7, 23

Demosthenes, 55, 62, 100, 117, 176
  Against Timocrates, 141–42
  De corona, 117n21
  On the False Embassy, 112
  Orations, 92
Digesta (Digest), 140n36, 159n27, 176n42
Dio, Cassius: *Roman History*, 157n14
Diogenes Laertius: *Lives and Opinions of Eminent Philosophers*, 146n6
Dionysius, 80n24, 151n33

Empedocles, 111n10
Ennius, Quintus: *Annals*, 141
Epicharmus of Kos: *Fragments*, 18, 52, 191
Erasmus of Rotterdam, ix, xi–xii, xviii, xxii, xxv
  Adages, xxvi, 9n16, 19n16, 20, 71n45, 85, 121n5, 142, 177, 201n3, 204n11
  Annotationes in Novum Instrumentum, xiin7

Euripides, 8, 94, 175n36, 189
  Fragments, 177
  Hippolytus, 171n11, 202–3n7, 220n5
  Palamedes, 172n19
  The Phoenician Women, 189
  Telephus, 19n16

Gellius, Aulus: *Attic Nights*, 183
Gregory of Nazianzus: *Poems*, 56, 118

Herodotus: *Histories*, 124, 125n18, 128, 130, 175, 189n42
Hesiod, 7n9, 8
  Works and Days, 88n15, 137
Homer, 7-8
  Iliad, 11, 176
  Odyssey, 51, 187
Horace:
  Epistles (*Letters*), 18, 117, 128, 145, 187, 193
  Satires, 116, 214

Irenaeus of Lyon: *Against Heresies*, 174n27
Isocrates, 23n34, 172n19

Jerome: *Epistles*, 217n57
John Chrysostom: *Hom. XXV in loco N. T.: In Ac. 9:1* (*De mutatione nominum*), 44
Julian the Apostate, emperor, xxiv, 6–9, 23–24
  Against the Galileans, 6, 23n34
Junius, Hadrianus: *Adagiorum centuriae VIII*, 56n30
Justinian I, emperor:
  Corpus Juris Civilis, 92n7, 159
  Pandectae or *Digestum*, 159n27
Juvenal: *Satires*, 20, 56, 81, 86

Lactantius: *Divine Institutes*, 7–8, 92n8
Laelius, Gaius, 12
Livy: *History of Rome*, 171
Lucan:
   On the Civil War, 66, 93
   The Dance, 134n9
Luther, Martin, ix, xiv, xix, 20n21, 146n8, 181n72
   Lectures on Genesis, 82n27
   Letter to Emperor Charles V (28 April 1521), 143n44
   Operationes in Psalmos, xiiin15
   Preface to His German Works, 190n50
   On Temporal Authority, 107n44

Major, Georg, xix–xx
   On the Authority and Origin of the Word of God, 52n8
   Vita S. Pauli, Apostoli, xix
Martial: *Epigrams*, 87n7, 87n10, 117, 129, 217
Melanchthon, Philip:
   Apology of the Augsburg Confession, 163n2
   Commentary on Romans, ix, xv, 166n20
   De officio principum, 160n33
   Explicatio Proverbiorum Salomonis in Schola VVitebergensi recens dictata a Philippo Melanthone, xxi
   Interpretatio Orationis Demosthenis De Corona, 92n9
   Loci communes theologici, xvii, xviiin27, xxiin38, 52n8, 120n30, 160n33
   Nova Scholia Philippi Melanchthonis, in Proverbia Salomonis, ad iusti penè commentarij modum conscripta, xv
   ΠΑΡΟΙΜΙΑΙ, sive Proverbia Solomonis filii Davidis, Cum Adnotationibus, xivn17
   Philosophiae moralis epitome, 48n14
   Scholia in Epistolam Pauli ad Colossenses, xiv
Menander, 170–71, 202, 215, 220
   Paidion, 179

Nicholas of Lyra, 105n37
   Postilla super Bibliam, 131n30, 221n9

Oppian (Pseudo-Oppian), 46
   The Chase, 46
   Cynegetica, 46n5, 46n6
Ordinary Gloss (*Glossa ordinaria*), 40n14, 131n30
Ovid, 51–52, 145
   Art of Love, 18, 51–52, 78, 121, 122, 191, 213
   Letters from the Black Sea, 183, 191
   Love's Cure, 121
   Metamorphoses, 48n19
   Sorrows, 145, 177, 183, 186

Pandectae (Pandects), 140, 159, 176. See also Corpus Juris Civilis, Digest
Persius: *Satires*, 116
Peter Lombard: *Sentences*, xxii

Index of Authors and Works before 1600

Peucer, Caspar: *Operum ... Philippi Melanthonis pars secunda*, xvin22, xxv
Phocylides, xxiv, 6–7, 8, 17, 22–24, 88, 213n39
  Poem of Admonition, 177
Phocylides (Pseudo-): *Sentences*, 207n2
Pindar, 8
  Pythian Odes, 129–30, 176, 209
Plato, 71, 110n5, 172n19
  Apology, 87n11
  Charmides, 9n16
  Epinomis, 96n29
  Letters, 218
  Republic, 134n9, 149n26, 185n15, 201n3
  Timaeus, 208n6
Plautus, Titus Maccius:
  The Haunted House, 137
  Poenulus (*The Little Carthaginian*), 170, 203
  Pseudolus, 19
Pliny the Elder: *Natural History*, 9n16, 164
Pliny the Younger: *Epistles*, 187
Plutarch, 215n49
  Morals, 19n16, 188
  Parallel Lives, 145n2, 146n5, 150n28, 150n29, 195n9, 220n4
  To an Uneducated Ruler, 148, 170
Prudentissimus, Julius Paulus:
  Opinions, 159n28
Publilius (Publius) Syrus, 137
  Sentences, 18, 121, 169
Pythagoras, 94n16
  Golden Verses, 129

Quintilian, Marcus Fabius, xxiin38
  Institutes of Oratory, 79
Rashi, Schlomo Itzhaki, 221n9
Ripensis, Johannes Franciscus:
  "Domino Martino Themmio et Dorothea Sponsae," 118n26
Sallust (Gaius Sallustius Crispus):
  Jugurthine War, 56n35
Semonides of Amorgos: *Types of Women*, 221n10
Seneca the Younger, 217n57
  Agamemnon, 146–47, 150
  On Anger, 186–87, 187n27
  On Benefits, 152
  Epistles, 188
  Hercules on Oeta, 57, 137
  Sibylline Oracles, 207n2
Simonides of Ceos, 48n14, 208, 221
  Fragments, 90, 217
Socrates, 18n8, 87n11, 171, 172, 208n6
Solon, 7, 8, 11–12, 146, 218
Sophocles, 8, 190
  Ajax, 128
  Oedipus Rex, 45n3
Spalatin, George, xii
  Herrn Doctor Caspar Creutzigers auslegung uber Sanct Paulus spruch zum Thimotheo, wie die Eheweiber selig warden, 221n11
Stigel, Johann, xvin23, 129, 188n33
Stobaeus, Johannes: *Anthologium* (*Florilegium*), 93–94, 94n17, 175n36, 221n10
Suetonius: *The Twelve Caesars*, 19, 46n7

Synesius of Cyrene: *Epistles* (Letters), 190

Terence, xin6
  Brothers, 186
  The Eunuch, 70n38
  Phormio, 128–29
Tertullian: *Against Praxeas*, 143
Thales of Miletus, 7, 9n16, 23–24
Theocritus: *Idylls*, 18, 21n23
Theognis of Megara, xxiv, 7, 8, 17, 22–24
  Elegiac Poems, 90, 189, 214
Thucydides, 110n4, 129, 194
  Funeral Oration of Pericles, 177
  Peloponnesian Wars, 92n6, 110n4, 129, 194
Timon of Phlius, 111n10
Tremellius, Immanuel: *Biblia Sacra*, 24n38

Virgil, 21n23, 51–52, 88n15
  Aeneid, 13n29, 51n3, 191, 202
  Ecloga, or *Bucolica*, 21n23
  Georgics, 71n43, 88

Xenophon: *Hellenica*, 142, 194

Zenobius, 194

Sources in Early Modern Economics, Ethics, and Law

Titles Available in the Second Series

On the Law of Nature: A Demonstrative Method
Niels Hemmingsen

On the Duty to Keep Faith with Heretics
Martinus Becanus

The Right Use of Moral Philosophy
Pierre de la Place

Deliberation on the Cause of the Poor
Domingo de Soto

Commentary on Proverbs
Philip Melanchthon

Titles Available in the First Series

A Treatise on the Alteration of Money
Juan de Mariana

On the Law in General
Girolamo Zanchi

On Law and Power
Johannes Althusius

On Exchange and Usury
Thomas Cajetan

On Righteousness, Oaths, and Usury: A Commentary on Psalm 15
Wolfgang Musculus

On Exchange: An Adjudicative Commentary
Martín de Azpilcueta

A Treatise on Money
Luis de Molina

The Mosaic Polity
Franciscus Junius

Of the Law of Nature
Matthew Hale

On Sale, Securities, and Insurance
Leonardus Lessius

www.ingramcontent.com/pod-product-compliance
Lightning Source LLC
Chambersburg PA
CBHW060516080526
44586CB00012B/504